SDN and NFV

A New Dimension to Virtualization

World Scientific Series on Future Computing Paradigms and Applications

Series Editor: Brij B Gupta (*Asia University, Taichung, Taiwan*)

Published:

Vol. 3   *Distributed Intelligent Circuits and Systems*
by Balwinder Raj, Brij B Gupta, Shalendra Singh and
Monirujjaman Khan

Vol. 2   *SDN and NFV: A New Dimension to Virtualization*
by Brij B Gupta, Amrita Dahiya and Elhadj Benkhelifa

Vol. 1   *Big Data Management and Analytic*
by Brij B Gupta and Mamta

World Scientific Series on
Future Computing Paradigms
and Applications – **Vol. 2**

SDN and NFV

A New Dimension to Virtualization

Brij B Gupta

Asia University, ROC

Amrita Dahiya

Thapar Institute of Engineering and Technology, India

Elhadj Benkhelifa

Staffordshire University, UK

World Scientific

NEW JERSEY · LONDON · SINGAPORE · BEIJING · SHANGHAI · HONG KONG · TAIPEI · CHENNAI · TOKYO

Published by

World Scientific Publishing Co. Pte. Ltd.

5 Toh Tuck Link, Singapore 596224

USA office: 27 Warren Street, Suite 401-402, Hackensack, NJ 07601

UK office: 57 Shelton Street, Covent Garden, London WC2H 9HE

Library of Congress Cataloging-in-Publication Data
Names: Gupta, Brij, 1982–   author. | Dahiya, Amrita, author. | Benkhelifa, Elhadj, author.
Title: SDN and NFV : a new dimension to virtualization / Brij B Gupta, Asia University, Taiwan,
    Amrita Dahiya, Thapar Institute of Engineering and Technology, India,
    Elhadj Benkhelifa, Staffordshire University, UK.
Description: New Jersey : World Scientific, [2024] | Series: World Scientific series on future
    computing paradigms and applications ; 2 | Includes bibliographical references and index.
Identifiers: LCCN 2023027037 | ISBN 9789811254871 (hardcover) |
    ISBN 9789811255984 (ebook) | ISBN 9789811255991 (ebook other)
Subjects: LCSH: Software-defined networking (Computer network technology) |
    Computer network architectures. | Virtual computer systems. | Cloud computing.
Classification: LCC TK5105.5833 .G87 2024 | DDC 004.6--dc23/eng/20231020
LC record available at https://lccn.loc.gov/2023027037

British Library Cataloguing-in-Publication Data
A catalogue record for this book is available from the British Library.

For any available supplementary material, please visit
https://www.worldscientific.com/worldscibooks/10.1142/12794#t=suppl

Desk Editors: Nambirajan Karuppiah/Amanda Yun

Typeset by Stallion Press
Email: enquiries@stallionpress.com

*Dedicated to my parents and family for their
constant support during the course of this book*
— Brij B. Gupta

*Dedicated to my parents, beloved husband, my daughter,
and my mentor for their motivation throughout the journey of
completion of this book*
— Amrita Dahiya

*Dedicated to my family for their constant support
during the course of this book*
— Elhadj Benkhelifa

Preface

Software Defined Networking (SDN) is the technology that makes networks more programmable and automated by separating the control plane from the underlying data plane. Separating the data plane from the control plane is the most common way to automate network management and to provision or deprovision resources; however, the functionality of SDN is more than that. For example, a combination of 5G technology and SDN can provide sustainable prices and lower latency to end-users, resulting in a better user experience across many platforms. Moreover, it can be well integrated with various cutting-edge technologies, such as edge computing, the Internet of Things (IoT), intent-based networking, and remote accessing. It can also help leverage cloud computing.

This book provides an overview of the basic concepts of modern networking and the key technologies behind them. This book illustrates the fundamentals and evolution of SDN and how this technology can be utilised to solve traditional networking challenges. In this book, the authors have emphasised the importance of virtualisation and how it forms the basis of SDN and Network Functions Virtualization (NFV). Further, detailed descriptions of components of the SDN control plane and application planes have been described in the book, along with a chapter completely dedicated to virtualised services. Moreover, this book illustrates the security issues and challenges related to SDN and NFV. Finally, this book covers various issues and challenges encountered by different platforms, including cloud computing, IoT, and cellular networks to be integrated with SDN and NFV.

This book is designed for readers with an interest in networking and its related concepts, including researchers who are exploring different dimensions associated with virtualisation, developers and professionals who are focusing on developing SDN controllers and applications to provide vendor independent networking services, industrialists who are keen on promoting their SDN/NFV services with more programmable features and flexibility, and faculty members across different universities.

This book contains 10 chapters, with each chapter focusing on providing an understanding and knowledge of SDN and NFV, along with their integration with cutting-edge technologies. The following list provides a detailed overview of the topics covered by each chapter.

Chapter 1: Elements of Modern Networking: This chapter introduces the concept of modern networking and the key technologies that play a key role in making networking programmable and automated.

Chapter 2: Introduction to Networking Concepts: This chapter showcases basic networking terminologies and concepts that a reader must know before diving deep into virtualisation-based SDN and NFV. This chapter illustrates networking planes that offer background on the core ideas behind contemporary state-of-the-art Internet switches. These concepts are crucial to comprehending how SDN executes these essential operations in a way that differs significantly from traditional switch architecture.

Chapter 3: SDN and NFV: Introduction, History, and Evolution: This chapter highlights the traditional and conventional methods of networking and their associated weaknesses. Further, this chapter discusses the history, evolution, and use cases of SDN and NFV and how the weaknesses of traditional networking are addressed by these two.

Chapter 4: SDN Basic Architecture: This chapter discusses the three architectural layers of the SDN framework, along with the interfaces between these layers. Next, it discusses how the decoupling of the control plane from the data plane makes SDN a preferable choice for programmable and automated networks. Finally, this chapter highlights SDN operations, such as maintaining a global view of the network, and SDN devices, i.e., software and hardware switches.

Chapter 5: SDN Controllers: This chapter specifically focuses on the SDN controller, as it is considered the brain of an SDN-enabled network. This chapter discusses the main components of the SDN controller and its related functionalities. Next, this chapter discusses and compares the SDN solutions provided by two leading networking companies, i.e., VMware and Cisco. Further, this chapter showcases a detailed comparative analysis of various other major SDN controllers.

Chapter 6: The OpenFlow Switch: This chapter illustrates the OpenFlow protocol, which is prominently and widely utilised as the southbound connection between the SDN controller and the switch. This chapter illuminates the concepts related to the OpenFlow switch, i.e., OpenFlow ports and tables, pipeline processing, packet matching, group tables, flow entry format, etc. Next, this chapter highlights the evolution of the OpenFlow protocol from V1.0 to V1.5.1.

Chapter 7: SDN Application Plane: This chapter specifically focuses on the application layer of the SDN framework. Apart from the SDN framework proposed by the SDNRG, this chapter illustrates the significance of abstraction and how abstractions are achieved in an SDN network. Next, this chapter highlights traffic engineering as the main application of SDN and discusses various factors that contribute to this functionality.

Chapter 8: Network Function Virtualisation: This chapter discusses how heterogeneous and proprietary networking devices have rendered network operation, management, and service deployment very cumbersome tasks. In the same direction, this chapter illustrates how NFV can be utilised to provide infrastructure virtualisation, resulting in efficient use of the resources available.

Chapter 9: SDN Security and Challenges: This chapter highlights the vulnerabilities and security issues introduced by the SDN platform. These include an increased risk of denial-of-service (DoS) attacks due to network device centralised control, flow-table limitations, a lack of trust between network elements due to the open programmability of the network, and a lack of best practices related to SDN functions and components.

x SDN and NFV: A New Dimension to Virtualization

Chapter 10: SDN and NFV with Other Technologies: This chapter discusses the integration of SDN/NFV with other cutting-edge technologies, such as cloud computing, IoT, and 5G. This chapter highlights the benefits provided by SDN to these platforms, along with the challenges and issues that hinder the seamless implementation of SDN in these particular domains.

Acknowledgements

First of all, we would like to express our gratitude to God by bowing our heads for lavishing upon us continuous blessings and enthusiasm for completing this book. Writing a book is not the work of an individual; rather, it is the outcome of the incessant support of our loved ones. This book is the result of inestimable hard work, continuous efforts, and the assistance of loved ones. Therefore, we would like to express our gratitude to each one of them who is linked with this book directly or indirectly for their exquisite cooperation and creative ideas for meliorating the quality of this book. Along with this feeling, we would like to appreciate and thank World Scientific Publishing and their staff for their assistance and persistent support.

We are grateful, from the bottom of our hearts, to our family members for their absolute love and uncountable prayers. This experience is both internally challenging and rewarding. Therefore, once again, special thanks to all who helped us make this happen.

About the Authors

Brij B. Gupta is the Director of the International Center for AI and Cyber Security Research and Innovations and a Distinguished Professor at the Department of Computer Science and Information Engineering (CSIE), Asia University, Taiwan. In more than 17 years of his professional experience, he has published over 500 papers in journals/conferences, including 35 books and 12 Patents with over 25,000 citations. He has received numerous national and international awards, including the Canadian Commonwealth Scholarship (2009), the Faculty Research Fellowship Award (2017), the Visvesvaraya Young Faculty Research Fellowship Award from the Indian Ministry of Electronics and Information Technology, Government of India, the IEEE GCCE outstanding and Women in Engineering (WIE) paper awards, and National Institute of Technology Kurukshetra, India's Best Faculty Award (2018 and 2019), respectively. Prof. Gupta was selected for Clarivate's Web of Science Highly Cited Researchers in Computer Science (top 0.1% researchers in the world) consecutively in 2022 and 2023. He was also listed in Stanford University's ranking of the world's top 2% of scientists in 2020, 2021, 2022, and 2023.

Dr Gupta is also a visiting/adjunct professor with several universities worldwide and an IEEE Senior Member (2017). He was selected as the 2021 Distinguished Lecturer in IEEE Consumer Technology Society (CTSoc). Dr Gupta is also serving as a Member-at-Large of IEEE Consumer Technology Society's Board of Governors (2022–2024). He is also the Editor-in-Chief of the *International Journal on Semantic Web and Information Systems, International Journal of Software Science and*

Computational Intelligence, Sustainable Technology and Entrepreneurship, and International Journal of Cloud Applications and Computing, the Lead Editor of a Book Series with CRC and IET Press, and the Associate/Guest Editor of various journals and transactions. He also served as a member of the technical program committee of more than 150 international conferences. His research interests include information security, cyber physical systems, cloud computing, blockchain technologies, intrusion detection, AI, social media, and networking.

Amrita Dahiya is currently working in the Thapar Institute of Engineering and Technology (TIET), Patiala, as an Assistant Professor in the Computer Science and Engineering Department. She completed her PhD at the National Institute of Technology (NIT), Kurukshetra, India, in 2021. She completed her dissertation at Jawaharlal Nehru University (JNU), Delhi. Her research interests include information and cybersecurity, web security, denial-of-service attacks, Internet of Things (IoT), and Software Defined Networking (SDN). She has published several papers in reputed journals and conferences.

Elhadj Benkhelifa is a full professor of computer science and the head of professoriate at Staffordshire University. He is also the founding director of the Smart Systems, AI and Cybersecurity Research Centre. Elhadj's research areas cover cloud computing and applications in their centralised and decentralised forms (fog/edge computing, cloudlets, blockchain, etc.), software-defined systems. service computing, cybersecurity, data (governance, semantics, analytics, social networks), artificial intelligence, and software engineering methods. Elhadj has delivered more than 40 keynote talks internationally and has edited a number of conference proceedings and special editions of scientific journals. He has published more than 150 research papers in conferences and journals and has been the principal investigator of a number of collaborative projects. Elhadj has chaired many prominent IEEE conferences in different parts of the world. Elhadj is currently the chair of the IEEE UK&I Section's Education Office and sits on the West Midlands Cyber Resilience Centre's Advisory Board. Elhadj is a senior member of IEEE, a fellow of the UK Higher Education Academy, and a Prince2 practitioner.

Contents

List of Figures

List of Tables

Chapter 1

Elements of Modern Networking

1.1 Introduction

Networking technologies are the core of any technology and have been for a very long time. Technologists are trying to push everything towards cloud, 5G, and Big Data, which ultimately puts a lot of pressure on networking technologies to be efficient, robust, and fast. Modernising IT infrastructure is not easy, as it faces hindrances such as legacy networking infrastructure, interoperability issues with integration platforms, and the abundance and diversification of mobile and networking devices. A modern networking ecosystem [1–5] has been developed by virtualising data centres and their related infrastructure. Analytics is also another feature which, when combined with virtualisation, makes applications or technologies satisfy increasing new demands. Earlier, a single vendor provided all hardware, software, communication, and networking devices and services to an enterprise. In the current scenario, organisations or users face heterogeneous and complex environments which require elegant and advanced solutions.

SDN and NFV are among the technologies that have attained a significant level of maturity after emerging from lab environments. These technologies have made it possible to have separate control and data planes as well as decouple network functions from hardware [6–8]. When these technologies are integrated with data centres, it leads to faster adoption of cloud computing. Virtualisation, programmability, and automation are going to be the three pillars of a new networking ecosystem. Allowing network automation to drive programmability through the command line has already made its mark in the new ecosystem.

1

The main aim of a networking ecosystem is to provide services to the end user in an efficient way. In its very basic structure, users access content or an application provider through multiple network access facilities. These network access facilities include cellular and wireless networks, cable modems, and digital subscriber lines (DSLs). Next, users are broadly interested in three main categories: content, application, and application service provider [9, 86]. The content provider is the entity with the data that are to be consumed by the end user. Next, the application provider provides applications to be installed on the user's platform [10, 11, 87]. Finally, the application service provider is the entity that provides services and resources for application development.

1.2 Elements of Modern Infrastructure

Ethernet [12], Wi-Fi [13–15], and 4G/5G cellular networks [16] have grown to accommodate extremely high data rates for a variety of multimedia applications demanded by businesses and consumers while also placing significant demands on network hardware and management facilities. Now, we discuss the main elements of modern networking, their evolution, and their application.

1.2.1 Ethernet

XEROX PARC, today known simply as PARC (Palo Alto Research Centre), developed and launched the Ethernet concept. A coaxial cable-based method for connecting computers and other electronic devices was proposed by this organisation [17, 18, 88]. In 1972, Bob Metcalfe and D. R. Boggs began developing Ethernet. In 1980, industry standards based on their work were established under the IEEE 802.3 set of specifications. Figure 1.1 shows the broad classification of Ethernet. Further, Figure 1.2 shows the evolution of Ethernet, i.e., it started at 10 Mbps and today has reached 100 Gbps and continues to evolve towards higher and higher speeds and better performance [89].

1.2.1.1 *Applications of Ethernet*

The growing availability of high-speed, low-cost Wi-Fi on computers, tablets, smartphones, routers, and other devices has reduced the

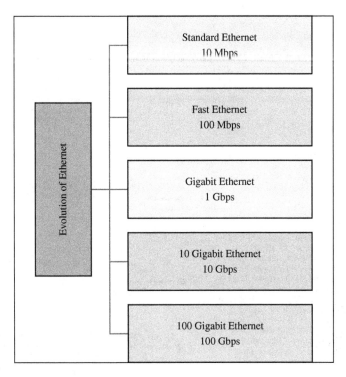

Figure 1.1.   Broad classification of Ethernet.

dependence on Ethernet in homes [19]. Nonetheless, almost all home networking setups make use of Ethernet in some way. Powerline carrier (PLC) and power over Ethernet (PoE) are two recent Ethernet extensions that have increased and expanded the use of Ethernet in the home. Powerline modems leverage existing power lines to send Ethernet packets over the power signal, while PoE distributes power across the Ethernet data wire in a complementary manner to simplify the cabling for devices, such as PCs and televisions [20]. Ethernet will maintain a significant presence in home networking with all of these Ethernet solutions, augmenting the benefits of Wi-Fi.

In the office, Ethernet has always been the standard network technology for wired local-area networks (LANs). Features such as simplicity, performance, and widespread availability have made Ethernet technology dominate its contemporary technologies, including IBM's Token Ring LAN and the Fiber Distributed Data Interface (FDDI) [21]. Wi-Fi

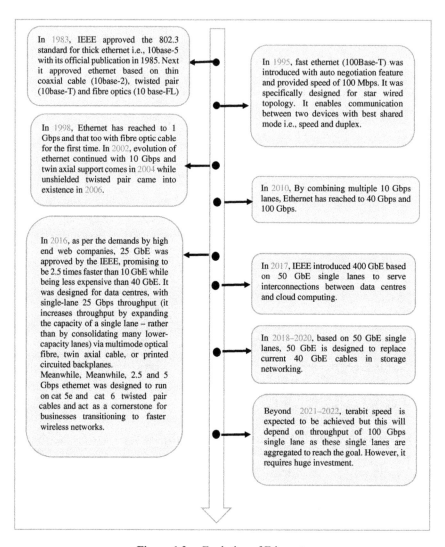

Figure 1.2.   Evolution of Ethernet.

currently accounts for a large portion of traffic in a typical workplace setting, especially to support mobile devices. Ethernet's popularity continues to grow because it can accommodate a large number of devices at fast speeds, is immune to interference, and offers security against eavesdropping attacks. As a result, the most popular architecture is a mix of Ethernet and Wi-Fi.

The ability to scale the network in terms of distance and data throughput with the same Ethernet protocol and accompanying quality of service (QoS) and security requirements is a huge benefit of Ethernet. For many years, Ethernet evolution was defined by the "demand for speed," as networks and data centres sought ever-increasing throughput. However, Ethernet has found its way into applications that the original specification's creators had not anticipated, resulting in a diverse Ethernet ecosystem [22–27]. Today, the need to incorporate the benefits of Ethernet into new applications involves a new strategy in which the needs of the application are emphasised while developing new Ethernet manifestations.

In smart vehicles, the IEEE 802.3bw-2015 100BASE-T1 [12, 28] and IEEE 802.3bp-2016 1000BASE-T1 [12, 29] standards provide 100 Mbps and 1000 Mbps Ethernet over a single twisted pair copper cable, respectively, and mark the introduction of Ethernet into vehicular applications to connect the growing number of intelligent devices. These two new Ethernet specifications demonstrate the application-driven approach for the automotive sector, which necessitates lightweight cabling and ruggedness in the face of adverse weather conditions.

The current infrastructure demands of business campus applications have prompted a need for higher speeds, as Ethernet has moved into new application domains. IEEE Std 802.3bz-2016 [30] specifies 2.5 and 5 Gbps MAC operating rates, as well as 2.5 GBASE-T and 5 GBASE-T physical layers (PHYs) for use over category 5e, category 6, or superior cables to meet this demand. The technology is already in use on devices, allowing consumers to get more data bandwidth from the 70 billion metres of established cable while also enabling PoE for our favourite wireless access points. The Internet of Things (IoT) will undoubtedly drive new Ethernet applications due to its various, even unimagined, networking requirements.

1.2.2 Wi-Fi

IEEE 802.11, also known as Wi-Fi [31], has expanded from 2 Mbps to over gigabit speeds in the past 20 years, a 1000-fold growth in throughput. The standard has evolved over time, with additional protocols, such as IEEE 802.11n [32], IEEE 802.11ac [33], and IEEE 802.11ax [34], being introduced (Wi-Fi 6). Higher-order modulation methods, such as 64 QAM, 256 QAM, and 1024 QAM, are supported by the new standards.

These new standards also allow numerous streams to be sent to a single client or several clients at the same time. In this section, we discuss its applications and classification.

1.2.2.1 *Wi-Fi Evolution*

Since Wi-Fi was originally introduced to the public in 1997, its standards have been steadily improving, resulting in faster speeds and better network/spectrum performance. As new features are introduced to the original 802.11 standard, they are referred to as "amendments" (IEEE 802.11b [35], IEEE 802.11g [36], etc.) [37]. Table 1.1 lists some milestone improvements in the 802.11 standard and summarises the complete evolution of Wi-Fi.

1.2.2.2 *Wi-Fi Applications*

There is no denying the fact that Wi-Fi has enormous applications in our daily lives, ranging from homes, public places to enterprises. Therefore, in this section, we discuss the benefits and applicability of Wi-Fi 6E. Wi-Fi 6E devices will operate in 14 additional 80 MHz channels and 7 more 160 MHz channels due to an additional 1200 MHz of spectrum available in the 6 GHz band for Wi-Fi applications. This expanded spectrum simplifies network architecture and provides optimum Wi-Fi performance with better throughput and wider channels while removing the requirement to support legacy devices, resulting in reduced network congestion [46]. W-Fi 6E upgrades 802.11ax by providing an enhanced network user experience with more reliable Wi-Fi networks that are resilient, scalable, and built for high-bandwidth multimedia applications, such as streaming, videoconferencing, and phone conversations. Wi-Fi 6E can provide a platform for artificial intelligence (AI)-aided media devices, such as high-resolution cameras [47–49], augmented reality (AR)/virtual reality (VR) [50, 51] goggles, and projectors that are bandwidth intensive and latency sensitive to reach a near-real-time experience. Another area of benefit is Industrial Internet of Things (IIoT) applications [52], such as cameras and other real-time instrumentation that need more predictable network behaviour to fulfil quality and safety standards in manufacturing lines, refinery operations, and other areas. These applications are just the tip of the iceberg, and the evolution of this technology still continues.

Table 1.1. Evolution of Wi-Fi.

IEEE 802.11 Protocol	Year	Frequency Band	Bandwidth	Max. Throughput	Description
802.11-1997	1997	2.4 MHz	22	2 Mbps	• This protocol featured three physical layer technologies: infrared with a 1 Mbps data rate, frequency hopping spread spectrum (FHSS) with a 1 Mbps and optional 2 Mbps data rate, and direct sequence spread spectrum (DSSS) with both 1 and 2 Mbps data rates.
802.11b	1999	2.4 MHz	22	11 Mbps	• 802.11b is used in point-to-multipoint communication, in which an access point communicates with mobile clients within its range [38].
802.11a	1999	5 MHz	20	54 Mbps	• The 5 GHz spectrum gives 802.11 a considerable advantage because the 2.4 GHz band is becoming crowded, but the effective overall range is less than 802.11b/g due to the high carrier frequency [39].
802.11g	2003	2.4 GHz	20	54 Mbps	• It offers a maximum theoretical rate of 54 Mbps, just like 802.11a. However, like 802.11b, it runs in the saturated 2.4 GHz band, making it sensitive to interference. • 802.11g is backwards compatible with 802.11b. • Using 802.11a and 802.11b/g, 802.11g could support dual-band or dual-mode access points [40].
802.11n (Wi-Fi 4)	2009	2.4/5 GHz	20/40	600 Mbps	• MIMO and 40 MHz channels are implemented in the PHY, and frame aggregation is added to the MAC layer to achieve this speed [41]. • 802.11n is backwards compatible with 802.11g, 11b, and 11a.

(*Continued*)

Table 1.1. (*Continued*)

IEEE 802.11 Protocol	Year	Frequency Band	Bandwidth	Max. Throughput	Description
802.11ac (Wi-Fi 5)	2013	2.4/5 GHz	20/40/80/160	6.8 Gbps	• 802.11ac boosted Wi-Fi speeds to gigabits per second by extending 802.11n principles, such as greater bandwidth (up to 160 MHz), additional MIMO spatial streams (up to eight), downlink multi-user MIMO (up to four clients), and high-density modulation (up to 256 QAM) [42]. • All legacy clients work properly with 802.11ac routers because they are backwards compatible with 802.11b, 11g, 11a, and 11n.
802.11ax (Wi-Fi 6) [43]	2019	2.5/5 GHz	20/40/80/160	10 Gbps	• Denser modulation (1024 QAM), (OFDMA), shorter subcarrier spacing (78.125 kHz), and plan-based resource allocation are used in 802.11ax to achieve these features. • 802.11ax was designed for maximum compatibility, coexisting efficiently with 802.11a/g/n/ac clients. • Overlapping basic service set (OBSS), a feature in Wi-Fi 6, further optimises for crowded environments, and it is proving very beneficial for critical and time-sensitive applications.
Wi-Fi 6E	2021	6 GHz	It can access up to seven 160 MHz channels	10.8 Gbps	• High-data-rate applications, particularly those with high-definition video components, will increasingly benefit from this additional capacity. • Virtual reality and augmented reality will also benefit [44].
Wi-Fi 7 [45]	2023	—	—	—	—

1.2.3 4G/5G Cellular Network

Cellular technology is the backbone of mobile wireless communications, allowing users to connect in places where wired networks aren't readily available. The fundamental technology enabling mobile phones, personal communications systems, wireless Internet, and wireless web applications, among other things, is cellular technology. This section examines how cellular technology has progressed through four generations and is about to enter a fifth.

1.2.3.1 *Evolution of 4G/5G Cellular Network*

Like wired communication, the sole purpose of wireless communication is to deliver high-quality, secure communication, and each new generation marks a significant step forward in that regard [53]. Due to rapid advancements in mobile technology, mobile communication has grown in popularity in recent years. Table 1.2 shows the complete evolution description of cellular networks.

1.2.3.2 *Applications of Cellular Networks*

In this section, we discuss the applications of 5G specifically to keep up with technological advancements. 5G technology will underpin a wide range of future businesses, including retail, education, transportation, and entertainment, as well as smart homes and healthcare. It will make mobile technology even more important than it is now. 5G will transform the mobile experience with a supercharged wireless network capable of supporting data download speeds ranging from 10 to 20 Gbps [54–57]. It is analogous to a fibre-optic Internet connection that can be accessed wirelessly. In comparison to traditional mobile cellular technologies, 5G allows for the efficient delivery of voice and high-speed data. Figure 1.3 shows the applications of cellular networks, specifically 5G.

1.2.4 Cloud Computing

Cloud computing is the delivery of computer services via the Internet in order to provide resources on demand and scale economies [58–60]. It provides the users with the flexibility of plugging into infrastructure

Table 1.2.   Evolution of cellular networks.

Attribute	1G	2G	3G	4G	5G
Introduction year	1970–1984	1980–1999	1990–2002	2000–2010	2010–2015
Standard	AMPS	GSM, CDMA, GPRS, EDGE	WCDMA	LTE, WiMax	MIMO, mm waves
Technology used	Analog cellular	Digital cellular	Broad bandwidth, CDMA, IP network	Digital broadband, LTE, Wi-Max	Unified IP and seamless combination of broadband and wireless technologies like wwww, LAN, IEEE 802.11, WAN, and PAN.
Core network	PSTN	PSTN	Packet network	Internet	Internet
Switching type	Circuit	Circuit	Both circuit and packet switching	Packet	Packet
Handoff	Horizontal	Horizontal	Horizontal	Horizontal and vertical	Horizontal and vertical
Multiplexing	FDMA	TDMA, CDMA	CDMA	OFDM	OFDM based waveform
Data rate	2 Kbps	14.4–64 Kbps	2 Mbps	200Mbps-1 Gbps	>1 Gbps

Internet service	Narrowband	Narrowband	Broadband	Ultra-broadband	Wireless world wide web
Bandwidth	Analog	25 MHz	25 MHz	100 MHz	30–300 GHz
Applications	Voice calls	Voice calls, SMS, partial browsing	Videoconferencing, mobile TV, GPS	High-speed applications, mobile TV, wearable devices	High-resolution video streaming smart home, transportation, and healthcare
Advantages	Low complexity	Multimedia features (SMS, MMS), Internet access, and SIM introduced	High-security international roaming	Global mobility, high-speed handoffs	Extremely high speed, critical, time-sensitive, and real applications handling
Disadvantages	Limited capacity, unreliable handoff, poor voice links, less secure	Low network range, slow data rate	High cost of spectrum license, low network coverage, low battery life	Infrastructure overhead	Limited global coverage, initial costs of implementation are high

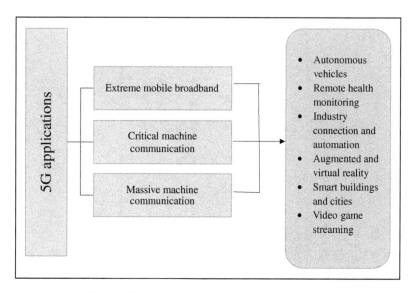

Figure 1.3.   Applications of cellular network (5G).

through the Internet and using computing resources without investing in and maintaining them on premises. Google Drive is by far the most popular cloud storage service in the world, with a use rate of 94.44% [61, 90]. Yet amazingly, with a 66.2% use rate, Dropbox, the finest cloud storage for collaboration, comes in second, followed by OneDrive (39.35%) and iCloud (38.89%) [61, 91].

The COVID-19 pandemic had a significant impact on many aspects of our lives, including employment. Faced with lockdowns, social isolation, and other restrictions, a significant segment of the workforce had no choice but to go online. According to remote work statistics, around 34% of employees prefer to work in the cloud and will hunt for a new job if they are obliged to return to the office [62].

1.2.4.1 *Evolution of Cloud Computing*

The business world is growing more complicated and competitive. Customers' expectations are also growing at the same time. The old computing paradigm appears to be insufficient as organisations seek innovative methods to improve the quality of their products and services through IT [63]. Using the traditional strategy for sourcing and implementing IT systems and solutions necessitates huge expenditures in IT infrastructure

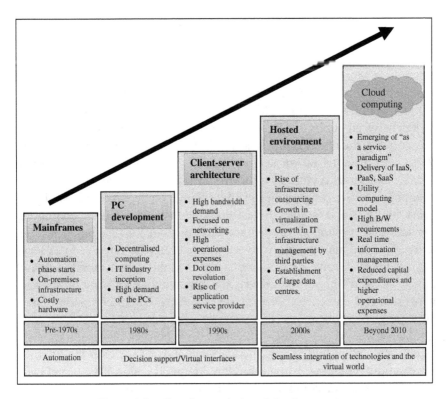

Figure 1.4.   Complete evolution of cloud computing.

but may not result in efficient resource usage. In this way, cloud computing has proven its worth over the years and paved an easy way for other technologies to seamlessly integrate [64]. Figure 1.4 shows the complete evolution description of cloud computing [92].

1.2.4.2 *Applications of Cloud Computing*

Cloud computing has emerged as a fundamental computing paradigm, enabling ubiquitous, on-demand access to a pool of configurable and shared computer resources through the Internet. Cloud computing can be categorised into three categories based on deployment model: public, private, and hybrid. Third-party cloud service providers own, run, and manage public clouds, which supply computing resources, i.e., ranging from software (software as a service, or SaaS) applications to virtual machines and bare metal hardware over the Internet, for example, Microsoft Azure and IBM Cloud. In a private cloud, a company implements its own cloud architecture and hosts cloud services within its own data centres, for example, VMware and OpenStack. It is used by enterprises to meet their regulatory compliance requirements. Hybrid clouds combine the features of both public and private clouds by allowing data and applications to switch between public and private clouds to provide more flexibility to the business. On the other hand, cloud computing can also be categorised into three categories based on service model: SaaS, platform as a service (PaaS), and infrastructure as a service (IaaS). SaaS is a technique of distributing software programmes via the Internet on demand and usually by subscription, for example, Salesforce and Netsuite. Cloud computing services that provide an on-demand environment for designing, testing, delivering, and maintaining software applications are referred to as PaaS [94]. It helps developers construct web or mobile apps rapidly without having to worry about the underlying infrastructure of servers, storage, networks, and databases, for example, DevOps. Cloud computing has a large range of applications [65–71].

IaaS gives pay-as-you-go access to basic computing resources, such as physical and virtual servers, networking, and storage over the Internet, for example, Google Compute Engine. Figure 1.5 shows the broad classification of cloud computing models based on deployment point and

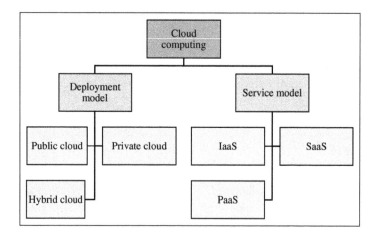

Figure 1.5.   Classification of cloud computing models based on deployment and service type.

service type. Following are some of the important features of cloud computing [72, 73]:

- **Cost:** Cloud computing eliminates the capital investment of purchasing hardware and software as well as establishing and operating on-site data centres — the racks of servers, electricity consumption, and IT experts to manage the infrastructure. It quickly adds up.
- **Scalability:** The capacity to scale elastically is one of the advantages of cloud computing services. That implies delivering the proper amount of IT resources, for example, more or less computing power, storage, and bandwidth, at the right time and at the right geographic location.
- **Performance:** The largest cloud computing services are delivered through a global network of secure data centres that are continually upgraded to the most recent generation of hardware. This has various advantages over a single corporate data centre, including lower network latency for applications and larger cost savings.
- **Reliability:** Multiple copies of data are maintained on redundant sites on the cloud provider's network; therefore, cloud computing enables data backup, disaster recovery, and easier business continuity.
- **Payment scheme:** Used resources are calculated at a granular level that allows users to only pay for the resources that they have actually used.
- **Multi-tenancy and resource pooling:** Multi-tenancy allows multiple clients to share the same physical infrastructure or apps while maintaining their own privacy and security. Cloud providers use resource pooling to provide resources to several clients using the same physical resources. The cloud providers' resource pools should be large and flexible enough to accommodate the needs of various customers.

1.2.5 Internet of Things

The IoT is a massive network of inter-connected things and people that collect and share data on how they are utilised and the world around them. Devices and items with built-in sensors are connected to an IoT platform, which combines data from various devices and applies analytics to share the most useful information with apps tailored to individual needs [74]. These sophisticated IoT solutions can detect precisely which data are useful and which may be safely ignored. These data can be used to spot patterns, make recommendations, and identify potential issues before they arise.

1.2.5.1 *IoT Evolution*

The IoT definition is complex, multifaceted, and even debatable. The Institute of Electrical and Electronics Engineers (IEEE) published a white paper titled "Towards a Definition of the IoT" in May 2015 [75, 76]. According to the IEEE, IoT consists of enabling technologies, components, and processes to successfully integrate these components. This frequently refers to a network that facilitates the integration of many parts, ranging from mobile phones to autonomous sensors. Figure 1.6 shows the evolution of the IoT.

The idea of a network of smart devices was initially suggested in 1982, and the first Internet-driven appliance was a customised Coke machine at Carnegie Mellon University [77]. A number of publications were released in various scholarly journals throughout the 1990s. Through the Auto-ID Centre at MIT and related market-analysis studies, the idea of the IoT first gained popularity in 1999. A British professor at MIT named Kevin Ashton popularised the term "IoT." He envisaged vendors integrating intelligence into physical products or things by the beginning of the millennium, essentially anything that could handle a sensor and connecting these via networks. LG announced ambitions to construct an internet-enabled refrigerator in 2000. From 2003 to 2004, the term "IoT" appeared in mainstream newspapers, such as *The Guardian*, *Scientific American*, and *The Boston Globe*; it also appeared in book titles for the first time. The International Telecommunications Union (ITU) of the United Nations (UN) published its first study on IoT in 2005, confirming the technology's continued global popularity.

1.2.5.2 *IoT: Design, Features and Applications*

An IoT architecture is a collection of components that include protocols, actuators, sensors, cloud services, and layers. In addition to devices and sensors, the IoT architecture layers are separated by protocols and gateways that track the consistency of a system [78]. Researchers have presented a variety of architectures, and there is no single IoT architecture

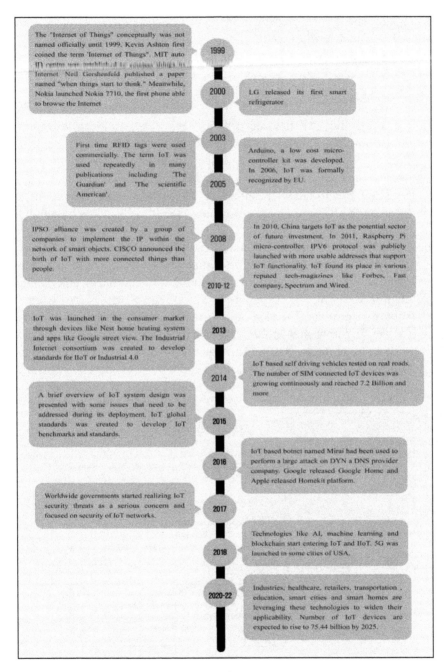

The "Internet of Things" conceptually was not named officially until 1999. Kevin Ashton first coined the term 'Internet of Things'. MIT auto ID centre was established to explore things via Internet. Neil Gershenfeld published a paper named "when things start to think." Meanwhile, Nokia launched Nokia 7710, the first phone able to browse the Internet — **1999**, **2000**

LG released its first smart refrigerator — **2000**

2003

First time RFID tags were used commercially. The term IoT was used repeatedly in many publications including 'The Guardian' and 'The scientific American'. — **2005**

Arduino, a low cost micro-controller kit was developed. In 2006, IoT was formally recognized by EU. — **2005**

IPSO alliance was created by a group of companies to implement the IP within the network of smart objects. CISCO announced the birth of IoT with more connected things than people. — **2008**

In 2010, China targets IoT as the potential sector of future investment. In 2011, Raspberry Pi micro-controller. IPV6 protocol was publicly launched with more usable addresses that support IoT functionality. IoT found its place in various reputed tech-magazines like Forbes, Fast company, Spectrum and Wired. — **2010-12**

IoT was launched in the consumer market through devices like Nest home heating system and apps like Google street view. The Industrial Internet consortium was created to develop standards for IIoT or Industrial 4.0 — **2013**

IoT based self driving vehicles tested on real roads. The number of SIM connected IoT devices was growing continuously and reached 7.2 Billion and more — **2014**

A brief overview of IoT system design was presented with some issues that need to be addressed during its deployment. IoT global standards was created to develop IoT benchmarks and standards. — **2015**

IoT based botnet named Mirai had been used to perform a large attack on DYN a DNS provider company. Google released Google Home and Apple released Homekit platform. — **2016**

Worldwide governments started realizing IoT security threats as a serious concern and focused on security of IoT networks. — **2017**

Technologies like AI, machine learning and blockchain start entering IoT and IIoT. 5G was launched in some cities of USA. — **2018**

Industries, healthcare, retailers, transportation, education, smart cities and smart homes are leveraging these technologies to widen their applicability. Number of IoT devices are expected to rise to 75.44 billion by 2025. — **2020-22**

Figure 1.6.   Evolution of Internet of Things (IoT).

that is universally accepted. A three-layer design is the most basic configuration, which is discussed in Figure 1.7.

Any IoT device, as a design standard, includes some common set of functions, such as connection, analytics, and endpoint management. This section discusses some features of the IoT ecosystem one by one [79]:

- **Connectivity:** IoT devices can be networked using radio waves, Bluetooth, Wi-Fi, Li-Fi, and other technologies. Various protocols of Internet connectivity can be leveraged in order to enhance efficiency and develop generic communication between IoT ecosystems.
- **Sensing:** Electrochemical, pressure, gyroscope, light sensors, GPS, pressure, RFID, and other sensors are used to collect data based on a specific problem.
- **Scalability:** IoT devices should be built in a way that allows them to be readily scaled up or down on demand. IoT is being used in a wide range of applications, from smart home automation to automating huge factories and workstations; therefore, the use cases are diverse.
- **Dynamic nature:** The first and most important step in any IoT use case is to gather and process data in a fashion that allows business choices to be made from it. Throughout this process, many IoT components must change their states dynamically. A temperature sensor's

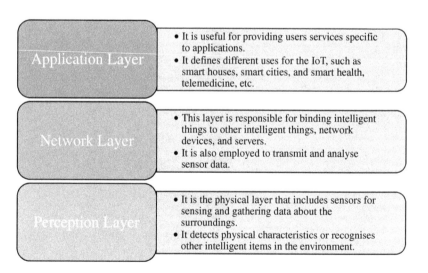

Figure 1.7.   Architectural layers of IoT.

input, for example, will change over time depending on weather conditions, location, and other factors.

- **Intelligence:** Various machine learning and deep learning models are designed to analyse the data collected by IoT sensors and devices to extract useful insights. These useful insights would help in real-time decision making to yield better performance and productivity of the system.
- **Energy:** IoT devices are battery-constrained; therefore, IoT devices are embedded with a sleep mode. A number of studies have been conducted to improve the battery life and minimise the energy consumption of the whole IoT ecosystem.

1.2.6 SDN and NFV

We will discuss the evolution, concepts, and features of SDN and NFV in detail in the upcoming chapters.

1.2.7 Network Convergence

Network convergence brings together multimedia, voice, and data services on a single network instead of utilising separate networks [80, 81]. Multiple communication modalities on the same network provide ease and flexibility that separate infrastructures cannot provide. Network convergence includes texting, web surfing, voice over IP (VoIP), streaming media, videoconference applications, online gaming, and E-commerce.

Many services utilise multiple network infrastructures, hardware, and protocols to establish connections with servers before network convergence. Consumers, corporations, educational institutions, and government organisations now use a wider range of media and data [93]. Businesses and IT managers desire low costs, regulatory compliance, customisations, ease of updating technology using legacy infrastructure, security, and privacy while end users demand high QoS and robustness of experience [82, 95].

Given the wide range of services with which workers engage, it makes technological sense for all of them to share the same infrastructure. Network convergence encourages standardisation of TCP/IP, Ethernet, and Wi-Fi because it provides a consistent and predictable user experience, allows for the integration of various products and suppliers, and makes network management easier. There are many advantages and disadvantages to network convergence. This section discusses each of them one by one. Following are some of the advantages:

- **Consistent performance:** Network convergence guarantees consistent performance to a great extent since all media types are delivered through the same network.
- **Global security:** Network convergence also enables major corporate, government, and university IT departments to implement firewall rules, automated and comprehensive antivirus and malware scanners, and other security controls for all data connections on a global scale.

There also exist many challenges in network convergence. Following are some of the major ones [83]:

- **Monitoring:** To run all of a company's communications and cloud-based services via a converged network, IT professionals must carefully manage the changing bandwidth requirements of various services across a wide range of devices.
- **Security:** If a cybercriminal is able to breach the security mechanisms of a converged network, all elements of the network, not just one segregated sector, may be vulnerable.
- **Regulatory issue:** Historically, legislation governing separate spectrum bandwidths or frequencies for different technologies has hampered converged network systems. There are currently conflicting networking standards that enterprises must follow. For video, text, data, and voice transmissions; fibre connections, broadband, DSL, Wi-Fi, Ethernet, WAN/SAN, vWAN/vSAN, SD-WAN, and mobile might have different requirements.

1.2.8 Unified Communication

The integration of multiple enterprise communication tools, such as voice calling, videoconferencing, instant messaging (IM), presence, and content sharing, into a single, streamlined interface with the goal of improving user experience (UX) and productivity is known as unified communication (UC) [84, 85]. UC technology enables a user to smoothly switch from one method of communication to another within the same session, whether on a desktop computer, laptop, tablet, or smartphone. Many UC systems also collaborate with third-party business tools, such as project management software, to enable information and resource centralisation as well as more efficient workflows. UC technology allows software that supports both real-time communication (RTC) and asynchronous communication to be integrated so that the end user has easy and immediate access to all resources, irrespective of location or type of digital device. It yields better productivity, reduced costs, better performance, and a greater user experience. UC tools provide a single interface for seamless interaction throughout the digital workforce distributed globally. UC tools provide easy project monitoring, fast access to expertise, and easy documentation and reporting. For example, a web conference would utilise an audio conference mechanism, which would provide an interface for chat, talk, and video via a mere click.

Exercises

Q.1.   What do you understand by networking ecosystem? According to you, what are its other components apart from the ones mentioned in the book?

Q.2.   How does the evolution of switches play an important role in developing Ethernet to its current state?

Q.3.   How has the advent of low-cost and high-speed Wi-Fi reduced the dependence of businesses on Ethernet?

Q.4.   Discuss the current status of Wi-Fi evolution and the benefits that it could offer to end users.

Q.5.   Discuss augmented reality and how Wi-Fi is contributing to it.

Q.6.   Discuss the evolution of cellular networks and what services 6G can provide to its users which 5G is unable to.

Q.7.   Discuss smart living and remote health monitoring as real-time applications of 6G.

Q.8.   Discuss in detail the broad classification of cloud computing into deployment and service models.

Q.9.   Discuss some important features of cloud computing and how it offers virtualisation to end users.

Q.10. Briefly discuss the architectural model of IoT and some issues it faces during its deployment.

Q.11. Discuss the applications of deep learning in the IoT.

Q.12. Discuss network convergence and how a business can reduce its CAPEX and OPEX through network convergence and unified communication.

Q.13. Discuss some challenges one can face in executing network convergence. Explain it with an example.

Q.14. Discuss unified communication and how it contributes as an element to modern networking.

References

[1] Stallings, W. (2015). *Foundations of Modern Networking: SDN, NFV, QoE, IoT, and Cloud.* Addison-Wesley Professional, Boston, MA.

[2] Shahraki, A., Taherkordi, A., Haugen, Ø., & Eliassen, F. (2020). A survey and future directions on clustering: From WSNs to IoT and modern networking paradigms. *IEEE Transactions on Network and Service Management, 18*(2), 2242–2274.

[3] Dy-Liacco, T. E. (1994). Modern control centers and computer networking. *IEEE Computer Applications in Power, 7*(4), 17–22.

[4] Smeliansky, R. L. (2014). SDN for network security. In 2014 *International Science and Technology Conference (Modern Networking Technologies, MoNeTeC)*, 28–29 Oct. 2014, Moscow, Russia (pp. 1–5). IEEE.

[5] Dajani, K., Owor, R., & Okonkwo, Z. (2010). The relevance of quantum cryptography in modern networking systems. *Neural, Parallel and Scientific Computations, 18*(3), 391.

[6] Barakabitze, A. A., Ahmad, A., Mijumbi, R., & Hines, A. (2020). 5G network slicing using SDN and NFV: A survey of taxonomy, architectures and future challenges. *Computer Networks, 167,* 106984.

[7] Ordonez-Lucena, J., Ameigeiras, P., Lopez, D., Ramos-Munoz, J. J., Lorca, J., & Folgueira, J. (2017). Network slicing for 5G with SDN/NFV: Concepts, architectures, and challenges. *IEEE Communications Magazine, 55*(5), 80–87.

[8] Haleplidis, E., Joachimpillai, D., Salim, J. H., Lopez, D., Martin, J., Pentikousis, K., Denazis, S., & Koufopavlou, O. (2014). Forces applicability to SDN-enhanced NFV. In *2014 Third European Workshop on Software Defined Networks*, 1–3 Sept. 2014, Budapest, Hungary (pp. 43–48). IEEE.

[9] Tao, L. (2001). Shifting paradigms with the application service provider model. *Computer, 34*(10), 32–39.

[10] Smith, M. A. & Kumar, R. L. (2004). A theory of application service provider (ASP) use from a client perspective. *Information & Management, 41*(8), 977–1002.

[11] Jiang, X. & Xu, D. (2003). Soda: A service-on-demand architecture for application service hosting utility platforms. In *High Performance Distributed Computing, 2003. Proceedings. 12th IEEE International Symposium*, 22–24 June 2003, Seattle, WA (pp. 174–183). IEEE.

[12] Cable, Single Twisted-Pair Copper. IEEE Standard for Ethernet.

[13] Noerenberg, J. W. (2001). Bridging wireless protocols. *IEEE Communications Magazine, 39*(11), 90–97.

[14] Khorov, E., Kiryanov, A., Lyakhov, A., & Bianchi, G. (2018). A tutorial on IEEE 802.11 ax high efficiency WLANs. *IEEE Communications Surveys & Tutorials, 21*(1), 197–216.

[15] Hiertz, G. R., Denteneer, D., Stibor, L., Zang, Y., Costa, X. P., & Walke, B. (2010). The IEEE 802.11 universe. *IEEE Communications Magazine, 48*(1), 62–70.

[16] Giust, F., Verin, G., Antevski, K., Chou, J., Fang, Y., Featherstone, W., Fontes, F., Frydman, D., Li, A., Manzalini, A., Purkayastha, D., Sabella, D., Wehner, C., Wen, K.-W., & Zhou, Z. (2018). MEC deployments in 4G and evolution towards 5G. *ETSI White Paper, 24*(2018), 1–24.

[17] Shoch, J. F., Dalal, Y. K., Redell, D. D., & Crane, R. C. (1982). Evolution of the Ethernet local computer network. *Computer, 15*(08), 10–27.

[18] Law, D., Dove, D., D'Ambrosia, J., Hajduczenia, M., Laubach, M., & Carlson, S. (2013). Evolution of Ethernet standards in the IEEE 802.3 working group. *IEEE Communications Magazine, 51*(8), 88–96.

[19] Feng, W. C., Balaji, P., Baron, C., Bhuyan, L. N., & Panda, D. K. (2005). Performance characterization of a 10-Gigabit Ethernet TOE. In *13th Symposium on High Performance Interconnects (HOTI'05)*, 17–19 Aug. 2005, Stanford, CA (pp. 58–63). IEEE.

[20] Ciobotaru, M., Stancu, S., LeVine, M., & Martin, B. (2006). GETB-A gigabit ethernet application platform: Its use in the ATLAS TDAQ network. *IEEE Transactions on Nuclear Science, 53*(3), 817–825.

[21] Duelk, M. & Zirngibl, M. (2006). 100 Gigabit Ethernet-applications, features, challenges. In *Proceedings IEEE INFOCOM 2006. 25TH IEEE International Conference on Computer Communications*, 23–29 April 2006, Barcelona, Spain (pp. 1–5). IEEE.

[22] Norris, M. (2003). *Gigabit Ethernet Technology and Applications*. Artech House, London, UK.

[23] Steinbach, T., Korf, F., & Schmidt, T. C. (2011). Real-time Ethernet for automotive applications: A solution for future in-car networks. In *2011 IEEE International Conference on Consumer Electronics-Berlin (ICCE-Berlin)*, 6–8 Sep. 2011, New York (pp. 216–220). IEEE.

[24] Piggin, R. & Brandt, D. (2006). Wireless ethernet for industrial applications. *Assembly Automation, 26*(3), 205–215.

[25] Hank, P., Müller, S., Vermesan, O., & Van Den Keybus, J. (2013). Automotive ethernet: In-vehicle networking and smart mobility. In *2013*

Design, Automation & Test in Europe Conference & Exhibition (DATE), 18–22 March 2013, Grenoble, France (pp. 1735–1739). IEEE.

[26] Sun, Y., Lingle, R., Inniss, D., & Shubochkin, R. (2021). High speed Ethernet transmission over multicore fibers for data center applications. In *2021 IEEE Photonics Conference (IPC)*, 18–21 Oct. 2021, Vancouver, BC, Canada (pp. 1–2).

[27] Udren, E. A., Vandiver, B., Anderson, J., Antonova, G., Apostolov, A., Beaumont, P., Beresh R., & Tengdin, J. T. (2021). Application of ethernet networking devices used for protection and control applications in electric power substations: Report of working group P6 of the power system communications and cybersecurity committee of the power and energy society of IEEE. In *2021 74th Conference for Protective Relay Engineers (CPRE)*, 22–25 March 2021, College Station, TX (pp. 1–88). IEEE.

[28] IEEE Standard for Ethernet Amendment 1: Physical Layer Specifications and Management Parameters for 100 Mb/s Operation over a Single Balanced Twisted Pair Cable (100BASE-T1). IEEE, NewYork.

[29] ISO/IEC/IEEE International Standard — Information technology — Telecommunications and information exchange between systems — Local and metropolitan area networks — Specific requirements — Part 3: Standard for Ethernet Amendment 4: Physical Layer Specifications and Management Parameters for 1 Gb/s Operation over a Single Twisted-Pair Copper Cable. In ISO/IEC/IEEE 8802-3:2017/Amd.4:2017(E), 8 March 2018, New York (pp. 1–214). IEEE. doi: 10.1109/IEEESTD.2018.8314566.

[30] IEEE Standard for Ethernet Amendment 7: Media Access Control Parameters, Physical Layers, and Management Parameters for 2.5 Gb/s and 5 Gb/s Operation, Types 2.5GBASE-T and 5GBASE-T.

[31] Hiertz, G. R., Denteneer, D., Stibor, L., Zang, Y., Costa, X. P., & Walke, B. (2010). The IEEE 802.11 universe. *IEEE Communications Magazine*, *48*(1), 62–70.

[32] IEEE Standard for Information technology — Local and metropolitan area networks — Specific requirements — Part 11: Wireless LAN Medium Access Control (MAC) and Physical Layer (PHY) Specifications Amendment 5: Enhancements for Higher Throughput.

[33] IEEE Standard for Information technology — Telecommunications and information exchange between systems–Local and metropolitan area networks — Specific requirements — Part 11: Wireless LAN Medium Access Control (MAC) and Physical Layer (PHY) Specifications — Amendment 4: Enhancements for Very High Throughput for Operation in Bands below 6 GHz.

[34] IEEE Standard for Information Technology — Telecommunications and Information Exchange between Systems Local and Metropolitan Area Networks — Specific Requirements Part 11: Wireless LAN Medium

Access Control (MAC) and Physical Layer (PHY) Specifications Amendment 1: Enhancements for High-Efficiency WLAN.

[35] IEEE 802.11b-1999: IEEE Standard for Information Technology — Telecommunications and Information exchange between systems — Local and Metropolitan networks — Specific requirements — Part 11: Wireless LAN Medium Access Control (MAC) and Physical Layer (PHY) specifications: Higher Speed Physical Layer (PHY) Extension in the 2.4 GHz band.

[36] IEEE 802.11 g Working Group. (2003). IEEE 802.11 g-2003-further higher data rate extension in the 2.4 GHz band.

[37] Sun, W., Lee, O., Shin, Y., Kim, S., Yang, C., Kim, H., & Choi, S. (2014). Wi-Fi could be much more. *IEEE Communications Magazine, 52*(11), 22–29.

[38] Velayos, H. & Karlsson, G. (2004). Techniques to reduce the IEEE 802.11 b handoff time. In *2004 IEEE International Conference on Communications (IEEE Cat. No. 04CH37577)*, June, Paris (Vol. 7, pp. 3844–3848). IEEE.

[39] Doufexi, A., Armour, S., Butler, M., Nix, A., Bull, D., McGeehan, J., & Karlsson, P. (2002). A comparison of the HIPERLAN/2 and IEEE 802.11 a wireless LAN standards. *IEEE Communications Magazine, 40*(5), 172–180.

[40] Vassis, D., Kormentzas, G., Rouskas, A., & Maglogiannis, I. (2005). The IEEE 802.11 g standard for high data rate WLANs. *IEEE Network, 19*(3), 21–26.

[41] Perahia, E. (2008). IEEE 802.11 n development: History, process, and technology. *IEEE Communications Magazine, 46*(7), 48–55.

[42] Kaewkiriya, T. (2017). Performance comparison of Wi-Fi IEEE 802.11ac and Wi-Fi IEEE 802.11n. In *2017 2nd International Conference on Communication Systems, Computing and IT Applications (CSCITA)* (pp. 235–240). Doi: 10.1109/CSCITA.2017.8066560.

[43] Khorov, E., Kiryanov, A., Lyakhov, A., & Bianchi, G. (2018). A tutorial on IEEE 802.11 ax high efficiency WLANs. *IEEE Communications Surveys & Tutorials, 21*(1), 197–216.

[44] Wang, P., Zhang, M., Bai, Z., Guo, H., & Tan, E. K. (2021). Wi-Fi 6E test challenges on ATE. In *2021 China Semiconductor Technology International Conference (CSTIC)*, March, Shanghai, China (pp. 1–4). IEEE.

[45] Garcia-Rodriguez, A., Lopez-Perez, D., Galati-Giordano, L., & Geraci, G. (2021). IEEE 802.11 be: Wi-Fi 7 strikes back. *IEEE Communications Magazine, 59*(4), 102–108.

[46] Pahlavan, K. & Krishnamurthy, P. (2021). Evolution and impact of Wi-Fi technology and applications: A historical perspective. *International Journal of Wireless Information Networks, 28*(1), 3–19.

[47] Loukatos, D. & Arvanitis, K. G. (2019). Extending smart phone based techniques to provide AI flavored interaction with DIY robots, over Wi-Fi and LoRa interfaces. *Education Sciences*, *9*(3), 224.

[48] Tseng, C. L., Cheng, C. S., Hsu, Y. H., & Yang, B. H. (2018). "An IoT-based home automation system using Wi-Fi wireless sensor networks. In *2018 IEEE International Conference on Systems, Man, and Cybernetics (SMC)*, 7–10 Oct. 2018, Miyazaki, Japan (pp. 2430–2435). IEEE.

[49] Ding, Y. R. & Cheng, Y. J. (2019). A tri-band shared-aperture antenna for (2.4, 5.2) GHz Wi-Fi application with MIMO function and 60 GHz Wi-Gig application with beam-scanning function. *IEEE Transactions on Antennas and Propagation*, *68*(3), 1973–1981.

[50] Deng, C., Fang, X., Han, X., Wang, X., Yan, L., He, R., Long, Y., & Guo, Y. (2020). IEEE 802.11 be Wi-Fi 7: New challenges and opportunities. *IEEE Communications Surveys & Tutorials*, *22*(4), 2136–2166.

[51] Zhao, J., Chen, K., Yuan, Z., & Lu, S. (2019). High-performance intelligent Wi-Fi multicast for VR/AR applications.

[52] Maldonado, R., Karstensen, A., Pocovi, G., Esswie, A. A., Rosa, C., Alanen, O., Kasslin, M., & Kolding, T. (2021). Comparing Wi-Fi 6 and 5G downlink performance for industrial IoT. *IEEE Access*, *9*, 86928–86937.

[53] Bhandari, N., Devra, S., & Singh, K. (2017). Evolution of cellular network: From 1G to 5G. *International Journal of Engineering and Techniques*, *3*(5), 98–105.

[54] Fülöp, A. & Horváth, A. (2021). Application of cellular neural networks in semantic segmentation. In *2021 IEEE International Symposium on Circuits And Systems (ISCAS)*, 22–28 May 2021, Daegu, Korea (pp. 1–5). IEEE.

[55] Bakare, B. I., Abayeh, O. J., & Orike, S. (2022). Application of frequency reuse technique for the management of interference in cellular network in Port Harcourt. *American Journal of Engineering Research*, *11*(1), 16–24.

[56] Zhang, K., Chuai, G., Zhang, J., Chen, X., Si, Z., & Maimaiti, S. (2022). DIC-ST: A hybrid prediction framework based on causal structure learning for cellular traffic and its application in urban computing. *Remote Sensing*, *14*(6), 1439.

[57] Wang, W., Zhu, K., Liu, J., Hu, J., Raganvan, V., Xu, J., & Song, X. (2022). Traffic speed mapping with cellular network signaling data by FOSS4G. *Spatial Information Research*, *30*(1), 131–142.

[58] da Cunha Rodrigues, G., Calheiros, R. N., Guimaraes, V. T., Santos, G. L. D., De Carvalho, M. B., Granville, L. Z., Rockenbach Tarouco, L. M., & Buyya, R. (2016). Monitoring of cloud computing environments: Concepts, solutions, trends, and future directions. In *Proceedings of the 31st Annual ACM Symposium on Applied Computing*, 4–8 April 2016, Pisa, Italy (pp. 378–383).

[59] Buyya, R., Broberg, J., & Goscinski, A. M. (Eds.) (2010). *Cloud Computing: Principles and Paradigms.* John Wiley & Sons, Hoboken, NJ.

[60] Buyya, R., Vecchiola, C., & Selvi, S. T. (2013). *Mastering Cloud Computing: Foundations and Applications Programming.* Newnes, Southampton Street, London.

[61] Sumina, V. 26 cloud computing statistics, facts & trends for 2022. Cloudwards. Available at: https://www.cloudwards.net/cloud-computing-statistics/#:~:text=With%20an%20overwhelming%2094.44%20percent, and%20iCloud%20(38.89%20percent) (Accessed on 28 July 2022).

[62] Simovic, D. The ultimate list of remote work statistics-2022 edition. Available at: https://www.smallbizgenius.net/by-the-numbers/remote-work-statistics/#gref. (Last accessed on 28 July 2022).

[63] Böhm, M., Leimeister, S., Riedl, C. H. R. I. S. T. O. P. H., & Krcmar, H. (2010). Cloud computing and computing evolution. *Technische Universität München (TUM).* Germany.

[64] Varghese, B. & Buyya, R. (2018). Next generation cloud computing: New trends and research directions. *Future Generation Computer Systems, 79,* 849–861.

[65] Bo, Y. & Wang, H. (2011). The application of cloud computing and the internet of things in agriculture and forestry. In *2011 International Joint Conference on Service Sciences,* 25–27 May 2011, Taipei, Taiwan (pp. 68–172). IEEE.

[66] Wang, B. & Xing, H. (2011). The application of cloud computing in education informatization. In *2011 International Conference on Computer Science and Service System (CSSS),* June, Nanjing, China (pp. 2673–2676). IEEE.

[67] Vinoth, S., Vemula, H. L., Haralayya, B., Mamgain, P., Hasan, M. F., & Naved, M. (2022). Application of cloud computing in banking and e-commerce and related security threats. *Materials Today: Proceedings, 51,* 2172–2175.

[68] Chen, C. L., Huang, P. T., Deng, Y. Y., Chen, H. C., & Wang, Y. C. (2020). A secure electronic medical record authorization system for smart device application in cloud computing environments. *Human-centric Computing and Information Sciences, 10*(1), 1–31.

[69] Sun, L., Jiang, X., Ren, H., & Guo, Y. (2020). Edge-cloud computing and artificial intelligence in internet of medical things: Architecture, technology and application. *IEEE Access, 8,* 101079–101092.

[70] Aksoy, B. & Salman, O. K. M. (2021). Detection of COVID-19 disease in chest X-ray images with capsul networks: Application with cloud computing. *Journal of Experimental & Theoretical Artificial Intelligence, 33*(3), 527–541.

[71] Kanimozhi Suguna, S. & Nanda Kumar, S. (2019). Application of cloud computing and internet of things to improve supply chain processes. In *Edge Computing* (pp. 145–170). Springer, Cham.

[72] Son, J. & Buyya, R. (2018). A taxonomy of software-defined networking (SDN)-enabled cloud computing. *ACM Computing Surveys (CSUR)*, *51*(3), 1–36.

[73] Padhy, R. P. & Patra, M. R. (2012). Evolution of cloud computing and enabling technologies. *International Journal of Cloud Computing and Services Science*, *1*(4), 182.

[74] Mrabet, H., Belguith, S., Alhomoud, A., & Jemai, A. (2020). A survey of IoT security based on a layered architecture of sensing and data analysis. *Sensors*, *20*(13), 3625.

[75] Minerva, R., Biru, A., & Rotondi, D. (2015). Towards a definition of the Internet of Things (IoT). *IEEE Internet Initiative*, *1*(1), 1–86.

[76] Wang, J., Lim, M. K., Wang, C., & Tseng, M. L. (2021). The evolution of the Internet of Things (IoT) over the past 20 years. *Computers & Industrial Engineering*, *155*, 107174.

[77] Abuagoub, A. M. (2019). IoT security evolution: Challenges and counter-measures review. *International Journal of Communication Networks and Information Security*, *11*(3), 342–351.

[78] Evolution of Internet of Things (IoT): Past, present and future, Techahead. Available at : https://www.techaheadcorp.com/knowledge-center/evolution-of iot/#:~:text=The%20evolution%20of%20IoT%20started,internet%20 of%20things%20was%20paved (Accessed on 28 July 2022).

[79] Hassan, W. H. (2019). Current research on Internet of Things (IoT) security: A survey. *Computer Networks*, *148*, 283–294.

[80] Lee, S. K., Bae, M., & Kim, H. (2017). Future of IoT networks: A survey. *Applied Sciences*, *7*(10), 1072.

[81] Moyer, S. & Umar, A. (2001). The impact of network convergence on telecommunications software. *IEEE Communications Magazine*, *39*(1), 78–84.

[82] Hanrahan, H. (2007). *Network Convergence: Services, Applications, Transport, and Operations Support*. John Wiley & Sons, Hoboken, NJ.

[83] Tiao-Wei, Y. U. A. N., Jin-Bei, Z. H. A. N. G., & Jian-Bei, Y. A. O. (2010). Present status and development of network convergence. *Journal of Beijing University of Posts and Telecommunications*, *33*(6), 1.

[84] Gaber, A., ElBahaay, M. A., Mohamed, A. M., Zaki, M. M., Abdo, A. S., & AbdelBaki, N. (2020). 5G and satellite network convergence: Survey for opportunities, challenges and enabler technologies. In *2020 2nd Novel Intelligent and Leading Emerging Sciences Conference (NILES)*, 24–26 Oct. 2020, Giza, Egypt (pp. 366–373). IEEE.

[85] Evans, D. (2004). An introduction to unified communications: Challenges and opportunities. In *Aslib Proceedings*, October (Vol. 56, no. 5, pp. 308–314). Emerald Group Publishing Limited.

[86] Baraković Husić, J., Baraković, S., Cero, E., Slamnik, N., Oćuz, M., Dedović, A., & Zupčić, O. (2020). Quality of experience for unified communications: A survey. *International Journal of Network Management*, *30*(3), e2083.

[87] Gupta, B. B., Perez, G. M., Agrawal, D. P., & Gupta, D. (2020). *Handbook of Computer Networks and Cyber Security* (Vol. 10, pp. 978–983). Springer, New York.

[88] Sharma, K. & Gupta, B. B. (2018). Taxonomy of distributed denial of service (DDoS) attacks and defense mechanisms in present era of smartphone devices. *International Journal of E-Services and Mobile Applications (IJESMA)*, *10*(2), 58–74.

[89] Gupta, B. B. & Badve, O. P. (2017). GARCH and ANN-based DDoS detection and filtering in cloud computing environment. *International Journal of Embedded Systems*, *9*(5), 391–400.

[90] Stergiou, C., Psannis, K. E., Kim, B. G., & Gupta, B. (2018). Secure integration of IoT and cloud computing. *Future Generation Computer Systems*, *78*, 964–975.

[91] Plageras, A. P., Psannis, K. E., Stergiou, C., Wang, H., & Gupta, B. B. (2018). Efficient IoT-based sensor BIG data collection–processing and analysis in smart buildings. *Future Generation Computer Systems*, *82*, 349–357.

[92] Chui, K. T., Arya, V., Peraković, D., & Alhalabi, W. (2023). A novel attack detection technique to protect AR-based IoT devices from DDoS attacks. In *International Conference on Cyber Security, Privacy and Networking (ICSPN 2022)*, February (pp. 361–373). Springer International Publishing, Cham.

[93] Gaurav, A., Psannis, K., & Peraković, D. (2022). Security of cloud-based medical internet of things (miots): A survey. *International Journal of Software Science and Computational Intelligence (IJSSCI)*, *14*(1), 1–16.

[94] Sharma, S. & Singh, S. K. (2022). IoT and its uses in security surveillance. Insights2Techinfo, p.1. Available at: https://insights2techinfo.com/iot-and-its-uses-in-security-surveillance/.

[95] Bhatnagar, R. & Sinha, D. (2021). Smart adoption of IoT in COVID-19 pandemic paves new era of sustainable future world. Insights2Techinfo, p. 1. Available at: https://insights2techinfo.com/smart-adoption-of-iot-in-covid-19-pandemic-paves-new-era-of-sustainable-future-world/.

Chapter 2

Introduction to Networking Concepts

In this chapter, we showcase the data plane, control plane, and management plane, which offer background on the core ideas behind contemporary state-of-the-art Internet switches. These ideas are crucial to comprehending how SDN executes these essential operations in a way that differs significantly from traditional switch architecture. We also cover how forwarding decisions of data packets are made in current Internet implementations and how this condition restricts the administrator to adapt to the network according to the constantly changing conditions. Then, how the separation of control and data planes addresses the above-mentioned issue is also illustrated.

2.1 Packet Switching

This section defines basic packet switching terminologies, which help the reader in understanding how SDN evolves and how it is different from traditional networking. First, we discuss the types of networks, the OSI model and its related terminologies.

A wide area network (WAN) is a computer network that spans a vast geographic area, often more than one metropolitan area [1, 2]. A local area network (LAN) is a computer network that covers a small geographic area, i.e., a few thousand square metres [3, 4]. A metropolitan area network (MAN), which is larger than a LAN, is geographically even smaller than a WAN [5, 6]. A wireless local area network (WLAN) is a collection of co-located computers or other devices that form a network via radio signals as opposed to conventional or physical connections. A Wi-Fi network is a sort of WLAN.

The open systems interconnection (OSI) model is the conceptual framework that contains a set of protocols and is used to describe the working of a networking system, i.e., how a packet travels from one node to another [7, 8]. This model has seven layers in which the lowest layer is the physical layer that deals with hardware specifications for data transfer. In this layer, data travel through an electrical or an optical medium in the form of bits. Next, the data link layer which is the second lowest layer in the OSI model allows data to be transferred from one computer to another within a LAN. Multiple network segments are connected via repeaters to form a single LAN segment. This data link layer is divided into two parts: the logical link control (LLC) layer and the medium access control (MAC) layer [9]. The LLC layer is responsible for finding out sequencing and bit errors, in the bit transmission, occurring in the physical layer. It is also responsible for flow control and multiplexing to allow multiple protocols to work smoothly within a single multiple access point network. On the other hand, the MAC layer is responsible for managing medium access by multiple devices. A cable wire carries data to and from several computers. Now, if multiple signals travel at the same time on a single wire, then collision would occur, resulting in data loss [10]. This problem is resolved by the MAC layer by detecting collision and managing medium access through carrier sense multiple access with collision detection (CSMA/CD) mechanism.

Now, the next layer is the network layer that actually sends and receives data through multiple intermediate networks [7]. This is the layer where the Internet comes into the picture via the router. It is responsible for routing and forwarding data packets across the network. Next, a port is a virtual point where network connections begin and stop. Ports are software managed by the operating system of a computer. A process or service is coupled with each port. Emails, for example, use a different port than webpages, despite the fact that they both reach a computer via the same Internet connection [11, 12].

A frame is the unit of data transferred on layer 2. A packet is the unit of data transferred on layer 3. A packet is always the payload of a frame when the distinction is needed. A MAC address, also known as a media access control address, is a unique identifier issued to network interface cards (NICs) and is used to identify an equipment globally. It is sometimes referred to as a physical or hardware address usually used at layer 2 [13].

An IP address is the unique identifier used in communication based on the Internet Protocol (IP) at layer 3. The original IP is IPv4 in which the IP address is 32 bits. IPv6 is the new protocol offering 128 bits long IP addresses with much larger address space than IPv4 [14, 15].

A switch is a networking device operated at layer 2 and is used to expand a LAN. A switch has multiple ports to which computers are connected and when a data packet arrives at a port, the switch checks the destination MAC address before forwarding it [16]. Circuit switching is a switching mechanism in which data travel through a dedicated communication line. Resources along the path are reserved for the circuit for the entire duration of the connection [17]. In packet switching, every data packet is considered as an individual packet and is allowed to take its own path to reach its destination [18]. Packet switching can be of two types: connection-oriented and connectionless. In connection-oriented data transfer, there is some kind of contextual information related to a particular connection present in intermediate switches, which is used to forward the data packet [19]. Circuit switching can be considered as an example of connection-oriented data transfer. In the connectionless paradigm, there is no such contextual information present at switches, i.e., there is no reservation of resources. Every packet tends to travel independent of the path taken by other data packets belonging to the same connection.

A router is a layer 3 device that is responsible for data transfer between LANs and WANs, and tends to forward the data packets by checking its IP address.

2.2 Conventional Switch Architecture

In this section, we discuss the traditional switch architecture and what factors contributed to the evolution of this traditional switch to today's modern complex switch architecture. First, we discuss networking planes and their three types, including data, control and management planes.

2.2.1 Introduction to Networking Planes

There exist three dimensions to a network called planes: data, control and management planes [20, 21]. It is very important to understand these terminologies to comprehend the evolution of traditional switch architecture to the SDN-enabled modern switch architecture. Following are the three types of networking planes [22]:

1. **Data plane:** The data plane is in command of all of the various aspects of message forwarding. The data plane is commonly referred to as the forwarding plane as it involves receiving, processing, and forwarding information. The data are forwarded according to the information fed by the network administrator into the lookup tables. Encrypting traffic, network address translation, traffic filtering with ACLs, and encapsulating and decapsulating as packets transit up and down the OSI model are all functions here [23]. The control plane directs the data plane to the port to which data are forwarded. The response time of a switch depends on the line speed.
2. **Control plane:** The control plane is where all of the decisions are made. It includes routing protocols, STP, IPv4 ARP, IPv6 neighbour node discovery and learning MAC addresses. It refers to the methods used to manage the data flow or how the device determines where information should be forwarded. Parameters like quality of service (QoS) and virtual LANs are implemented on this plane. It need not be operated at line speed.
3. **Management plane:** We can configure and monitor the network device in the management plane (e.g., switch or router). A shell, command-line interface (CLI), or web interface can be used to configure the switch. The management plane and the control plane are normally on the same processor.

2.2.2 Traditional Switch Architecture

A traditional non-SDN switch is composed of the following components: transceiver, application-specific integrated circuit (ASIC), layer 2 and layer 3 tables. Apart from these, certain functions have been added to provide better isolation of the network traffic, for example, virtual LANs (VLANs), virtual routing functions (VRF), access control and QoS [24]. These features have been configured at the manufacturing side according to the requirements of the client. New features like VLANs or virtual networking functions (VNFs), such as access management, QoS, and port groups, have been added for greater isolation of hosts or virtualised machines to meet the demands of virtualised servers and so on.

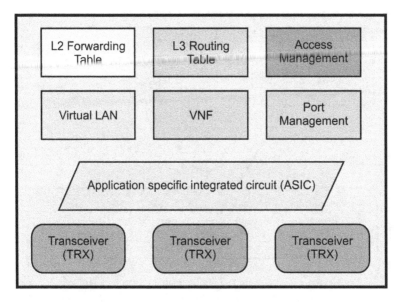

Figure 2.1. Traditional non-SDN switch architecture.

The majority of these functionalities must be adjusted manually and in varying ways for different providers [25, 71, 72]. Figure 2.1 shows the traditional non-SDN switch architecture in a more detailed way.

Now, we examine the integration of traditional non-SDN switches with the networking planes. The transceivers and ASIC together form a data plane. The processor hosts the control plane as well as the management plane. Now, if a packet arrives at the switch, then the packet is first handled by the data plane where the forwarding rules of the packet will be searched according to the header information [26]. If there exists some rule that matches the header information, then the packet will be forwarded to the corresponding port stored. If no match is found, the packet is transferred to the control plane for routing (layer 3) before being forwarded again by the data plane to the appropriate output port. Following that, the control plane inserts the new forwarding rule into the layer 2 forwarding table, making subsequent similar packets to be sent at wire speed with no delay [27]. Figure 2.2 shows different planes in a generic switch.

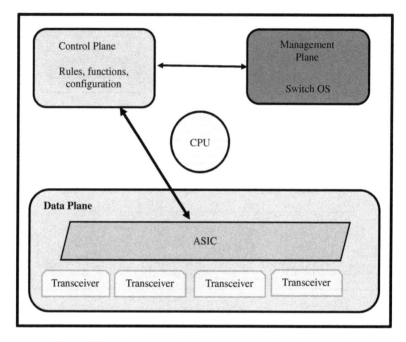

Figure 2.2.   Data, control and management planes in a switch.

Now, we look at what will happen to a switch when a new packet arrives. The process a newly arrived packet goes through can be seen in Figure 2.3. Following are the important steps:

1. A new packet arrives at the input port and gets stored in the buffer.
2. The data plane does not find any forwarding rule regarding this packet and hence forwards this to the control plane.
3. The control plane receives the packet from the data plane and starts processing it for the routing function.
4. Afterwards, when the control function goes through all calculations regarding packet routing and forwarding, i.e., it comes up with the output port and stores this information to ternary content-addressable memory (TCAM) for fast lookup so that the next packet belonging to the same connection need not go through the control plane.
5. The data plane retrieves the rule stored by the control plane and applies it on the packet.
6. The data plane now forwards this packet to the intended output port.
7. The output port then transfers the packet over the route.

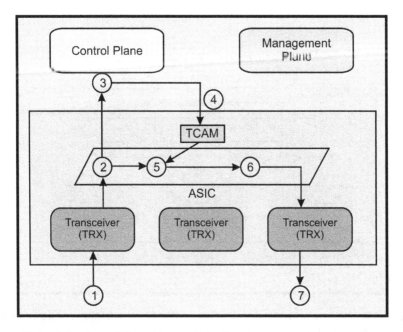

Figure 2.3.   Steps followed by a switch when a new network packet arrives.

Now, we see what happens to a subsequent data packet coming from a stored connection with a known forwarding rule, as shown in Figure 2.4.

1. The packet arrived.
2. It will get matched with the rules stored in TCAM.
3. The data plane will forward the packet to the output port.
4. The output port then transfers the packet over the route.

In the late 1980s, the advent of the Internet as a viable commercial network was a strong platform for the commercial networking sector. By this time, routers are not limited to serving military and research purposes only; commercial routers had started to come into the market. Cisco and many other start-ups were taking the lead and trying to provide customised routers to the clients. Meanwhile, continuous research was being made to improvise connection-oriented packet switching, such as X.25 and ATM and connectionless Internet architecture. Eventually, the connectionless router triumphed in the packet switching realm.

Prior to this, there existed general-purpose software-based routers operated by Unix machines that analysed a packet arriving on one

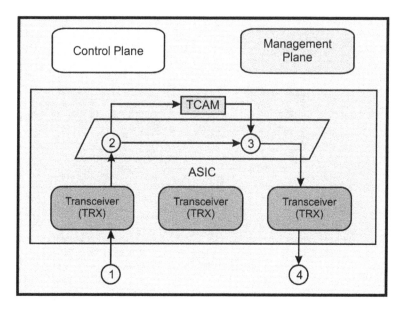

Figure 2.4.   Steps followed by a switch when a network packet from a known forwarding rule arrives.

interface and sought up the destination IP address by looking into a data type that could be searched efficiently, i.e., hierarchical tree structure. This data structure had been named as the routing table [28]. The packet would be delivered on the designated outgoing interface based on the entry found during this search. Instead of being routed through the routing table, control data packets would be routed to the proper Unix control processes [29]. Apart from layer 3 routers, layer 2 bridges were also a very predominant technology in the networking domain. Bridges are layer 2 hardware devices used to create bridged LAN networks.

2.3 Packet Forwarding

ASICs are major hardware-driven utilities in the packet switching and forwarding domain. This is in sharp contrast to a central processing unit (CPU) or even a graphics processing unit (GPU). A CPU is developed and manufactured for general-purpose processing and can handle a wide range of tasks. On the other hand, computer graphics workloads are accelerated by GPUs [30]. ASICs, unlike CPUs and GPUs, are designed with a specific purpose in mind. Google tensor processing units (TPU), which are used to accelerate machine learning operations, are excellent examples [31]. ASICs only contain the hardware elements necessary for their purpose, their total size and power consumption can be decreased. The disadvantage is that you must embed many of your features in hardware, and whenever a new technology or specification emerges, any chips designed without it will be unable to support it (VXLAN, for example).

In networking, ASICs are in charge of packet switching and routing as well as serving as the first line of defence (in the form of a stateless firewall). Fast memory access is a significant challenge due to the sheer speed with which packets are exchanged [32]. TCAM is a type of memory that will be used in most ASICs. Lookup tables of various types will be stored in this memory. These tables could be forwarding tables (where does this packet go?), ACL tables (is this packet authorised?), or CoS tables (class of service) tables (which priority should be given to this packet?) [33]. Content-addressable memory (CAM) and its more evolved version, TCAM, are the types of memory that operate in ways that are very different from regular random access memory (RAM). A memory address is needed to access data in RAM, CAM and TCAM to allow direct access to the information. It is the physical embodiment of a key-value store [34].

Initially, a switch is used to distinguish hardware-based lookup, i.e., the bridge at layer 2 from the software-based lookup tables, i.e., the router at layer 3. Even today, routers are still used in software form because ASICs are not capable enough to perform packet header modification required for layer 3 switching. Moreover, address lookup at layer 2 is more straightforward relatively as only a 48-bit MAC address needs to be considered for packet switching. However, CAM capabilities steadily increased, and within a few years, there were layer 3 routers capable of hardware lookup of the destination layer 3 address. The line between router and switch began to fade at this point, and the terms "layer 2 switch" and "layer 3 switch" became commonplace.

2.4 Evolution of Forwarding Rules

Many packets that must be processed by a switch require more complex treatment than merely being sent to a different interface than the one from which they originated. This can be resolved by pushing more intelligence towards the forwarding plane so that packets can be processed at the line rate [35–37]. In the traditional networking architecture, routers tend to decrement the time to live (TTL) field as well as swap the MAC address embedded in the IP packet with the MAC address of the next hop. Further, the packet needs to be replicated multiple times in case of broadcast and multicast. With time, switches evolve to support technologies like VLAN and it requires more complex header information to get processed. In this scenario, programmable switches come into picture where some of the complex information processing can be encoded as rules in the forwarding table so that incoming packets can be forwarded at the line rate.

2.4.1 Static and Dynamic Forwarding Tables

In this section, we discuss how the forwarding table at layer 2 is different from the same at layer 3. What are the major challenges in both layers and what are the state-of-the-art protocols that have been proposed to resolve the issues?

2.4.1.1 *Layer 2 Forwarding Table*

A layer 2 forwarding table is a lookup table that is referenced by the destination MAC address and specifies which switch port will be used to forward the packet [39–41]. A layer 2 switch can learn the MAC address in two ways: statically and dynamically.

First, we discuss static learning of MAC addresses by layer 2 switch. The switch learns and maintains the MAC addresses of all connected devices in order to make accurate forwarding and filtering decisions. The learnt MAC addresses are saved in a table known as the CAM table on the switch. Earlier, when bridges are used to connect two LAN segments [41]. When the first frame is received for the first time on a specific interface, the switch can learn the sender's MAC address and location, and update its forwarding table accordingly. When the frame designated for that address comes up, it might utilise the forwarding table to route it to the appropriate port. If the bridge receives an unknown destination MAC address, it can send it out over all interfaces, knowing that it will be dropped on all connected networks except the one where it has been received [42]. This approach cannot be used in the situation where multiple bridges are connected to form a network of inter-connected bridges.

Moreover, bridges are replaced by switches [43]. In the static learning of MAC addresses, the network admin has to add the MAC addresses manually. On the other hand, in the dynamic option, the switch learns the MAC address automatically as soon as the packet arrives.

If the switch cannot find an entry for the source MAC address, it generates a new entry in the table. An entry includes three components: the source MAC address, the port or interface on which the frame came up, and the time when the frame arrived. If the switch discovers an entry for the source MAC address, it updates it and resets the timer for that entry. Each entry in the CAM table is assigned a timer by the switch [44]. This timer is used to remove old entries from the CAM table, freeing up space for new entries. The switch can no longer store new addresses once the CAM table is full. This problem is solved by removing old entries from the CAM table automatically. It keeps the MAC addresses of the devices that are constantly sending the frames.

Layer 2 switching is prone to switching loops as there is no field like TTL in MAC header that determines the fixed number of hops to be passed to reach the destination. It is very important to avoid switching loops as it renders the network to a complete deadlock and resources are wasted in forwarding a packing in the loop again and again [45]. Moreover, broadcasting at layer 2 worsens the situation even more as many control frames need to be sent to all MAC addresses in a network and it gets received again by the switch that had already broadcasted it. This problem is solved by the spanning tree protocol (STP) specified in IEEE 802.1D [46, 47], in which loops are prevented by forwarding all packets through a spanning tree, i.e., from the source MAC address (root) to every destination MAC address (leaf). With time and advancements in technology, many protocols have been proposed to resolve the same issue, namely, Shortest Path Bridging (SPB) [48] and the Transparent Interconnection of Lots of Links (TRILL) [50, 51] protocols.

2.4.1.2 *Layer 3 Forwarding Table*

Unlike layer 2 forwarding table which finds out the MAC address or a specific device to which the packet is directed, layer 3 routing table is the lookup table that finds out the network address to which the packet should be forwarded [52]. All hosts in a destination network have the same network address in the router's forwarding table. Static or dynamic routes are listed in this table. The router looks for the destination IP address in the IP routing table when an IP packet arrives [53, 54]. If the target IP isn't identified in the table, the packet is dropped unless the router is programmed with the default route.

A layer 3 switch works in the same way as the router as it has the same IP routing table for lookups. However, it is still somewhat different from the router in the following ways [55, 56]:

- Layer 3 switch appears like a switch as it contains more than 24 ethernet ports with no WAN interface.
- If the devices are on the same network, then layer 3 switch will act like a switch.
- A layer 3 switch functions like a switch with built-in routing intelligence.

In other words, we can say that layer 3 switch is a high-speed router only with no WAN interfaces or ports. Here, the question arises as to why would we want to embed the routing functionality in a switch when we don't have WAN connectivity. Layer 3 switch's routing functionality is used to route traffic between multiple subnets or VLANs on a campus LAN or any other big LAN [57, 58]. As a result, layer 3 switch is best suited for large Ethernet networks that require subnetting into smaller networks. VLANs are commonly used to do this. In the following, we discuss the differences between layer 3 switch and router:

- **Hardware:** Layer 3 switching can be divided into two categories: hardware and software. An ASIC (a dedicated chip) is used to accomplish the function in a hardware-based solution. On the contrary, with software implementation, the device performs the function using a computer processor and some built-in functions or scripts. In general, layer 3 switches and high-end routers employ hardware (ASICs) to route packets, whereas general-purpose routers use software. Layer 3 switches integrate the hardware of traditional switches and routers, enhancing some of the router's software logic with integrated circuit technology to improve the data transfer for LAN.
- **Interfaces:** The next difference lies in the number and type of interface supported. An L3 switch supports interfaces like ethernet (RJ45) and single or multimode fibre. A router, on the other hand, has a wider range of possibilities, such as SDH, SONET, E1/T1, and so on. Furthermore, switches were simply LAN devices, while routers connected the LAN to the WAN.

- **Working principle:** The layer 3 switch examines the destination host's MAC address and sends the frame solely to that address. While a router uses the target IP address, it can perform tasks such as IP address assignment (DHCP) and firewall filtering in addition to packet routing [59]. Table 2.1 shows the comparison between layer 3 switch and router.

We discuss various types of routing protocols in Table 2.2.

The protocols we have compared in Table 2.2 are just the tip of the iceberg. There co-exist numerous control protocols, some of which are standard and some others proprietary, which are used to bombard the control plane of the switch or the router at the same time with so much data [65, 66]. A modern router will very certainly support LDP [16] for transferring information about MPLS labels as well as IGMP [68], MSDP [69], and PIM [70] for multicast routing in addition to those already mentioned.

Table 2.1. Comparison between layer 3 switch and router.

Feature	Layer 3 Switch	Router
Main functionality	Routes on a campus LAN that connect distinct subnets or VLANs	A router communicates and routes across different WANs
Scope	LANs for campus, office and data centre	WANs for campus, office and data centre
Routing table size	Small	Comparatively large
Network boundary technologies support	Not supported	Firewalls, NAT, tunnelling, IPSec
Supported interfaces	Ethernet	Ethernet ports (copper/fibre), interfaces like SONT, OC-N, T1/T3, etc.
Forwarding decision	Embedded in ASICs	Software logic
Switching capacity	Very high	Comparatively lower
Throughput	Very high	Comparatively lower
Port density	High	Low
WAN support	No	Yes
QoS features	No	Yes
Traffic management	Yes	Yes

Table 2.2.   Comparative analysis of various routing protocols.

Features	RIP [60]	IGRP [61]	EIGRP	OSPF [62]	IS-IS [63]	BGP [64]
Deployment point	Interior	Interior	Interior	Interior	Interior	Exterior
Type	Distance vector	Distance vector	Hybrid	Link-state	Link-state	Path-vector
Metric	Hop (max 15)	Bandwidth and delay (hop count 100, max hop count: 224)	Bandwidth and delay	Cost	Cost	Path attributes (usually AS-Path)
Administrative distance	120	100	5 (summary) 90 (internal) 170 (external)	110	115	200 (internal) 20 (external)
Convergence	Slow	Slow	Very fast	Fast	Fast	Average
Routing updates	Every 30 seconds Full table Multicast address: 224.0.0.9	Every 90 seconds Full Table Broadcast: 224.0.0.10	Multicast address: 224.0.0.10 Or unicast only when any change occurs	Only when change occurs. Multicast address: 224.0.0.5-6	Only when there is a change in the network	Unicast updates and that too when change occurs in the system
Classless	Yes	No	Yes	Yes	Yes	Yes
VLSM support	Yes	No	Yes	Yes	Yes	Yes
Algorithm	Bellman–Ford	Bellman–Ford	Diffusing update algorithm (DUAL)	Dijkstra	Dijkstra	Best path selection
Scalability	No	Yes, to an extent	Yes	Less scalable	Less scalable	Highly scalable
Routing loop	Not protected	Prone to race conditions	Prone to race conditions	Protected against loops	Protected against loops	Protected against loops

These control protocols are distributed protocols, which means that they need time to converge to a set of consistent forwarding tables whenever an intentional change is made, such as the addition of a new server or the removal of a communications link. This can cause temporary chaos within the data centre. It is a matter of fact that today scalability of the network is much more than the size of the network these protocols are designed for and these protocols take a very large time to converge to a stable state of the network. Therefore, network management with these protocols is a nightmare, and moreover, data centre networking with virtualisation is an altogether different domain where VMs get created, merged and migrated within a few seconds. Thus, SDN emerged out of these desires, where it offers flexibility for the researchers to customise networking protocols as per the requirements.

Exercises

Q.1.   Discuss packet switching and how it differs from circuit switching.
Q.2.   Discuss the OSI reference model and functionalities of each layer.
Q.3.   How are the networking planes different in modern switch architecture than in traditional switch architecture?
Q.4.   Discuss why functionalities like virtual LANs (VLANs) and virtual routing functions are not possible in traditional switch architecture.
Q.5.   Discuss the steps followed by a switch when a new packet and a packet from a known connection entry arrive at the switch interface.
Q.6.   Discuss the various types of memories used for storing flow tables in a switch.
Q.7.   How is layer 2 forwarding different from layer 3 forwarding in a switch?
Q.8.   Discuss the differences between layer 3 router and switch.
Q.9.   Discuss the application of border gateway protocol (BGP) in cloud computing.
Q.10. Compare the various routing protocols along with their issues and deployment challenges.

References

[1] Cahn, R. (1998). *Wide Area Network Design: Concepts and Tools for Optimization*. Morgan Kaufmann, United States.

[2] Balakrishnan, H., Stemm, M., Seshan, S., & Katz, R. H. (1997). Analyzing stability in wide-area network performance. In *Proceedings of the 1997 ACM SIGMETRICS International Conference on Measurement and Modeling of Computer Systems*, June, Seattle, WA (pp. 2–12).

[3] Fowler, H. J., & Leland, W. E. (1991). Local area network characteristics, with implications for broadband network congestion management. *IEEE Journal on Selected Areas in Communications, 9*(7), 1139–1149.

[4] Boden, N. J., Cohen, D., Felderman, R. E., Kulawik, A. E., Seitz, C. L., Seizovic, J. N., & Su, W. K. (1995). Myrinet: A gigabit-per-second local area network. *IEEE Micro, 15*(1), 29–36.

[5] Sze, D. (1985). A metropolitan area network. *IEEE Journal on Selected Areas in Communications, 3*(6), 815–824.

[6] Cho, D. H., Song, J. H., Kim, M. S., & Han, K. J. (2005). Performance analysis of the IEEE 802.16 wireless metropolitan area network. In *First International Conference on Distributed Frameworks for Multimedia Applications*, 06–09 February, Besancon, France (pp. 130–136). IEEE.

[7] Stallings, W. (1987). *Handbook of Computer-communications Standards; Vol. 1: The Open Systems Interconnection (OSI) Model and OSI-related Standards*. Macmillan Publishing Co. Inc., United States.

[8] Alani, M. M. (2014). *Guide to OSI and TCP/IP Models*. Springer, United Germany.

[9] Black, U. (1993). *Data Link Protocols*. Prentice-Hall Inc., United States.

[10] Jurdak, R. (2007). Data link layer. In *Wireless Ad Hoc and Sensor Networks: A Cross-Layer Design Perspective* (pp. 17–44). Springer, United Germany.

[11] Saxena, P. (2014). OSI reference model — A seven layered architecture of OSI model. *International Journal of Research, 1*(10), 1145–1156.

[12] Zhao, Jinxiong, Jing Bai, Qin Zhang, Fan Yang, Zhiru Li, Xun Zhang, Xiaoqin Zhu, & Runqing Bai (2018). The discussion about mechanism of data transmission in the OSI model. In *2018 International Conference on Transportation & Logistics, Information & Communication, Smart City (TLICSC 2018)*, December (pp. 1–4). Atlantis Press.

[13] Cohe, D., Postel, J. B., & Rom, R. (1992). IP addressing and routing in a local wireless network. In *Proceedings IEEE INFOCOM'92: The Conference on Computer Communications*, 04–08 May, Florence, Italy (pp. 626–632). IEEE.

[14] Graham, B. (2001). *TCP/IP Addressing: Designing and Optimizing Your IP Addressing Scheme*. Morgan Kaufmann, United States.

[15] Semeria, C. (1996). Understanding IP addressing: Everything you ever wanted to know. NSD Marketing, 3Com Corporation.

[16] Fernández, P. M. (2003). Circuit switching in the internet (Doctoral dissertation, Stanford University).

[17] Broomell, G. & Heath, J. R. (1983). Classification categories and historical development of circuit switching topologies. *ACM Computing Surveys (CSUR)*, *15*(2), 95–133.

[18] Roberts, L. G. (1978). The evolution of packet switching. *Proceedings of the IEEE*, *66*(11), 1307–1313.

[19] Baran, P. (2002). The beginnings of packet switching: Some underlying concepts. *IEEE Communications Magazine*, *40*(7), 42–48.

[20] Nisar, K., Jimson, E. R., Hijazi, M. H. A., Welch, I., Hassan, R., Aman, A. H. M., Sodhro, A. H., Pirbhulal, S., & Khan, S. (2020). A survey on the architecture, application, and security of software defined networking: Challenges and open issues. *Internet of Things*, *12*, 100289.

[21] Haji, S. H., Zeebaree, S. R., Saeed, R. H., Ameen, S. Y., Shukur, H. M., Omar, N., Sadeeq, M. A. M., Ageed, Z. S., Ibrahim, I. M., & Yasin, H. M. (2021). Comparison of software defined networking with traditional networking. *Asian Journal of Research in Computer Science*, 1–18.

[22] Farrington, N., Rubow, E., & Vahdat, A. (2009). Data center switch architecture in the age of merchant silicon. In *2009 17th IEEE Symposium on High Performance Interconnects*, August, United States (pp. 93–102). IEEE.

[23] Chen, S., Chen, X., Yao, Z., Yang, J., Li, Y., & Wu, F. (2020). Evolving switch architecture toward accommodating in-network intelligence. *IEEE Communications Magazine*, *58*(1), 33–39.

[24] Lin, B. & Keslassy, I. (2010). The concurrent matching switch architecture. *IEEE/ACM Transactions on Networking*, *18*(4), 1330–1343.

[25] Vickers, R. & Wernik, M. (1988, 08–10 March). Evolution of switch architecture and technology. In *1988 International Zurich Seminar on Digital Communications-Mapping New Applications onto New Technologies. Proceedings*, 08–10 March, Zurich, Switzerland (pp. 185–190). IEEE.

[26] Kuo, F. C., Chang, Y. K., & Su, C. C. (2013). A memory-efficient TCAM coprocessor for IPv4/IPv6 routing table update. *IEEE Transactions on Computers*, *63*(9), 2110–2121.

[27] Briscoe, N. (2000). Understanding the OSI 7-layer model. *PC Network Advisor*, *120*(2), 13–15.

[28] Sarrar, N., Feldmann, A., Uhlig, S., Sherwood, R., & Huang, X. (2010). Towards hardware accelerated software routers. In *Proceedings of the ACM CoNEXT Student Workshop*, November, United States (pp. 1–2).

[29] Qiu, L., Varghese, G., & Suri, S. (2001). Fast firewall implementations for software-based and hardware-based routers. In *Proceedings of the 2001*

ACM SIGMETRICS International Conference on Measurement and Modeling of Computer Systems, June, United States (pp. 344–345).

[30] Casado, M., Koponen, T., Moon, D., & Shenker, S. (2008). Rethinking packet forwarding hardware. In *HotNets*, November, Calgary, Alberta, Canada (pp. 1–6).

[31] Jouppi, N., Young, C., Patil, N., & Patterson, D. (2018). Motivation for and evaluation of the first tensor processing unit. *IEEE Micro, 38*(3), 10–19.

[32] McGeer, R. & Yalagandula, P. (2009). Minimizing rulesets for TCAM implementation. In *IEEE INFOCOM 2009*, 19–25 April, Rio de Janeiro, Brazil (pp. 1314–1322). IEEE.

[33] Pontarelli, S., Bonola, M., Bianchi, G., Capone, A., & Cascone, C. (2015). Stateful openflow: Hardware proof of concept. In *2015 IEEE 16th International Conference on High Performance Switching and Routing (HPSR)*, 01–04 July, Budapest, Hungary (pp. 1–8). IEEE.

[34] Zheng, K., Hu, C., Lu, H., & Liu, B. (2006). A TCAM-based distributed parallel IP lookup scheme and performance analysis. *IEEE/ACM Transactions on Networking, 14*(4), 863–875.

[35] Degermark, M., Brodnik, A., Carlsson, S., & Pink, S. (1997). Small forwarding tables for fast routing lookups. *ACM SIGCOMM Computer Communication Review, 27*(4), 3–14.

[36] Zhao, X., Liu, Y., Wang, L., & Zhang, B. (2010). On the aggregatability of router forwarding tables. In *2010 Proceedings IEEE INFOCOM*, 14–19 March, San Diego, CA (pp. 1–9). IEEE.

[37] Bux, W., Denzel, W. E., Engbersen, T., Herkersdorf, A., & Luijten, R. P. (2001). Technologies and building blocks for fast packet forwarding. *IEEE Communications Magazine, 39*(1), 70–77.

[38] Rai, S., Mukherjee, B., & Deshpande, O. (2005). IP resilience within an autonomous system: Current approaches, challenges, and future directions. *IEEE Communications Magazine, 43*(10), 142–149.

[39] Stott, D. T. (2002). Layer-2 path discovery using spanning tree MIBs. Avaya Labs Research, Avaya Inc., 233.

[40] Bianco, A., Birke, R., Giraudo, L., & Palacin, M. (2010). Openflow switching: Data plane performance. In *2010 IEEE International Conference on Communications*, 23–27 May, Cape Town, South Africa (pp. 1–5). IEEE.

[41] Hadzic, I. (2001). Hierarchical MAC address space in public Ethernet networks. In *GLOBECOM'01. IEEE Global Telecommunications Conference (Cat. No. 01CH37270)*, 25–29 November, San Antonio, TX (Vol. 3, pp. 1563–1569). IEEE.

[42] Buchanan, W. J. (2004). Network design, switches and vLANs. In *The Handbook of Data Communications and Networks* (pp. 807–823). Springer, Boston, MA.

[43] Spangler, R. (2003). Packet sniffing on layer 2 switched local area networks. *Packetwatch Research*, 1–5.

[44] Myers, A., Ng, E., & Zhang, H. (2004). Rethinking the service model: Scaling Ethernet to a million nodes. In *Proc. HotNets*, November.

[45] Joseph, D. A., Tavakoli, A., & Stoica, I. (2008). A policy-aware switching layer for data centers. In *Proceedings of the ACM SIGCOMM 2008 Conference on Data Communication*, August (pp. 51–62).

[46] Pustylnik, M., Zafirovic-Vukotic, M., & Moore, R. (2007). Performance of the rapid spanning tree protocol in ring network topology. RuggedCom, Inc.

[47] Kasu, S., Hash, L., Marsh, J., & Bull, R. (2015). Spanning tree protocol (Doctoral Dissertation).

[48] Allan, D., Ashwood-Smith, P., Bragg, N., Farkas, J., Fedyk, D., Ouellete, M., Seaman, M., & Unbehagen, P. (2010). Shortest path bridging: Efficient control of larger ethernet networks. *IEEE Communications Magazine*, *48*(10), 128–135.

[49] Farkas, J. & Arató, Z. (2009). Performance analysis of shortest path bridging control protocols. In *GLOBECOM 2009–2009 IEEE Global Telecommunications Conference*, 30 November 2009–04 December 2009, Honolulu, HI (pp. 1–6). IEEE.

[50] Touch, J. & Perlman, R. (2009). *Transparent Interconnection of Lots of Links (TRILL): Problem and Applicability Statement* (No. rfc5556).

[51] Eastlake 3rd D., Senevirathne, T., Ghanwani, A., Dutt, D., & Banerjee, A. (2014). *Transparent Interconnection of Lots of Links (TRILL) Use of IS-IS* (No. rfc7176).

[52] Ichiriu, M. (2000). High performance layer 3 forwarding. *White Paper, NetLogic Microsystems*.

[53] Degermark, M., Brodnik, A., Carlsson, S., & Pink, S. (1997). Small forwarding tables for fast routing lookups. *ACM SIGCOMM Computer Communication Review*, *27*(4), 3–14.

[54] Yu, J. T. & Liu, C. (2006). Applications and performance analysis of bridging with Layer-3 forwarding on wireless LANs. In *Advanced Int'l Conference on Telecommunications and Int'l Conference on Internet and Web Applications and Services (AICT-ICIW'06)*, February, Guadeloupe, French Caribbean (pp. 81–81). IEEE.

[55] Kawahara, K., Nakazawa, S., Takine, T., & Oie, Y. (2000). Performance analysis of layer3 switch: Case of flow-driven connection setup. *IEICE Transactions on Communications*, *83*(2), 130–139.

[56] Mellah, H. & Sanso, B. (2011). Routers vs switches, how much more power do they really consume? A datasheet analysis. In *2011 IEEE International Symposium on a World of Wireless, Mobile and Multimedia Networks*, June, Lucca, Italy (pp. 1–6). IEEE.

[57] Garimella, P., Sung, Y. W. E., Zhang, N., & Rao, S. (2007). Characterizing VLAN usage in an operational network. In *Proceedings of the 2007 SIGCOMM Workshop on Internet Network Management*, August, Kyoto, Japan (pp. 305–306).

[58] Sun, X., Sung, Y. W., Krothapalli, S. D., & Rao, S. G. (2010). A systematic approach for evolving VLAN designs. In *2010 Proceedings IEEE INFOCOM*, 14–19 March, San Diego, CA (pp. 1–9). IEEE.

[59] Vuppala, V. & Ni, L. M. (1999). Layer-3 switching using virtual network ports. In *Proceedings Eight International Conference on Computer Communications and Networks (Cat. No. 99EX370)*, 11–13 October, Boston, MA (pp. 642–648). IEEE.

[60] Hedrick, C. L. (1988). *Routing Information Protocol* (No. rfc1058).

[61] Savage, D., Ng, J., Moore, S., Slice, D., Paluch, P., & White, R. (2016). *Cisco's Enhanced Interior Gateway Routing Protocol (EIGRP)* (No. rfc7868).

[62] Moy, J. (1997). *OSPF Version 2* (No. rfc2178).

[63] Oran, D. (1990). *OSI IS-IS Intra-domain Routing Protocol* (No. rfc1142).

[64] Rekhter, Y., Li, T., & Hares, S. (2006). *A Border Gateway Protocol 4 (BGP-4)* (No. rfc4271).

[65] Manzoor, A., Hussain, M., & Mehrban, S. (2020). Performance analysis and route optimization: Redistribution between EIGRP, OSPF & BGP routing protocols. *Computer Standards & Interfaces, 68*, 103391.

[66] Black, U. D. (2000). *IP Routing Protocols: RIP, OSPF, BGP, PNNI, and Cisco Routing Protocols*. Prentice Hall Professional, United States.

[67] Andersson, L., Minei, I., & Thomas, B. (2007). LDP specification, RFC 3036. Internet Engineering Task Force.

[68] Cain, B., Deering, S., Kouvelas, I., Fenner, B., & Thyagarajan, A. (2002). *Internet Group Management Protocol, Version 3, RFC 3376*. Internet Engineering Task Force, United States.

[69] Fenner, B. & Meyer, D. (2003). *Multicast Source Discovery Protocol (MSDP), RFC 3618*. Internet Engineering Task Force, United States.

[70] Fenner, B., Handley, M., Holbrook, H., & Kouvelas I. (2006). *Protocol Independent Multicast — Sparse Mode (PIM-SM): Protocol Specification (Revised), RFC 2362*. Internet Engineering Task Force, United States.

[71] Adat, V., Dahiya, A., & Gupta, B. B. (2018). Economic incentive based solution against distributed denial of service attacks for IoT customers. In *2018 IEEE International Conference on Consumer Electronics (ICCE)*, 12–14 January, Las Vegas, NV (pp. 1–5). IEEE.

[72] Vinoth, R., Deborah, L. J., Vijayakumar, P., & Gupta, B. B. (2022). An anonymous pre-authentication and post-authentication scheme assisted by cloud for medical IoT environments. *IEEE Transactions on Network Science and Engineering, 9*(5), 3633–3642.

Chapter 3

SDN and NFV: Introduction, History, and Evolution

Companies and organisations are always driven by competitive forces. Further, traditional business models are being wreaked by the massive development in multimedia content, the explosion of cloud computing, the impact of growing mobile usage, and continued commercial pressures to cut costs while revenues remain static. To maintain the swiftness among these factors, companies have started moving towards software-defined networking (SDN) and network function virtualisation (NFV) to automate and dynamize network design and operations. Every company has to balance the advantages and disadvantages of different types of networks when it comes to establishing their own network. With increasing customer demands and the need for flexibility, some cons turn out to be heavier than others. Physical infrastructure, particularly hardware and equipment that require manual configuration, cannot keep up their transformation pace with giant developments in technologies. Traditional infrastructure systems are unable to handle the increasing demands of modern users. Therefore, companies that desire as little disruption as possible in legacy systems are frequently switching to SDN and NFV.

3.1 Introduction

Software-defined networks and network function virtualisation are two technology trends that are revolutionising network management, particularly in highly distributed networks that use public, private, or hybrid cloud services [1–5]. SDN and NFV technologies, when combined, make it easier to deploy network resources, lowering capital and operating expenses and offering greater network flexibility. The increasing usage of network function virtualisation is one of the primary factors facilitating SDN adoption. The services provided by SDN and NFV are complementary, with NFV delivering many of the real services controlled in a software-defined network. SDN is concerned with the control plane, whereas NFV is concerned with optimising the actual network services that manage data flows. Devices such as routers, firewalls, and VPN terminators are replaced with virtual devices that run on commodity hardware in NFV physical networking [6]. In many aspects, this resembles a typical "as-a-service" model of cloud services. These virtual devices can be accessed on-demand by communication, network, or data centre providers.

SDN is a promising technology that has drawn attention globally as it is an emerging networking paradigm that offers scope for improvement over current issues in network infrastructure. It is a novel idea that allows easy provisioning, flexible configuration, scalable automation, and greater programmability of the network. SDN allows software applications to programme network behaviour in a centrally controlled manner by utilising open APIs. SDN helps with provisioning automation and policy-based network management by decoupling or separating the network control plane from the forwarding plane [7, 8].

On the contrary, NFV allows communication services to be separated from specialised hardware, such as routers and firewalls. Because of this separation, network operations can supply new services dynamically and without the need for new hardware [9]. NFV is utilised to deploy network components that could take a few hours rather than months, as in traditional networking. Furthermore, virtualised services can run on less-expensive generic servers rather than specialised hardware [10].

3.2 Advantages of SDN and NFV

For the deployment of 4G-based services, LTE service quality is very critical. There are users who want to utilise its basic services, such as voice calls and banking transactions, and those who want to use its premium services, such as high-speed Internet downloads and streaming services. Network operators are not supposed to employ expensive proprietary hardware for supplying network chains to implement NFV and SDN [11]. Also, cost reduction is critical as we progress from one generation of technological improvement to the next, which uses minimal network bandwidth and increases latency [12]. Following are the four critical areas in which SDN and NFV are making a difference for an organisation:

(a) **Network abstraction:** The underpinning technologies and hardware that provide networking capabilities are isolated from services and applications running on SDN technology [13]. APIs facilitate the path of communication to applications, which is contrary to the monolithic applications that run on tightly bound hardware [14].

(b) **Intelligent and logically centralised control:** SDN is based on logically centralised network topologies that allow for intelligent network resource provisioning and management. In traditional networks, control methods are distributed in nature, where network entities function with autonomous capabilities having meagre knowledge of the state of the network [15]. Unlikely, apart from bandwidth management, security, and restoration, SDN provides centralised control, which helps make policies intelligent and optimised [16].

(c) **Openness:** SDN has revolutionised the term "openness" by allowing multi-vendor operability as well as strengthening a vendor-neutral environment. APIs are designed in a way to support a wide range of applications, such as services and cloud orchestration. Additionally, intelligent software provides a platform for hardware from multi-vendors to collaborate with each other, for example, OpenFlow [17, 18].

(d) **Network programmability:** SDN has a new feature called "network programmability," in which network behaviour can be modelled to support a new range of services and sometimes even individual customers. By separating the hardware layer from software, service providers can introduce new services without worrying about proprietary platforms and hardware [19, 20].

(e) **Granular security:** Firewalls and content filtering have been made more challenging by virtual machines, which are exacerbated by personal devices. The central control point of SDN proves to be a boon for companies as they can regulate and provision the security policies for every device with more granularity [21–24].

(f) **Reduced operating costs:** SDN paved a feasible path for easy network administration, efficient server utilisation, and better virtualisation control, resulting in reduced operating and management costs. It helps in growing administrative savings [25–27].

(g) **Comprehensive enterprise management:** The network of an organisation is expected to be flexible enough to handle the constantly changing demands of its users. SDN enables the organisation to scale the network without significant changes in the network. Unlike Simple Network Management Protocol (SNMP), SDN can also manage virtual devices and switches very well [28].

(h) **Content delivery:** Another feature that renders SDN stand out from other network management technologies is the manipulation of data traffic. SDN makes it easier to achieve the required quality of service for multimedia transmissions, resulting in an improved user experience [29–31].

SDN has been majorly utilised by companies to deploy their application at reduced operating and deployment costs [32].

3.3 Difference between Traditional Networks and SDN and NFV

The distinguishing feature between SDN and traditional networks is that SDN is a completely software-based paradigm, whereas traditional networks are completely hardware based. Figure 3.1 shows the traditional network architecture, while Figure 3.2 shows the networking paradigm based on SDN. As SDN depends on software for network management and configuration, it offers more flexibility, greater control by users, and ease of maintaining virtual machines [33–35]. As far as traditional networks are concerned, they utilise switches, routers, and other hardware devices to run a network. Second, unlike traditional networks that are dependent on certain protocols for connection establishment, SDN utilises a northbound interface connected to APIs through which an application developer can programme the network according to his requirements [36]. SDN utilises software to configure new devices instead of using existing infrastructure, and thus, required services can be arranged proactively by the service provider.

NFV performs exactly what the name implies: It virtualises network operations such as application delivery controllers (ADCs) [37, 38] and

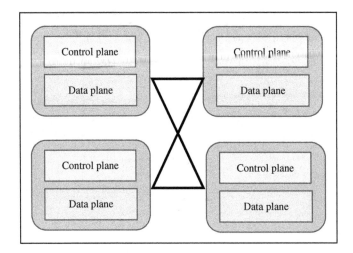

Figure 3.1. Traditional network architecture.

web application firewalls (WAFs) [39]. The use of software to accomplish network tasks eliminates the requirement for proprietary physical hardware and allows the network to benefit from the virtual nature of data centre installations. Through the use of NFV, virtualised ADC and WAF functions may now be more easily integrated into the rest of the infrastructure, allowing numerous network services to be chained together. By hosting these virtual appliances on a virtual server, you may construct a centrally controlled infrastructure that saves money by eliminating the need to maintain and support a large number of physical equipment. Configuration scripts regulated by version control techniques further improve reliability by reducing misconfigurations and operator errors.

Virtualisation is the next distinguishing feature that makes SDN and NFV stand out from traditional networks [40–42]. SDN has the capability to completely virtualise your underlying physical network, i.e., an abstract copy of the network can be created using SDN. This abstract copy of the network lets a user programme the network as per his requirements [43]. Moreover, granular manipulation or modification of network traffic can be done through SDN. This feature of SDN offers more flexibility to administrators to analyse the traffic and ensure the security of the network in a better way. Additionally, network segmentation can also be efficiently done as its centralised user interface

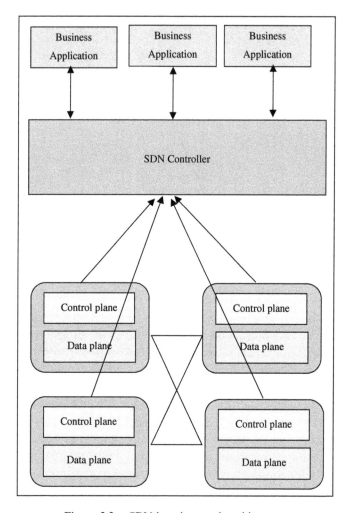

Figure 3.2.   SDN-based network architecture.

provides greater control to the user over traffic flow management [44, 45]. Currently, SDN has become a viable and reliable alternative to traditional networking methods, as it is a great way to provision bandwidth and resources, and that too without much investment in additional physical infrastructure [46]. Though the details of SDN architecture and its functionality will be explored in the upcoming chapters, Table 3.1 describes the key differences between SDN and traditional networking.

Table 3.1. Comparison between SDN and traditional network.

Key Feature	SDN	Traditional Network
Deployment	• Network management, provisioning, and configuration can be done through a single centralised point. • Abstraction concept is followed to configure the devices, resulting in accuracy, flexibility, and consistency.	• Manual configuration or device-by-device configuration of every physical device, such as switches and routers. • Siloed approach is followed while configuring devices to make them part of the network, resulting in inconsistencies and errors.
Operational simplification	• Data and control planes are separated, which facilitates the ease of maintaining and managing the network. It offers a single point of installation and customisable functionalities due to its flexible control and management plane.	• The data and control planes are located on the physical device itself. Traffic forward policies are configured at every device, as every device is not aware of the network topology and its features.
Programmability and automation	• Programmability and automation are easy as SDN is a centrally programmable network.	• These networks are inflexible, static, and not centrally programmable.
Attack detection	• It is easy to detect and mitigate cyberattacks on SDN.	• It is difficult to detect and mitigate cyberattacks on traditional networks.
Cloud deployment	• Organisations willing to deploy private cloud data centres, along with scalability of resources, also need to maintain a multi-tenant environment for the users, and that too with minimal impact on the IT infrastructure. SDN is well suited for this kind of environment.	• It is not easy to integrate with traditional networks to extend its functionalities.

(Continued)

Table 3.1. (*Continued*)

Key Feature	SDN	Traditional Network
New integrations	• New innovations such as network analytics, network insights, hypervisor integration, and micro-segmentation can be easily done on an SDN network.	• New integration platforms need to be developed separately to work on traditional systems.

3.4 Background Technologies Contributing to SDN and NFV

It's quite difficult to trace the origins of "software-defined networking," given that the underlying requirement of adding network programmability has existed since the advent of computer networks. However, the term was originally used in a 2009 paper to explain development on a standard called OpenFlow that allows network engineers to change network layout and traffic flow in real time by accessing flow tables in switches and routers from external computers [47]. Prior to SDN, technologies for central-ising network control, including programmability and virtualisation, existed and progressed to varied degrees of adoption among operators catering to specific application requirements. The following sections discuss some key technologies that contribute majorly to SDN:

- **Centralised network control:** At the very least, centralisation of network control dates all the way back to the early 1980s, when AT&T launched the network control point (NCP) [48], which pro-vided a centralised database of telephone connections and an out-of-band signalling mechanism for calling card machines. Separating the control and data planes was also employed in the early 1990s with BSD4.4 routing sockets [49, 50], allowing route tables to be con-trolled via a simple command line or a router daemon [51]. Another key milestone in the evolution of centralised network control is the ForCES project, which began as an Internet Engineering Task Force (IETF) working group in 2001 [52]. ForCES formulates the routing table in traffic forwarding elements using a control element [53–55]. Each control element communicates with one or more forwarding elements, which are in turn handled by a control and forwarding element manager that provides enhanced scalability. With the introduction and widespread use of generalised and multiprotocol label switching (G/MPLS), routers required complicated computations, including path selection, satisfying a variety of criteria ranging from backup route calculations to adhering to a particular bandwidth constraint [56]. Individual routers, on the other hand, lacked the computational capacity and network expertise necessary to design the requisite routes. As a result, the IETF's path computation engine (PCE) working group created a set of protocols that enable path computation by a client, such as a router, to obtain path information from the computation engine, which may be centralised or distributed across multiple routers [57, 58]. The technology has garnered considerable interest, with over 25 RFCs in existence at the time of writing. However, the approach lacks a specific control or PCE discovery mechanism and exposes information to computation clients only in a reactive or on-demand fashion. The Open Signaling (OPENSIG) working group was founded in 1995 with the goal of programmability and openness in ATM, Internet, and mobile networking [59, 60]. The group's goal was to enable access to network hardware via programmable interfaces, enabling the dispersed and scalable deployment of new services on current equipment. The IETF used this concept to define and specify the General Switch Management Protocol (GSMP), a protocol for controlling network switch ports, connections, and monitoring data, as well as upgrading and assigning switch resources via a controller [61]. The 4D project, which began in 2004, offered a network design that separated traffic routing logic and interelement communication protocols [62]. The concept offered a control or "decision" plane with a global view that is supported by planes further down the hierarchy that are responsible for delivering element status information and traffic routing. The Ethane project [63] was more recently completed and served as a direct precursor to enabling SDN technology. Proposed in 2007, Ethane's domain controller generated flow table entries based on access control policies and implemented traffic forwarding constructs using custom switches operating on OpenWRT [64], NetFPGA [65], and Linux platforms. However, due to the limits associated with having tailored hardware, Ethane was not adopted by as many industry vendors as planned. In comparison, the current SDN method utilises existing hardware and requires suppliers to offer interfaces to flow tables on switches via OpenFlow [66], which enables controller–switch communication. The growth of centralised network control has not occurred in isolation; there are efforts to automate and programme the network appliances discussed in the following section.

- **Network programmability:** Network administrators have long wished for better programmability of network devices, as the current way of setup (mostly via CLI), though effective, is very slow and involves painstaking effort when changing the configurations of the growing network. In the mid-1990s, the US Defense and Advanced Research Projects Agency (DARPA) identified the underlying issues associated with integrating new technology into conventional networking and the intricate and time-consuming reconfigurations required to accelerate innovation [67]. Around the same time, the phrase "active networks" was introduced, which advocated doing custom computations on packets in order to significantly restrict the programmability of individual devices [68]. Trace programmes running on routers and the concept of active nodes receiving new service instructions to act as a firewall or provide other application services were examples of this. However, due to the lack of a clear application at the time, such as cloud computing today, and a lack of affordable network infrastructure, the notion was never completely realised. In the mid-1990s, another network programming attempt was Devolved Control of ATM Networks (DCAN) [69]. DCAN's overarching objective was to build and create the infrastructure and services necessary for achieving scalability in controlling and programming ATM networks. The DCAN technology's underlying idea is that ATM switch control choices should be separated from devices and assigned to other organisations, specifically the DCAN management. The DCAN manager, in turn, manages the network parts by programming instructions, which is pretty similar to modern SDN. AT&T's GeoPlex [63, 70] was another such effort aiming at adding programmability to network parts. The project incorporated middleware capabilities into networking by utilising the Java programming language. GeoPlex was intended to be a service platform for controlling networks and services using operating systems running on machines linked to the Internet. However, the derived soft switch abstraction was unable to reconfigure physical devices due to its compatibility with proprietary operating systems.

Another critical addition to network programmability is the Extensible Message and Presence Protocol (XMPP) specified in RFC 6121 [71], which operates similarly to SMTP but is optimised for near real-time communication and includes presence monitoring in addition to messaging [72]. Each XMPP client establishes a connection with the network's server, which stores client contact addresses and may notify others when a contact becomes available. Messages are pushed (in real time) rather than polled as with SMTP/POP, and the protocol is increasingly being used to manage network elements in data centre networking and to encourage the Internet of Things (IoT) paradigm. Clients on the network have XMPP clients that respond to XMPP messages, including command-line interface management requests. XMPP has gained tremendous traction in the SDN (southbound API) area because of its widespread use in legacy computing systems.

From the standpoint of a network administrator or service provider, the Application Layer Traffic Optimisation (ALTO) protocol [73], which was originally developed by an IETF working committee to optimise P2P traffic by locating close peers, has been extended for locating resources in data centres [74]. Cisco and other technology companies have aimed to make it easier for programmers to create applications that interface with the network fabric. Cisco Open Network Environment Platform Kit (Cisco onePK) is a configurable framework that allows operators to adjust traffic flows and visualise network data for simpler deployment in response to changing business requirements [75]. Cisco's Application Centric Infrastructure (ACI) [76] now includes the framework, which aims to further integrate software and hardware based on functional requirements.

- **Network virtualisation:** The representation of one or more network topologies on the same infrastructure is known as "network virtualisation. Virtualisation has gone through several stages of implementation, from simple VLANs to intermediate technologies and test beds. Tempest, VINI, and Cabo are just a few of the notable ventures. Tempest was founded in 1998 at Cambridge, and it suggested the separation of the control framework from the switches as well as switch virtualisation [77]. Tempest was a pioneering attempt to decouple traffic forwarding and control logic, particularly in the setting of ATM networks. Tempest, like today's SDN, laid great emphasis on open programming interfaces and enhanced support for network virtualisation. The virtual network infrastructure (VINI), a slightly different strand centred on testing new protocols and services, was introduced in 2006, providing researchers with a virtual networking test bed to deploy and evaluate multiple ideas simultaneously on different network topologies using realistic routing software, user traffic, and networking events [78]. The VINI-enabled network also allowed operators to run numerous protocols on the same underlying physical network, with each virtual switch handling traffic forwarding on its own network device. The Cabo project advocated a separation of infrastructure and services in 2007 from the perspective of a service provider relying on hardware infrastructure from numerous infrastructure providers [79]. Cabo encourages infrastructure and service providers to be separated, allowing the latter to flexibly alter service provisioning for customers. Cabo allows service providers to deploy various services on networking equipment from different infrastructure suppliers using virtualisation and customisable traffic routing. Virtualisation can be perceived as a platform that provides sharing in terms of resource slicing or traffic forwarding utilities.

In addition to device virtualisation efforts, overlay technologies such as virtual extensible local area network (VXLAN) have been created to overcome the constraints of current networking technology, allowing for extensibility and applicability in bigger data centre and cloud deployments. VXLANs encapsulate traffic by using MAC-in-IP tunnelling to create stateless overlay tunnels between endpoint switches. Network virtualisation using GRE (NVGRE) [80] is similar to VXLAN. NVGRE also includes MAC-in-IP tunnelling, albeit the header structure differs slightly. To aid load balancing, VXLAN packets use UDP-over-IP packet formats broadcast as unicast between two endpoint switches, whereas NVGRE uses the GRE standard header. Stateless transport tunnelling (STT), which also uses MAC-in-IP tunnelling, is a modern virtualisation approach [81, 82]. While the concept of a virtual network is present in STT, it is encapsulated in a more general identifier known as a context ID. The 64-bit context IDs used by STT enable a substantially higher variety of virtual networks and service models. STT seeks to outperform NVGRE and VXLAN by taking advantage of the TCP segmentation offload (TSO) inherent in many servers' network interface cards (NICs). TSO reduces the overhead by allowing big packets of data to be transmitted from the server to the NIC in a single send request. STT utilises TCP in the stateless way (without the TCP windowing technique) associated with TSO. Along with network virtualisation, services such as DNS, access control, firewalls, and caching can be separated from the underlying virtual network and run as software programmes on specialised hardware and storage with high throughput. Virtualisation of network functionality (VNF) attempts to further reduce an organisation's operating and capital costs by lowering the need for dedicated hardware [83].

- **SDN requirement:** While network virtualisation technologies offered significant advantages over conventional and legacy protocols and architectures, the growth of the Internet, public and private network infrastructure, and an evolving range of applications necessitated a complete reimagining of the existing networking framework. The implementation of distributed protocols on the underlying conventional network is extremely complex, as these protocols support numerous services for traffic routing, switching, ensure quality of service applications, and provide authentication. When incredibly advanced policies are implemented using a confined set of low-level configuration commands, keeping track record of the states of numerous network devices and updating policies becomes even more tedious. Continuously changing traffic conditions necessitate regular manual interventions to reconfigure the network, which commonly results in misconfigurations; nevertheless, the tools provided may not be smart enough to give adequate granularity and automation to achieve optimal configurations.

3.5 Network Management

Network management has always been difficult. With an ever-increasing number of over-the-top (OTT) services and a growing user base, the difficulties have multiplied. This situation generates a slew of change requests, ranging from topology updates to routing tables and a variety of traffic engineering alterations. Due to the distributed structure of the network, there always exists a trade-off between ease of network management and the time it takes to implement new features. Moreover, cost is also a major consideration in geographically dispersed networks, such as mobile phone networks. SDN was born out of the need to balance all of these trade-offs in order to streamline network administration tasks. These trade-offs can be categorised into three primary objectives that create the underlying basis for SDN's requirement, as outlined in this section.

The operational issues of controlling a computer network are the most essential impetus for SDN. There are two operational challenges:

- **Time to reflect changes:** Due to the distributed nature of the network, it is difficult and time-consuming to make changes to the configuration of all network entities. It increases in proportion to the network's geographic reach and has a direct effect on operational costs.
- **Risk of malfunction:** This is related to the first difficulty. Due to the time and effort required for provisioning, it is becoming increasingly difficult to undo those modifications in the event of a network outage. Finally, this is the explanation for the network administrator's lack of innovation in optimising network performance.

SDN is a simple concept. It centralises the setup of network devices, rather than setting each intermediate device separately. Configuration functions in a computer network are primarily concerned with the control plane settings for packet routing. It is feasible to administer network devices remotely by transferring the control plane of each router to a central controller.

SDN and NFV do not have to be implemented together conceptually, but their capabilities complement one another and function well in support of a software-defined data centre. Implementing SDN concepts without virtualising network functions, for example, would bind the network to the hardware. This contradicts the concept of SDN, which focuses on embedding network intelligence in software.

3.6 Use Cases of SDN/NFV

In this section, we discuss the use cases of SDN/NFV architectures in domains such as mobile computing, wireless, and traffic engineering.

3.6.1 Virtualisation of Middleboxes

Middleboxes are usually deployed to increase the performance, i.e., functionalities such as traffic policing, shaping, load balancing, and security, i.e., functionalities such as firewalls, deep packet inspection, IDS, and IPS, of the network. However, hardware-based middleboxes have certain drawbacks [84]. To start with, the management complexity leads to hefty operating expenses (OPEX). Since these middleboxes are manufactured by different manufacturers, they require separate deployment, configuration, and management. Second, these hardware middleboxes sustain capital expenses (CAPEX). Due to the inflexibility of proprietary hardware that causes vendor lock-in and hinders innovation, businesses must buy one or more middleboxes whenever new network functionalities are required.

These challenges can be resolved by employing NFV/SDN architectural approaches. Primary goals include lowering capital and operating expenditures and speeding up the rollout of new network functionalities, flexibility, and service chaining. Service function chaining is made possible due to the collaboration of NFV and SDN, where NFV is responsible for virtual middleboxes and SDN is responsible for providing interconnection between different VNFs.

3.6.2 Traffic Steering

With traffic steering, requests from users can be sent to the most relevant services and content providers. It's possible that traffic steering could be affected by a number of factors, including accessible networking resources and the technical capabilities of the user and server, user access rights, and geographical location. A user may request a video streaming service with rigorous application requirements. In this situation, application-specific and on-demand traffic steering could ensure effective utilisation of network resources and an enhanced quality of experience (QoE) for the user [91, 92].

SDN can improve traffic steering between VNFs in the NFV-enabled framework, which supports dynamic service chaining. By decoupling the control and data planes, SDN enables services to better understand the overall network status and make informed decisions (to fulfil service requirements) on how to direct traffic through VNFs [93, 94].

3.6.3 Abstraction

For the purpose of providing a unified and centralised perspective on the entire network, this idea proposes implementing an abstraction layer over all available computing and network resources. The initial focus of NFV/SDN solutions was on developing an abstraction layer (AL) to deliver intelligent network services — in terms of performance and reliability — to various customer profiles, such as end, retail, and enterprise customers, as well as OTT providers and developers [85]. The AL performs two orchestration functions: resource orchestration and network service orchestration [86].

3.6.4 Wireless Networks

As wireless networks have grown in popularity, additional requirements have emerged, such as mobility support, programmability, rapid delivery of network services, performance, and security [87]. However, modern large-scale Wi-Fi network management and configuration are complicated and inflexible, failing to take either application requirements or user needs into account. In the case of a Wi-Fi network, different open software-defined wireless network (SDWN) solutions have been proposed [87, 88], where the research conducted on WLANs makes use of the virtual access point (VAP) abstraction by exporting the processing of the MAC layer or middleboxes to the cloud.

3.6.5 Wireless and Mobility Network

5GPPP is a collaborative effort between the European Commission (EC) and the European ICT sector to develop solutions, architectures, and standards that will place Europe at the forefront of 5G networks. The 5GPPP sponsors many projects, which have been discussed in the final chapter of this book. A 5G network must accommodate a wide range of industries, including automotive, eHealth, energy, factories, and media and entertainment [89]. New 5G technologies will affect all aspects of the mobile network, from endpoints to radio access, transport, and core networks all the way up to the cloud in order to serve a wide variety of use cases and performance needs. 5G networks should also provide multi-domain, multi-service, and multi-tenancy support to allocate logical networks, referred to as "network slices," to provide them the flexibility of customising their own networks according to their requirements. Infrastructure providers must offer end-to-end resource, infrastructure (resource abstraction and virtualisation layer), and service orchestration functionalities to reserve adequate computing and network resources from multiple administrative domains, keeping QoS customised to user demands [89].

To be effective in the radio access network (RAN), 5G architecture must be able to function across a wide range of frequencies and support a wide range of characteristion. It must also be able to efficiently transmit and process data while also accommodating the coexistence of multiple radio access technologies (5G, LTE, Wi-Fi, etc.). The essential enablers for achieving these functions are virtualisation, softwarisation, and pro-grammability capabilities, which can provide 5G networks with the appropriate level of flexibility. NFV and SDN will play a crucial role in 5G networks due to their ability to facilitate the rapid rollout of new ser-vices, paving the way for network slicing as well as the implementation and orchestration of mobile edge computing (MEC) [90].

3.6.6 Video Analytics

Video analytic systems and software are another technology that has grown immensely in utility since the advent of the IoT. Now, businesses can col-lect enormous volumes of data from their factories, stores, offices, and even farms utilising the IoT and smart devices. Video analytics is one example of a service that is particularly vulnerable to network delays, making end-to-end network latency one of the most pressing problems in today's networks. To address this issue, businesses are increasingly using NFV and SDN architectures to better manage network resources and decrease latency. Researchers believe that, in conjunction with the use of video analytics at the network edge, this could cut bandwidth utilisation by as much as 90%.

3.6.7 Orchestration Engines

Orchestration engines represent one of the most promising applications of NFV. Low adaptability, human error, and a lack of automated processes and alarms severely constrained the capabilities of traditional legacy net-works [94, 95]. Human error is a leading source of network outages; therefore, automated methods are in high demand. These engines also reduce the costs associated with maintenance and upkeep due to the fact that they require significantly less human interaction.

3.6.8 Security

Firewalls are just one type of security device that will be virtualised in the future with NFV and SDN, but several security firms are already delivering virtual firewalls to protect VMs [96]. The promise of unified management and uniform enforcement is a major selling point for virtualised security, which has led many organisations to investigate these types of solutions.

However, as the world becomes more virtual and NFV (and SDN) acquire more and more traction, we may soon see a day when virtual security, as well as the other use cases mentioned on this list, become the norm rather than the exception.

Exercises

Q.1.   Discuss the key technologies behind the development of SDN and NFV.

Q.2.   Discuss how virtualisation plays a very important role in both SDN and NFV.

Q.3.   Elaborate on how SDN and NFV complement each other using a real-time scenario.

Q.4.   Discuss the benefits rendered by SDN and NFV to businesses and enterprises. How do these technologies help businesses cut their operational and capital expenses?

Q.5.   How is an SDN network different from a traditional network?

Q.6.   How does SDN solve flexibility and scalability issues in legacy infrastructure?

Q.7.   How does SDN act as an add-on to cloud computing in terms of scalability and multi-tenancy?

Q.8.   Discuss why virtualisation of middleware is important to improving the programmability and scalability of a network.

Q.9.   How do SDN and NFV provide better ways of traffic engineering than conventional methods?

Q.10.   Elaborate on why abstraction is an important factor in network management with a suitable example.

Q.11.   How do SDN and NFV contribute towards wireless and mobility networks?

Q.12.   Discuss orchestration as one of the most important applications of NFV.

Q.13.   How has the security issue of legacy networks been addressed by SDN and NFV?

References

[1] Farris, I., Taleh, T., Khettab, Y., & Song, J. (2018). A survey on emerging SDN and NFV security mechanisms for IoT systems. *IEEE Communications Surveys & Tutorials, 21*(1), 812–837.

[2] Barakabitze, A. A., Ahmad, A., Mijumbi, R., & Hines, A. (2020). 5G network slicing using SDN and NFV: A survey of taxonomy, architectures and future challenges. *Computer Networks, 167*, 106984.

[3] Alam, I., Sharif, K., Li, F., Latif, Z., Karim, M. M., Biswas, S., Nour, B., & Wang, Y. (2020). A survey of network virtualization techniques for internet of things using SDN and NFV. *ACM Computing Surveys (CSUR), 53*(2), 1–40.

[4] Zhu, S. Y., Scott-Hayward, S., Jacquin, L., & Hill, R. (Eds.). (2017). *Guide to Security in SDN and NFV: Challenges, Opportunities, and Applications.* Springer, NewYork.

[5] Kaur, K., Mangat, V., & Kumar, K. (2020). A comprehensive survey of service function chain provisioning approaches in SDN and NFV architecture. *Computer Science Review, 38*, 100298.

[6] Kim, T., Koo, T., & Paik, E. (2015). SDN and NFV benchmarking for performance and reliability. In *2015 17th Asia-Pacific Network Operations and Management Symposium (APNOMS)*, 19–21 Aug. 2015, Busan, Korea (South) (pp. 600–603). IEEE.

[7] Chadha, R., Lapiotis, G., & Wright, S. (2002). Policy-based networking. *IEEE Network Magazine, 16*, 8–9.

[8] Krief, F. & Jrad, Z. (2002). An Intelligent Policy-based networking environment for dynamic negotiation, provisioning and control of QoS. In *International Conference on Network Control and Engineering for QoS, Security and Mobility*, October (pp. 285–290). Springer, Boston, MA.

[9] Herrera, J. G. & Botero, J. F. (2016). Resource allocation in NFV: A comprehensive survey. *IEEE Transactions on Network and Service Management, 13*(3), 518–532.

[10] Matias, J., Garay, J., Toledo, N., Unzilla, J., & Jacob, E. (2015). Toward an SDN-enabled NFV architecture. *IEEE Communications Magazine, 53*(4), 187–193.

[11] Dorsch, N., Kurtz, F., Georg, H., Hägerling, C., & Wietfeld, C. (2014). Software-defined networking for smart grid communications: Applications, challenges and advantages. In *2014 IEEE International Conference on Smart Grid Communications (SmartGridComm)*, 3–6 Nov. 2014, Venice, Italy (pp. 422–427). IEEE.

[12] Foresta, F., Cerroni, W., Foschini, L., Davoli, G., Contoli, C., Corradi, A., & Callegati, F. (2018). Improving OpenStack networking: Advantages and performance of native SDN integration. In *2018 IEEE International Conference on Communications (ICC)*, 20–24 May 2018, Kansas City, MO (pp. 1–6). IEEE.

[13] Kreutz, D., Ramos, F. M., Verissimo, P. E., Rothenberg, C. E., Azodolmolky, S., & Uhlig, S. (2014). Software-defined networking: A comprehensive survey. *Proceedings of the IEEE, 103*(1), 14–76.

[14] Karakus, M. & Durresi, A. (2017). A survey: Control plane scalability issues and approaches in software-defined networking (SDN). *Computer Networks, 112*, 279–293.

[15] Amin, R., Reisslein, M., & Shah, N. (2018). Hybrid SDN networks: A survey of existing approaches. *IEEE Communications Surveys & Tutorials, 20*(4), 3259–3306.

[16] Michel, O. & Keller, E. (2017). SDN in wide-area networks: A survey. In *2017 Fourth International Conference on Software Defined Systems (SDS)*, 8–11 May 2017, Valencia, Spain (pp. 37–42). IEEE.

[17] Anerousis, N., Chemouil, P., Lazar, A. A., Mihai, N., & Weinstein, S. B. (2021). The origin and evolution of open programmable networks and SDN. *IEEE Communications Surveys & Tutorials, 23*(3), 1956–1971.

[18] Ramirez-Perez, C. & Ramos, V. (2016). SDN meets SDR in self-organizing networks: Fitting the pieces of network management. *IEEE Communications Magazine, 54*(1), 48–57.

[19] Lopes, F. A., Santos, M., Fidalgo, R., & Fernandes, S. (2015). A software engineering perspective on SDN programmability. *IEEE Communications Surveys & Tutorials, 18*(2), 1255–1272.

[20] Nadeau, T. D. & Gray, K. (2013). *SDN: Software Defined Networks: An Authoritative Review of Network Programmability Technologies.* O'Reilly Media Inc., California.

[21] Shu, Z., Wan, J., Li, D., Lin, J., Vasilakos, A. V., & Imran, M. (2016). Security in software-defined networking: Threats and countermeasures. *Mobile Networks and Applications, 21*(5), 764–776.

[22] Al Hayajneh, A., Bhuiyan, M. Z. A., & McAndrew, I. (2020). Improving Internet of Things (IoT) security with software-defined networking (SDN). *Computers, 9*(1), 8.

[23] Ketel, M. (2018). Enhancing BYOD security through SDN. In *IEEE 2018 southeastCon 2018,* 19–22 April 2018, St. Petersburg (pp. 1–2). IEEE.

[24] Flauzac, O., González, C., Hachani, A., & Nolot, F. (2015). SDN based architecture for IoT and improvement of the security. In *2015 IEEE 29th International Conference on Advanced Information Networking and Applications Workshops*, 24–27 March 2015, Gwangju, Korea (South) (pp. 688–693). IEEE.

[25] Akyildiz, I. F., Lee, A., Wang, P., Luo, M., & Chou, W. (2014). A roadmap for traffic engineering in SDN-OpenFlow networks. *Computer Networks, 71*, 1–30.

[26] Hernandez-Valencia, E., Izzo, S., & Polonsky, B. (2015). How will NFV/SDN transform service provider opex? *IEEE Network, 29*(3), 60–67.

[27] Naudts, D., Kind, M., Verbrugge, S., Colle, D. & Pickavet, M. (2016). How can a mobile service provider reduce costs with software-defined networking? *International Journal of Network Management, 26*(1), 56–72.

[28] Benzekki, K., El Fergougui, A., & Elbelrhiti Elalaoui, A. (2016). Software-defined networking (SDN): A survey. *Security and Communication Networks, 9*(18), 5803–5833.

[29] Nam, H., Calin, D., & Schulzrinne, H. (2015). Intelligent content delivery over wireless via SDN. In *2015 IEEE Wireless Communications and Networking Conference (WCNC)*, 9–12 March 2015, New Orleans, LA (pp. 2185–2190). IEEE.

[30] Chang, D., Kwak, M., Choi, N., Kwon, T., & Choi, Y. (2014). C-flow: An efficient content delivery framework with OpenFlow. In *The International Conference on Information Networking 2014 (ICOIN2014)*, 10–12 Feb. 2014, Phuket, Thailand (pp. 270–275). IEEE.

[31] Jia, Q., Xie, R., Huang, T., Liu, J., & Liu, Y. (2017). The collaboration for content delivery and network infrastructures: A survey. *IEEE Access, 5*, 18088–18106.

[32] Parulkar, G. (2020). SDN fundamentals: Motivation, architecture, and benefits. *CSI Transactions on ICT, 8*(1), 7–9.

[33] Haji, S. H., Zeebaree, S. R., Saeed, R. H., Ameen, S. Y., Shukur, H. M., Omar, N., Sadeeq, M. A., Ageed, Z. S., Ibrahim, I. M., & Yasin, H. M. (2021). Comparison of software defined networking with traditional networking. *Asian Journal of Research in Computer Science, 9*(2), 1–18.

[34] Abdou, A., Van Oorschot, P. C., & Wan, T. (2018). Comparative analysis of control plane security of SDN and conventional networks. *IEEE Communications Surveys & Tutorials, 20*(4), 3542–3559.

[35] Gopi, D., Cheng, S., & Huck, R. (2017). Comparative analysis of SDN and conventional networks using routing protocols. In *2017 International Conference on Computer, Information and Telecommunication Systems (CITS)*, 21–23 July 2017, Dalian, China (pp. 108–112). IEEE.

[36] Haleplidis, E., Pentikousis, K., Denazis, S., Salim, J. H., Meyer, D., & Koufopavlou, O. (2015). Software-defined networking (SDN): Layers and architecture terminology. *RFC 7426.*

[37] Salchow Jr., K. (2007). Load balancing 101: The evolution to application delivery controllers. *F5 White Paper.*

[38] Filip, O. (2011). Optimization of application delivery controllers deployment.

[39] Moradi Vartouni, A., Teshnehlab, M., & Sedighian Kashi, S. (2019). Leveraging deep neural networks for anomaly-based web application firewall. *IET Information Security*, *13*(4), 352–361.

[40] Bizanis, N. & Kuipers, F. A. (2016). SDN and virtualization solutions for the Internet of Things: A survey. *IEEE Access*, *4*, 5591–5606.

[41] Li, J., Li, D., Yu, Y., Huang, Y., Zhu, J., & Geng, J. (2018). Towards full virtualization of SDN infrastructure. *Computer Networks*, *143*, 1–14.

[42] Jain, R. & Paul, S. (2013). Network virtualization and software defined networking for cloud computing: A survey. *IEEE Communications Magazine*, *51*(11), 24–31.

[43] Salazar-Chacón, G. D. & Marrone, L. (2020). OpenSDN southbound traffic characterization: Proof-of-concept virtualized SDN-infrastructure. In *2020 11th IEEE Annual Information Technology, Electronics and Mobile Communication Conference (IEMCON)*, 4–7 Nov. 2020, Vancouver, BC, Canada (pp. 0282–0287). IEEE.

[44] Mhaskar, N., Alabbad, M., & Khedri, R. (2021). A formal approach to network segmentation. *Computers & Security*, *103*, 102162.

[45] Kirkpatrick, K. (2013). Software-defined networking. *Communications of the ACM*, *56*(9), 16–19.

[46] Wu, J., Luo, S., Wang, S., & Wang, H. (2018). NLES: A novel lifetime extension scheme for safety-critical cyber-physical systems using SDN and NFV. *IEEE Internet of Things Journal*, *6*(2), 2463–2475.

[47] Hicham, M., Abghour, N., & Ouzzif, M. (2018). 5G mobile networks based on SDN concepts. *International Journal of Engineering and Technology (UAE)*, *7*(4), 2231–2235.

[48] Ronayne, J. P. (1986). *The Digital Network Introduction to Digital Communications Switching*, 1st edn. Howard W. Sams & Co., Inc, Indianapolis, IN.

[49] Innocente, R. & Adewale, O. S. Network buffers The BSD, Unix SVR4 and Linux approaches (BSD4. 4, SVR4. 2, Linux2. 6.2).

[50] Jeker, C. Network stack internals. OpenBSD. Link available: https://www.openbsd.org/papers/asiabsdcon08-network.pdf.

[51] Raymond, E. S. (2013). The art of Unix programming: Origins and history of Unix, 1969–1995, Online Book. Available at: http://www.catb.org/esr/writings/taoup/html/index.html.

[52] Haleplidis, E., Salim, J. H., Halpern, J. M., Hares, S., Pentikousis, K., Ogawa, K., Wang, W., Denazis, S., & Koufopavlou, O. (2015). Network programmability with ForCES. *IEEE Communications Surveys & Tutorials*, *17*(3), 1423–1440.

[53] ForCES. Available at: http://datatracker.ietf.org/doc/rfc3746.

[54] Bolla, R., Bruschi, R., Lamanna, G., & Ranieri, A. (2009). Drop: An open-source project towards distributed sw router architectures. In *GLOBECOM 2009 - 2009 IEEE Global Telecommunications Conference*, 30 Nov.–4 Dec. 2009, Honolulu, HI (pp. 1–6). IEEE.

[55] Wang, W. M., Dong, L. G., & Zhuge, B. (2008). Analysis and implementation of an open programmable router based on forwarding and control element separation. *Journal of Computer Science and Technology*, *23*(5), 769–779.

[56] De Ghein, L. (2006). *MPLS Fundamentals*, 1st edn. Cisco Press, Hoboken, NJ.

[57] Oki, E., Inoue, I., & Shiomoto, K. (2007). Path computation element (PCE)-based traffic engineering in MPLS and GMPLS networks. In *2007 IEEE Sarnoff Symposium*, April, Princeton, NJ (pp. 1–5). doi: 10.1109/SARNOF.2007.4567400. IEEE.

[58] PCE. Available at: http://datatracker.ietf.org/wg/pce/.

[59] Campbell, A. T., Katzela, I., Miki, K., & Vicente, J. (1999). Open signaling for ATM, internet and mobile networks (OPENSIG'98). *ACM SIGCOMM Computer Communication Review*, *29*(1), 97–108.

[60] Campbell, A. T., De Meer, H. G., Kounavis, M. E., Miki, K., Vicente, J. B., & Villela, D. (1999). A survey of programmable networks. *ACM SIGCOMM Computer Communication Review*, *29*(2), 7–23.

[61] Doria, A., Hellstrand, F., Sundell, K., & Worster, T. (2002). *RFC3292: General Switch Management Protocol (GSMP) V3*. RFC Editor, USA.

[62] Greenberg, A., Hjalmtysson, G., Maltz, D. A., Myers, A., Rexford, J., Xie, G., Yan, H., Zhan, J., & Zhang, H., (2005). A clean slate 4D approach to network control and management. *ACM SIGCOMM Computer Communication Review*, *35*(5), 41–54.

[63] Casado, M., Freedman, M. J., Pettit, J., Luo, J., McKeown, N., & Shenker, S. (2007). Ethane: Taking control of the enterprise. *ACM SIGCOMM Computer Communication Review*, *37*(4), 1–12.

[64] OpenWrt. Available at: https://openwrt.org/.

[65] Netfpga platform. Available at: http://netfpga.org

[66] OpenFlow Specification (ONF). Available at: https://www.opennetworking.org/images/stories/downloads/sdn-resources/onf-specifications/openflow/openflow-spec-v1.4.0.pdf.

[67] Tennenhouse, D. L. & Wetherall, D. J. (2002) Towards an active network architecture. In *Proceedings of the DARPA Active Networks Conference and Exposition (DANCE '02)*, May, Washington, DC (pp. 2–15).

[68] Shalimov, A., Zuikov, D., Zimarina, D., Pashkov, V., & Smeliansky, R. (2013). Advanced study of SDN/OpenFlow controllers. In *Proceedings of the 9th Central & Eastern European Software Engineering Conference in Russia*, 24–25 Oct. 2013, Moscow, Russia (pp. 1–6).

[69]   Devolved Control of ATM Networks. Available at: http://www.cl.cam.ac.uk/research/srg/netos/old-projects/dcan/#pub.

[70]   AT&T, AT&T Labs Internet Platforms The GeoPlex Project. Available at: http://www.geoplex.com.

[71]   Messaging, E. & Protocol, P. (2011). Internet Engineering Task Force (IETF) P. Saint-Andre Request for Comments: 6121 Cisco Obsoletes: 3921 March 2011 Category: Standards Track.

[72]   Saint-Andre, P. (2009). *XMPP The Definite Guide*. Safari Book, O'Reilly. California.

[73]   Alimi, R., Penno, R., Yang, Y., Kiesel, S., Previdi, S., Roome, W., Shalunov, S., & Woundy, R. (2014). Application-layer traffic optimization (ALTO) protocol. No. rfc7285. 2014.

[74]   Lee, Y., Bernstein, G., Dhody, D., & Choi, T. ALTO extension for collecting data center resource in real-time. ALTO. Available at: https://datatracker.ietf.org/doc/draft-lee-alto-ext-dc-resource/.

[75]   Cisco OnePK. Available at: https://developer.cisco.com/site/onepk/.

[76]   Cisco ACI. Available at: http://www.cisco.com/c/en/us/solutions/data-centervirtualization/application-centric-infrastructure/index.html.

[77]   Van der Merwe, J. E., Rooney, S., Leslie, I., & Crosby, S. (1998). The tempest — A practical framework for network programmability. *IEEE Network*, *12*(3), 20–28.

[78]   Bavier, A., Feamster, N., Huang, M., Peterson, L., & Rexford, J. (2006). In VINI veritas: Realistic and controlled network experimentation. *ACM SIGCOMM Computer Communication Review*, *36*(4), 3–14.

[79]   Feamster, N., Gao, L., & Rexford, J. (2007). How to lease the internet in your spare time. *SIGCOMM Computer Communication Review*, *37*(1), 61–64.

[80]   Sridharan, M., Duda, K., Ganga, I., Greenberg, A., Lin, G., Pearson, M., *et al.* (2011). *NVGRE: Network Virtualization Using Generic Routing Encapsulation*. Internet Engineering Task Force, California.

[81]   Davie, B. & Gross, J. (2012). *STT: A Stateless Transport Tunneling Protocol for Network Virtualization (STT)*. Internet Engineering Task Force, California.

[82]   Kawashima, R. & Matsuo, H. (2014). Implementation and performance analysis of STT tunneling using vNIC offloading framework (CVSW). In *2014 IEEE 6th International Conference on Cloud Computing Technology and Science*, 15–18 Dec. 2014, Singapore (pp. 929–934). IEEE.

[83]   Duan, Q., Yan, Y. H., & Vasilakos, A. V. (2012). A survey on serviceoriented network virtualization toward convergence of networking and cloud computing. *IEEE Transactions on Network and Service Management*, *9*(4), 373–392.

[84] Cziva, R., Jouet, S., White, K. J. S., & Pezaros, D. P. (2015). Container-based network function virtualization for software-dened networks. In *2015 IEEE Symposium on Computers and Communication (ISCC)* (pp. 415–420). http://dx.doi.org/10.1109/ISCC.2015.7405550.

[85] ETSI (2015). Network functions virtualisation (NFV) — Ecosystem — Report on SDN usage in NFV architectural framework. ETSI GS NFV-EVE 005 V1.1.1. Available at: http://www.etsi.org/deliver/etsi_gs/NFV-EVE/001_099/005/01.01.01_60/gs_nfv-eve005v010101p.pdf.

[86] ETSI (2014). Network functions virtualisation (NFV) — Management and orchestration. ETSI GS NFV-MAN 001 V1.1.1. Available at: http://www.etsi.org/deliver/etsi_gs/NFV-MAN/001_099/001/01.01.01_60/gs_NFV-MAN001v010101p.pdf.

[87] Schulz-Zander, J., Mayer, C., Ciobotaru, B., Schmid, S., & Feldmann, A. (2015). OpenSDWN: Programmatic control over home and enterprise WiFi. In *Proceedings of the 1st ACM SIGCOMM Symposium on Software Dened Networking Research (SOSR'15)* (pp. 1–12). ACM, New York, NY. Article No. 16, http://dx.doi.org/10.1145/2774993.2775002.

[88] Schulz-Zander, J., Mayer, C., Ciobotaru, B., Schmid, S., & Feldmann, A. (2017). Unied programmability of virtualized network functions and software-dened wireless networks. *IEEE Transactions on Network and Service Management, PP99*, pp. 1046–1060. http://dx.doi.org/10.1109/TNSM.2017.2744807.

[89] 5G PPP Architecture Working Group (2016). View on 5G architecture. Technical Report. Available at: https://5g-ppp.eu/wp-content/uploads/2014/02/5G-PPP-5G-Architecture-WP-July-2016.pdf.

[90] 5G PPP Architecture Working Group (2017). Vision on software networks and 5G. Technical Report. Available at: https://5g-ppp.eu/wp-content/uploads/2014/02/5G-PPP_SoftNets_WG_whitepaper_v20.pdf.

[91] Vinoth, R., Deborah, L. J., Vijayakumar, P., & Gupta, B. B. (2022). An anonymous pre-authentication and post-authentication scheme assisted by cloud for medical IoT environments. *IEEE Transactions on Network Science and Engineering*, 9(5), 3633–3642.

[92] Bhushan, K. & Gupta, B. B. (2019). Distributed denial of service (DDoS) attack mitigation in software defined network (SDN)-based cloud computing environment. *Journal of Ambient Intelligence and Humanized Computing, 10*, 1985–1997.

[93] Bhushan, K. & Gupta, B. B. (2018). Detecting DDoS attack using software defined network (SDN) in cloud computing environment. In *2018 5th International Conference on Signal Processing and Integrated Networks (SPIN)*, 22–23 Feb. 2018, Noida, India (pp. 872–877). IEEE.

[94] Gupta, B. B. & Chaturvedi, C. (2019). Software defined networking (SDN) based secure integrated framework against distributed denial of service

(DDoS) attack in cloud environment. In 2019 *International Conference on Communication and Electronics Systems (ICCES)*, 17–19 July 2019, Coimbatore, India (pp. 1310–1315). IEEE.

[95] Mishra, A., Gupta, B. B., Peraković, D., Yamaguchi, S., & Hsu, C. H. (2021). Entropy based defensive mechanism against DDoS attack in SDN-Cloud enabled online social networks. In *2021 IEEE International Conference on Consumer Electronics (ICCE)*, 10–12 Jan. 2021, Las Vegas, NV (pp. 1–6). IEEE.

[96] Prathiba, S. B., Raja, G., Bashir, A. K., AlZubi, A. A., & Gupta, B. (2021). SDN-assisted safety message dissemination framework for vehicular critical energy infrastructure. *IEEE Transactions on Industrial Informatics*, *18*(5), 3510–3518.

Chapter 4

SDN Basic Architecture

Switches, routers, firewalls, and load balancers are some of the common components used to build computer networks. These devices communicate with one another using a variety of industry-standard protocols. Network administrators are responsible for defining proper policies and controlling all network devices in order to respond to a wide range of network events. These difficult operations are often carried out manually using a relatively small set of tools. As a result, network maintenance, configuration, and performance tuning are time-consuming and possibly error-prone procedures. Another significant issue network operators are facing is "Internet ossification" [1]. The Internet, which has a vast and intricate deployment base, is one of the world's key infrastructures today. As a result, updating the Internet's core protocols and physical infrastructures is very complex and, in some cases, even impossible. To address these issues and assist in upgrading the Internet based on new applications and services, network programmability has been proposed. As a result, network design and management are greatly streamlined, with increased flexibility and agility. SDN provides a solution in this direction [2, 3].

In the previous chapters, we have discussed the various modern networking elements and the evidential evolution of switches and routers to the modern-day programmable switch. In this chapter, we discuss the basic architecture, software stack, and various other aspects of SDN which need to be understood before diving deep into SDN.

4.1 SDN Preliminaries

Unpredictable traffic patterns are being brought on by the massive growth in multimedia content, the effects of rising mobile usage, and the strong demand for cloud computing. Large data centres are required to find a solution to the problem of coping with unexpected traffic patterns [4, 5]. Moreover, they require a huge number of resources. This problem can be solved in either of the following ways:

- Scale the existing network infrastructure to meet the increasing demands.
- Program the network in such a way that it automatically copes with the increasing network requirements.

To implement both of these solutions, we have SDN. Figure 4.1 shows the basic architecture of an SDN switch.

In this section, we discuss the basic architecture of an SDN switch. A conventional representation of an SDN switch has three layers: data plane, control plane, and management plane. These layers tend to communicate with each other through southbound or northbound APIs. The purpose of SDN is to offer open interfaces that make it possible for software to be developed that can control the connectivity of network resources as well as the traffic flow through them. Moreover, it is also required that traffic flow be inspected and modified by the network administrator as per the requirement.

4.1.1 SDN Architecture

SDN has three layers: infrastructure, control, and application [6–9], as seen in Figure 4.1.

The three layers are described as follows:

1. **Infrastructure layer:** The bottom plane, also known as the data plane, is made up of networking equipment, including routers, real or virtual switches, and access points, that tend to process and forward the data packets [10]. This layer is responsible for collecting information, such as traffic flow statistics, network topology, and network usage. An SDN controller utilises a controller–data plane interface (C-DPI) to provide access to and control over these device(s) [11]. Secure connections, such as a TLS connection, may be used for communication

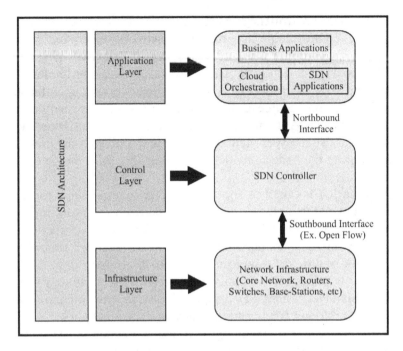

Figure 4.1. Architectural layers of SDN.

between the network components and controller(s). The most widely used C-DPI standard for establishing communication between controller(s) and data plane devices is the OpenFlow protocol [12].

2. **Control layer:** A controller handles the overall SDN operations in the control layer. This layer serves as a bridge between the infrastructure and application layers [13, 14]. The controller is in charge of managing the entire traffic flow through programming and is solely responsible for routing decisions, flow forwarding, and packet dropping. In a distributed environment, controllers communicate with one another via eastbound or westbound interfaces. The control and infrastructure layers communicate with one another using southbound APIs, such as OpenFlow [15, 16] and NetConf [17, 18].

Every network vendor is looking to develop their own SDN controller and framework products by embedding intelligence into this layer. A lot of business logic is implemented in the controller on this layer to retrieve and manage various types of network information, such as state details, topology details, and statistics details.

Since SDN controllers are used to manage networks, they must include control logic for real-time network functions, such as switching, routing, L2 and L3 VPNs, firewall security rules, DHCP, DNS, and clustering [19]. These use cases are being implemented in their SDN controllers by a number of networking manufacturers and even open-source groups. Once installed, these services are converted into APIs and provided to the application layer, which would assist network administrators in building, operating, and monitoring the underlying network using apps built on top of SDN controllers.

3. **Application layer:** The application layer is responsible for utilising all available network information regarding network topology, network state, network statistics, etc., to develop novel applications [20]. Numerous applications pertaining to network automation, network setup and management, network monitoring, network troubleshooting, network policy, and network security may be built into this layer. These SDN applications can offer numerous end-to-end solutions for business and data centre networks. Network manufacturers are developing their own collection of SDN apps to offer to various organisations and enterprises according to their requirements.

4.1.2 SDN Interfaces

There exist four prominent interfaces through which SDN interacts with the legacy network: northbound, southbound, eastbound, and westbound APIs. We discuss each interface in the following section one by one.

4.1.2.1 *Northbound APIs*

SDN permits information interchange with apps running on top of the network. This information interchange occurs between the SDN controller and an "application control plane" via a northbound API. Figure 4.2 shows the applications interfaced with a controller through a northbound API. There is no such thing as a uniform, standardised northbound API. Furthermore, information type, form, and frequency depend on the targeted application and network; therefore, such universal APIs are ineffective [21]. Standardisation of this interface makes sense only in common circumstances, assuming that all implementations remain open. While the

SDN controller can directly modify the network's behaviour, the application controller modifies the application's behaviour by utilising the network [22]. The northbound API exposes the information generated by the SDN controller to applications. The following API types are included in the northbound API:

(a) **Synchronous APIs:** The client initiates synchronous APIs, and the information is provided through the server in compliance with the API. It can be further divided into two categories: get/fetch and push/post/modify. In get/fetch, APIs collect network information without modifying the network's state. In push/post/modify, APIs alter the state of the network [23, 24]. Representational state transfer (REST) APIs are used to implement synchronous APIs using HTTP GET, POST, and DELETE methods. REST establishes a consistent interface between clients and servers while allowing them to exist independently without requiring state transfers [25]. Each time the information is desired, the client must make a new request via a fetch mechanism or a single API [26, 27]. Table 4.1 shows a list of synchronous APIs used in SDN.

(b) **Asynchronous APIs:** The availability of a resource, service, or data store may not be immediate in the case of asynchronous APIs. When the requested resource is ready, these APIs may send a callback to the requester. Asynchronous requests are beneficial for sustaining application functionality rather than tying up application resources while waiting on a request [28].

4.1.2.2 *Southbound APIs*

The interface between the control and data planes is represented by southbound APIs. It is essential to the corresponding SDN principle since it makes the externalisation of the control plane possible [29]. The manifestation of this principle occur through a standardised instruction set for networking hardware. The OpenFlow protocol and the IETF ForCES protocol are two implementation examples.

Its primary purpose is to make it possible for the physical and virtual switches, routers, and other network nodes to communicate with the SDN controller [30]. This allows the router to find out the topology of the network, create network flows, and carry out requests sent to it via northbound APIs.

Table 4.1. Synchronous APIs used in SDN.

API Name	Description
Switch API	It uses the HTTP GET method and returns information about switches in the network. Query parameters are **switch** and **switch?dpid**, which lists all switches present in the network and all switches associated with a specific dpid.
Host API	It uses the HTTP GET method to retrieve information about the hosts that are connected to the network. Examples of its query parameters are: • **Host:** Lists all hosts in the network. • **host?mac:** Lists all hosts associated with a specific MAC address. • **host?ip:** Lists all hosts associated with a specific IP address.
Flows API	It uses the HTTP GET method and returns information about the flows between applications and data processing engines (DPEs). Examples of its query parameters are: • **flows:** Lists all flows between applications and DPEs. • **flows?flow-group-id:** Lists all flows associated with a specific flow group. • **flows?flow-id:** Lists all flows associated with a specific flow ID.
Links API	It uses the HTTP GET method and returns information about the inter-switch links that create the network topology. Examples of its query parameters are: • **links:** Lists all links that make up the network topology.
Path API	It uses the HTTP GET method and returns information on the path between two ports (hosts) in the network. Using the Host API, it located the attachment point for each host, and then used the Path API to find the path between the two attachment points. Examples of its query parameters are: • **path?src-spid&src-port&dst-dpid&dst-port:** Lists a series of dpids and ports, which constitute the path between the source dpid/port and the destination dpid/port.
Flows API	The Flows API instals flows between applications and DPEs using the HTTP POST method. Examples of its output query parameters are: • **flow-group-id:** Flow group in which the new flows are installed. • **Flows:** List of new flows installed on the controller. • **flow-id:** ID of the new flow.

Table 4.1. (*Continued*)

API Name	Description
Flow update API	It uses the HTTP POST method and updates the list of actions that are installed on an existing flow. Examples of its query parameters are: • **flow-group-id:** Updates all flows associated with a specific flow-group ID.
Flow delete API	It uses the HTTP POST method to delete flows from the controller. Examples of its query parameters are: • **flow-group-id:** Deletes all flows associated with a specific flow-group ID. • **flow-group-id all:** Deletes all flows in the network.

4.1.2.3 *Eastbound APIs*

The eastbound APIs are used to communicate with the control planes of non-SDN domains, such as a multi-protocol label switching (MPLS) control plane [31]. The technology used in the non-SDN domain will determine how this interface is implemented. In essence, a translation module is needed between SDN and legacy technology. Both domains should ideally appear to be entirely compatible with one another in this way [32]. For instance, the SDN domain should be able to interact with the routing protocol used by non-SDN domains or respond to the Path Computation Element Protocol (PCEP) [33] signals from an MPLS domain requesting path arrangements.

4.1.2.4 *Westbound APIs*

Between the SDN control planes of various network domains, a westbound API acts as a conduit for information [34]. It permits the seamless establishment of network flows across many domains while also allowing the interchange of network status information to impact the routing decisions of each controller. Standard inter-domain routing protocols, such as BGP, could be utilised for the information exchange [35].

In Table 4.2, we have mapped these interfaces to various use cases of the SDN technology. We map each of the use cases in order to examine the value of SDN in terms of its interfaces and features for various

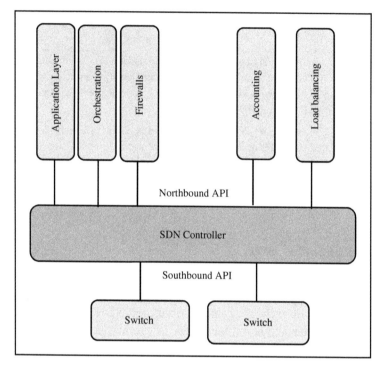

Figure 4.2.   Applications interfaced with SDN controller through a northbound API.

Table 4.2.   Use cases of SDN interfaces.

Use Cases	Northbound	Southbound	Eastbound	Westbound
Load balancing	✓	✓	✗	✓
Monitoring and measurement	✓	✓	✓	✓
Application awareness	✓	✗	✗	✗
Network management	✓	✓	✓	✗
Routing	✗	✓	✓	✓
Cloud orchestration	✓	✓	✗	✗

use cases. We can see in the table that the northbound interface supports load balancing, monitoring and management, application awareness, network management, and cloud orchestration. Further, the routing process relies on southbound, eastbound, and westbound interfaces. Monitoring and management are the use cases supported by all interfaces [36].

4.2 SDN Operations

SDN operations can be well understood by analysing them from bottom to top, starting from the SDN device, as we have discussed in the previous section about the infrastructure, control, and management planes. If we start by looking at devices, then devices are located at the infrastructure layer. SDN devices include forwarding functionality that determines what to do with each incoming packet [37]. The data that drive those forwarding decisions are likewise stored on the devices.

A flow is a sequence of packets sent from one network endpoint (or set of endpoints) to another endpoint (or set of endpoints). IP address–TCP/UDP port pairings, VLAN endpoints, layer-three tunnel endpoints, and input ports are examples of endpoints [38]. One set of rules specifies the forwarding actions that the device must take for all packets in that flow. A flow is unidirectional in the sense that packets moving in the opposite direction between the same two endpoints can each represent a separate flow. A flow entry represents a flow on a device [39].

The network device has a flow table that contains a number of flow entries and instructions for what to do when a packet of a particular flow enters. The SDN device searches its flow tables for a match when it receives a packet [40]. If a match is made, the SDN device performs the relevant configured action, which often involves sending the packet forward. If it does not find a match, the switch may drop the packet or forward it to the controller, depending on the version of OpenFlow and the switch's settings [41].

SDN refers to forwarding entities as OpenFlow switches, and all forwarding decisions are flow-based rather than destination-based, as in the conventional traditional network. A flow table with a logical data structure in an OpenFlow switch processes packets based on a list of prioritising entries [42]. In OpenFlow 1.10, typically a flow entry has 15 tuples; some fields are optional, but matching fields, action, statistical counter, priority, and timeout mechanism are typically used to analyse a packet. Matching fields are used to match packet metadata, such as MAC source and destination addresses, Ethernet type, and Internet protocol (IP) source and destination addresses [43]. These fields can be defined as exact-match or wildcard entries. The former indicates a single flow, whereas the latter depicts several flows, with any value indicated by an asterisk (*). Incoming packets are checked against the flow table, and if they match either the exact-match flow or the wildcard flow, the appropriate action is executed. The statistical count will be increased for any successful flow entry matched with arriving packets. Priorities are allocated to wildcard matching entries; if numerous packets match multiple wildcard flows, the higher priority will be assigned to the final match [44]. Exact-match flows are generally prioritised over wildcard flows. If the packet does not match any of the flows, it will be transmitted to the controller or dropped. Other operations/actions may be routed to a particular switch port number. Every arriving packet must perform a flow lookup. This can be performed by utilising a single or multiple flow tables that can be pipelined up to 255 tables [45].

OpenFlow 1.3 offers multiple flow table pipelining processing, which allows a packet to be processed by more than one flow table for efficiency and flexibility [46]. The four components present in both single and pipelining tables are matching field, action, statistic, priority, and timeout. In contrast to the single table, the matching procedure begins with the first flow table in the pipelining tables and may proceed to the next table until the matching flow entry is found. The process of checking the entry is carried out sequentially, and action is usually carried out at the end of the last table in the pipeline.

Depending on the configuration of the table-miss entry, the switch may drop the packet or send a packet-in message to the controller for a flow setup request. When a flow setup request packet is transmitted to the controller, the centralised controller computes a new flow entry and delivers a packet-out event to direct the switch to instal the appropriate entry in its flow table. With the presence of big flow arrivals, the controller will get frequent flow setup requests on a large scale [47]. Typical OpenFlow switch flow tables keep the rules in TCAM, a particular kind of high-speed memory that enables continuous flow entry lookup in just one clock cycle, i.e., $O(1)$. TCAM has already been discussed in the previous chapter. TCAM's capacity is limited to a few thousand entries despite the high-speed lookup. Increasing the TCAM size raises additional issues, such as higher cost and power requirements [48].

The SDN network devices are abstracted by the SDN controller, which provides this abstracted view of resources to the SDN applications that are operating above. The controller helps the SDN application respond to packets that are forwarded to it by the SDN devices and enables the SDN application to define flows on devices [49]. In Figure 4.3, we can see that the SDN controller maintains a complete view of the network on the right-hand side. This view helps the controller frame the rules that optimise the forwarding decisions in a deterministic way. On top of the controller, SDN applications are constructed. These applications are not to be confused with the application layer outlined in the seven-layer OSI computer networking model. This concept is unrelated to that of applications in the tight hierarchy of OSI protocol layers because SDN apps are essentially part of network levels two and three. The SDN application communicates with the controller, allowing it to configure

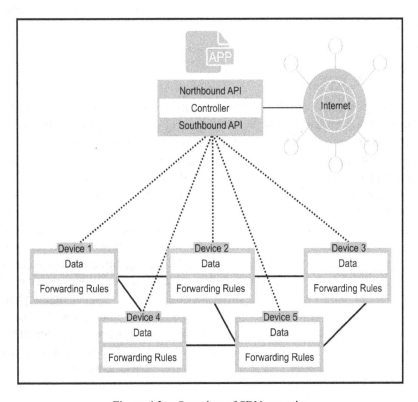

Figure 4.3. Overview of SDN operation.

proactive flows on devices and receive packets directed to the controller [50]. The application creates proactive flows; normally, the application will create these flows as the application starts up, and the flows will continue until some configuration change is made. This type of proactive flow is referred to as a static flow. Another type of proactive flow occurs when the controller decides to change a flow depending on the present traffic load being driven via a network device [51].

Some flows are defined in reaction to a packet passed to the controller, in addition to flows defined proactively by the application. When the SDN application receives inbound packets relayed to the controller, it instructs the controller on how to respond to the packet and, if necessary, creates new flows on the device to allow that device to respond locally the next time it gets a packet belonging to that flow. Such flows are known as reactive flows [52]. As a result, software programmes that implement forwarding, routing, overlay, multipath, and access control functionalities, among others, can now be easily implemented [53].

4.3 SDN Devices

An SDN device is composed of three entities: an API to interface with the controller, an abstraction layer, and a packet processing rule or function. Considering virtual switches, the packet processing module is itself implemented by the software, while in the case of physical switches, the packet processing rule is embedded into the hardware [54].

The mechanisms for taking action based on the outcomes of assessing incoming packets and identifying the highest-priority match comprise the packet-processing logic. Unless it is specifically routed to the controller, the incoming packet is analysed locally when a match is detected [55]. The packet might be copied to the controller for additional processing if there isn't a match. The abstraction layer includes the implementation of flow tables. Now, we discuss these modules one by one in detail [56]. Recently, a position for a pure software switch has emerged in data centres. Such a switch is typically implemented as a software programme that runs alongside a hypervisor in a data centre rack. We will discuss this switch later in the book. Now, we discuss the various constituent components of an SDN device.

4.3.1 Abstraction

The fundamental data structure of an SDN device is the flow table. In the past, networking devices tended to receive packets and assess them based on specific fields. Actions are then taken in accordance with that assessment. These options could include, among others, flooding the packet across all ports, discarding the packet, or forwarding it to a particular port [57]. With the exception of the fact that this fundamental operation has been made more general and programmable by the use of flow tables and related logic, an SDN device is not fundamentally different.

A flow table generally consists of two parts: fields and actions. Fields have the values that are used to compare against the incoming packet flow. The comparison has been performed in priority order, i.e., the action that corresponds to the first complete match is to be applied to the incoming packet [58]. Actions are the instructions followed by the network device if there is a match between the incoming packet and a flow table entry. In some cases, fields that are irrelevant to a specific match can have wildcards, for example, if an entry is configured to match only the IP address, subnet address, TCP/UDP port, or MAC address, then other fields need not match. Further, an entry could have no wildcard field if it considers all fields important to be matched with the incoming packet. We have discussed much about wildcard entries and exact matches in the previous section. Therefore, the flow tables, as a layer of abstraction, enable the developer to describe a wide range of possibilities for the incoming packet traffic.

4.3.2 Software Switches

The implementation of an SDN device in software form is the easiest way of implementing it, as it is easy for the developer to create flow tables and flow entries through data structures, such as arrays and hash tables [59]. Moreover, compatibility issues between two software SDN devices created by two vendors are less probable than those between two hardware-based SDN devices. However, the main drawback of software implementation is that the devices are relatively slower than hardware-driven SDN devices. The next important problem is that wildcard fields may pose issues when using hash tables to create flow tables. Therefore, in order to perform efficient lookups, the packet processing function needs a polished software logic [60]. Initially, there would be a large vari-ance in the performance of software SDN devices in terms of lookup efficiency. Eventually, software device implementation gets more sophis-ticated with time.

The positive aspects of using software SDN devices are as follows. These devices have fewer resource constraints. There is no need to specify processing power and memory size in the trivial implementation of soft-ware SDN devices [61]. Another important advantage is that software SDN devices can support a large number of flow entries as compared to hardware SDN devices. Further, they can support a wide range of actions and are flexible enough to support complex actions.

One of the most frequently witnessed SDN device implementations is the hypervisor in a virtualisation system. Multiple virtual machines are connected to the virtual network via hypervisors, which include a soft-ware switch implementation.

4.3.3 Hardware Switches

In contrast to software switches, hardware SDN devices or switches can be used in performance-driven environments as they are faster. We have already discussed CAMs and TCAMs that have been used for the hardware implementation of SDN switches [62]. These memories usually store layer-two and layer-three forwarding tables. A CAM is usually used to store simple flow tables, for example, when a packet is forwarded on the basis of a 48-bit MAC address. On the other hand, a TCAM is used to store more complex table entries, for example, exact matches and wildcard entries [63]. Apart from this, the possibility of TCAMs matching some but not all header fields of an incoming packet is a more significant and creative use of TCAMs. However, it poses some major challenges to the applicability of SDN. One of the major challenges faced by any SDN developer is deciding which flow entries should be handled by hardware and how many should be handled by software. Most implementations can perform some of the lookups with hardware, but others are passed to software to be handled there. Clearly, hardware will do flow lookups considerably faster than soft-ware; however, hardware tables have limits on the number of flow entries they can retain at any given time, while software tables could handle the overflow [64]. Second, it is difficult to modify an action or match field once it is configured on a TCAM. Thus, it may create a problem for the SDN developer to define a wide range of actions on the TCAM. These are some of the main issues that need to be considered while designing a SDN device.

4.3.4 Scalability of SDN Switches

The granularity of flow specifications will normally increase as the device carrying them approaches the network's boundary and decrease as the device approaches the core. Flows will enable different policies to be applied to individual users and even different kinds of traffic from the same user at the boundary. This may result in several flow entries for a single user in some circumstances [65]. This degree of flow granularity would simply not scale if used closer to the network core, where huge switches handle traffic for a large number of users simultaneously. The flow descriptions in the core devices will usually be coarser, where a single aggregated or consolidated flow entry will be defined that matches with the incoming traffic from a large number of users whose traffic has been aggregated in some fashion, such as a tunnel, a VLAN, or an MPLS LSP. Policies that are employed deep into the network are unlikely to be user-centric, but policies for aggregated flows are usually user-centric. One favourable outcome is that the number of flow entries in the core switches will not explode as a result of managing traffic from thousands of flows in the edge switches.

4.4 SDN Controllers

The controller maintains a unified picture of the network, implements policy choices, manages all SDN devices that make up the network architecture, and provides a northbound API for applications. When we indicated that the controller implements policy decisions regarding routing, forwarding, redirecting, load balancing, and the like, we meant both the controller and the network.

In this section, we discuss the architecture, core modules, interfaces, and other aspects related to SDN controllers.

4.4.1 SDN Controller Architecture

The controller, also known as a network operating system (NOS) in a software defined network, is the main and crucial component responsible for making decisions on traffic management on the underlying network. The basic structure of the controller does not get altered by the researchers; instead, they define the modules and capabilities differently. Generally, a basic SDN controller has the following core modules:

(a) **End-user device discovery module:** This module is responsible for discovering end-user devices, such as mobiles and laptops.
(b) **Network device discovery module:** It is responsible for the discovery of network devices that make up the infrastructure network components, including switches, routers, and wireless access points.
(c) **Topology management:** Keep records of the specifics of how network devices are connected to one another and to the end-user devices to which they are directly connected.
(d) **Flow management:** In order to ensure that the device flow entries are synchronised with the flow database stored on the controller, all essential coordination with the devices must be carried out.
(e) **Controller and switch management module:** The controller is shown as a container to which all switches are connected. The controller registers switch listeners and message listeners in order to notify them of switch changes and message arrivals. The model of the switch includes its input and output message streams and its state.
(f) **Packet processing module:** This module is responsible for processing the headers and payload of the data packets based on the network protocol. Each packet is modified by its source addresses, destination addresses, message type, and payload.
(g) **OpenFlow:** Every controller has an OpenFlow module that performs tasks such as sending and receiving OpenFlow messages, performing OpenFlow actions, entering and modifying flow rules, matching flow rules, and managing message queues and statistics.
(h) **Service abstraction module and plugins:** This layer is responsible for adding flexibility to the controller to add new devices to it.

The controller is primarily responsible for topology and traffic management. The external ports are polled often by the packet-out messages sent by the link discovery module. The controller can construct the network topology based on the responses to these packet enquiry messages in the form of packet-in messages. The topology manager is responsible for preserving the network's topology. This provides the deliberative module required to determine the best routes between network nodes. The pathways are constructed in such a way that various QoS and security policies can be implemented during path installation. In addition, the controller may feature a queue and statistics collector/manager to handle the incoming and outgoing packet queues and collect performance data of the network, respectively. The flow manager is a key component because it communicates with the flow entries and flow tables in the data plane. For this function, it makes use of the southbound interface.

4.4.2 SDN Controller Interfaces

Multiple layers and devices can communicate with the central controller via a variety of interfaces. The southbound interface specifies the processing rules that allow packet forwarding between controllers and forwarding devices. By providing this information to the controller, the southbound interface facilitates the intelligent provisioning of both physical and virtual network devices. The most widely deployed southbound interface and de facto industry standard is OpenFlow [66]. The primary function of OpenFlow is to create flows and categorise network traffic in accordance with a set of established rules. In contrast, the controller makes use of the northbound interface to facilitate application integration with the controller and data plane devices. Numerous northbound APIs are supported by controllers, with the REST API being the most common. The westbound interface facilitates communication between controllers. Since there is no standardised method of communication between controllers, each one must come up with its own solution. Also, heterogeneous controllers rarely communicate with one another. The controller's potential for communicating with legacy routers is augmented by the eastbound API. The most commonly used protocol for this use case is BGP.

The remaining topics related to SDN controllers will be studied in detail in the following chapter.

4.5 SDN Applications

The SDN controller acts as a relay between the SDN applications and their resource requests. SDN applications can take many forms and perform many tasks, including network administration, analytics, and the addition of security and common network services. The management of Internet Protocol addresses (IPAM), quality of service (QoS) management, load balancing, and the detection and mitigation of denial of service (DoS) cyberattacks are all examples [67, 68]. The application spends the majority of its processing time responding to events once the controller has finished initialising devices and has reported the network topology to the application. Application behaviour is influenced by both external inputs and controller events, even though the essential functionality of the application will differ from one application to the next. External inputs may include network monitoring systems, such as Netflow, IDS, or BGP. Whenever an event occurs, the controller triggers the concerned application by invoking the callback method. These events could be end-user discovery, network device discovery, network topology discovery, etc. We will study the application layer in detail in the upcoming chapters.

4.6 SDN through APIs

There's no denying that SDN is becoming more popular owing to the fact that it provides teams with the flexibility they desired in their old, rigid network setups. SDN provides a common platform for devices from different vendors to communicate with one another within the same network, freeing up administrators to focus on other tasks. They can establish a centralised policy that will apply to all the hardware in the data centre or over a wide area network. APIs play a very important role in implementing SDN [69]. APIs help network administrators reap the complete benefits of SDN through the following features:

(a) **Interoperability:** APIs enable the dissolution of barriers between various vendor technologies. By utilising APIs, controllers can exchange data with other programmes, such as IP address information, network orchestration data, and important virtualisation information, and push configuration and state to network devices, such as switches and routers.

(b) **Automation:** When it comes to maintaining and administering a network, rather than wasting time on recurring, routine operations, APIs allow users the power and flexibility to instantly automate processes.

(c) **Extensibility:** Having an open API makes it simple to add new features to your network with minimal effort. In other words, it makes your network design more resilient to change.

APIs can be implemented with SDN in the following four ways:

1. **Open SDN:** With Open SDN, the control plane is centralised, and the southbound API is OpenFlow. As a result, successful deployment must make use of evolutionary, hybrid approaches. We see it used effectively in ONOS and BigSwitch.
2. **API SDN:** It utilises a programmable southbound interface to manage the traffic between the data and control planes. SDN can be implemented in three ways: device, controller, and policy.
3. **SDN overlay model:** SDN is another type of networking that uses a virtual network to run on top of an existing hardware architecture, hence establishing dynamic tunnels to various on-premise and faraway data centres. The physical network is unaffected by the virtual network, which divides available bandwidth across several virtual channels and assigns specific devices to each channel.
4. **Hybrid SDN:** This approach integrates SDN with legacy networking protocols in a unified framework for comprehensive network support. Network managers can gradually incorporate SDN into a legacy system by having it take over responsibility for some traffic, while standard networking protocols continue to direct other traffic.

Exercises

Q.1. Discuss the architectural layers and various interfaces of an SDN network.

Q.2. Elaborate on how an SDN controller and the data plane interact to provide an SDN service to the user.

Q.3. Elaborate on how an SDN controller and the application layer interact to provide an SDN service to the user.

Q.4. Elaborate on the role of APIs in SDN networking and compare it with traditional networking.

Q.5. Discuss the role of northbound APIs in SDN networking. Also, elaborate on synchronous APIs, with more emphasis on REST APIs.

Q.6.   Discuss the role of southbound APIs in SDN networking, with more emphasis on the OpenFlow protocol.

Q.7.   Elaborate on the significance of eastbound and westbound interfaces in the SDN paradigm.

Q.8.   Maintaining the global view of the network is a very important SDN operation. Justify this statement.

Q.9.   Discuss the role of hardware and software switches in SDN networking. How are these different from each other?

Q.10. Discuss the core modules of an SDN controller and their functionalities.

Q.11. Discuss the ways in which SDN can be implemented through APIs.

References

[1] Alam, I., Sharif, K., Li, F., Latif, Z., Karim, M. M., Biswas, S., Nour, B., & Wang, Y. (2020). A survey of network virtualization techniques for internet of things using SDN and NFV. *ACM Computing Surveys (CSUR)*, *53*(2), 1–40.

[2] Farris, I., Taleb, T., Khettab, Y., & Song, J. (2018). A survey on emerging SDN and NFV security mechanisms for IoT systems. *IEEE Communications Surveys & Tutorials*, *21*(1), 812–837.

[3] Kaur, K., Mangat, V., & Kumar, K. (2020). A comprehensive survey of service function chain provisioning approaches in SDN and NFV architecture. *Computer Science Review*, *38*, 100298.

[4] Kim, T., Koo, T., & Paik, E. (2015). SDN and NFV benchmarking for performance and reliability. In *2015 17th Asia-Pacific Network Operations and Management Symposium (APNOMS)*, 19–21 Aug. 2015, Busan, Korea (South) (pp. 600–603). IEEE.

[5] Zhu, S. Y., Scott-Hayward, S., Jacquin, L., & Hill, R. (Eds.) (2017). *Guide to Security in SDN and NFV: Challenges, Opportunities, and Applications.* Springer, California.

[6] Zhang, H., Cai, Z., Liu, Q., Xiao, Q., Li, Y., & Cheang, C. F. (2018). A survey on security-aware measurement in SDN. *Security and Communication Networks*, *2018*, 2459154:1–2459154:14.

[7] Thirupathi, V., Sandeep, C. H., Kumar, N., & Kumar, P. P. (2019). A comprehensive review on SDN architecture, applications and major benefits of SDN. *International Journal of Advanced Science and Technology*, *28*(20), 607–614.

[8] Schriegel, S., Kobzan, T., & Jasperneite, J. (2018). Investigation on a distributed SDN control plane architecture for heterogeneous time sensitive networks. In *2018 14th IEEE International Workshop on Factory Communication Systems (WFCS)*, 13–15 June 2018, Imperia, Italy (pp. 1–10). IEEE.

[9] Raghunath, K. & Krishnan, P. (2018). Towards a secure SDN architecture. In *2018 9th International Conference on Computing, Communication and Networking Technologies (ICCCNT)*, 10–12 July 2018, Bengaluru, India (pp. 1–7). IEEE.

[10] Karakus, M. & Durresi, A. (2017). A survey: Control plane scalability issues and approaches in software-defined networking (SDN). *Computer Networks, 112,* 279–293.

[11] Amin, R., Reisslein, M., & Shah, N. (2018). Hybrid SDN networks: A survey of existing approaches. *IEEE Communications Surveys & Tutorials, 20*(4), 3259–3306.

[12] Lopes, F. A., Santos, M., Fidalgo, R., & Fernandes, S. (2015). A software engineering perspective on SDN programmability. *IEEE Communications Surveys & Tutorials, 18*(2), 1255–1272.

[13] Nadeau, T. D. & Gray, K. (2013). *SDN: Software Defined Networks: An Authoritative Review of Network Programmability Technologies.* O'Reilly Media, Inc. California.

[14] Shu, Z., Wan, J., Li, D., Lin, J., Vasilakos, A. V., & Imran, M. (2016). Security in software-defined networking: Threats and countermeasures. *Mobile Networks and Applications, 21*(5), 764–776.

[15] Lara, A., Kolasani, A., & Ramamurthy, B. (2013). Network innovation using openflow: A survey. *IEEE Communications Surveys & Tutorials, 16*(1), 493–512.

[16] Benton, K., Camp, L. J., & Small, C. (2013). OpenFlow vulnerability assessment. In *Proceedings of the Second ACM SIGCOMM Workshop on Hot Topics in Software Defined Networking*, 16 Aug. 2013, Hong Kong, China (pp. 151–152).

[17] Enns, R. (2006). *NETCONF Configuration Protocol (RFC 4741).* RFC Editor, p. 95.

[18] Enns, R., Bjorklund, M., Schoenwaelder, J., & Bierman, A. (2011). *Network Configuration Protocol (NETCONF) (RFC6241).* RFC Editor, p. 113.

[19] Flauzac, O., González, C., Hachani, A., & Nolot, F. (2015). SDN based architecture for IoT and improvement of the security. In *2015 IEEE 29th International Conference on Advanced Information Networking and Applications Workshops*, 24–27 March 2015, Gwangju, Korea (South) (pp. 688–693). IEEE.

[20] Dhamecha, K. & Trivedi, B. (2013). SDN issues — A survey. *International Journal of Computer Applications, 73*(18), 30–35.

[21] Akyildiz, I. F., Lee, A., Wang, P., Luo, M., & Chou, W. (2014). A roadmap for traffic engineering in SDN-OpenFlow networks. *Computer Networks*, *71*, 1–30.

[22] Al Hayajneh, A., Bhuiyan, M. Z. A., & McAndrew, I. (2020). Improving Internet of Things (IoT) security with software-defined networking (SDN). *Computers*, *9*(1), 8.

[23] Edwards, T. G. & Belkin, W. (2014). Using SDN to facilitate precisely timed actions on real-time data streams. In *Proceedings of the Third Workshop on Hot Topics in Software Defined Networking*, 17–22 Aug. 2014, Chicago, IL (pp. 55–60).

[24] ul Huque, T. I., Yego, K., Sioutis, C., Nobakht, M., Sitnikova, E., & den Hartog, F. (2019). A system architecture for time-sensitive heterogeneous wireless distributed software-defined networks. In *2019 Military Communications and Information Systems Conference (MilCIS)*, 12–14 Nov. 2019, Canberra, ACT, Australia (pp. 1–6). IEEE.

[25] Lara, A. & Quesada, L. (2018). Performance analysis of SDN northbound interfaces. In *2018 IEEE 10th Latin-American Conference on Communications (LATINCOM)*, 14–16 Nov. 2018, Guadalajara, Mexico. (pp. 1–6). IEEE.

[26] Hu, T., Zhang, Z., Yi, P., Liang, D., Li, Z., Ren, Q., Hu, Y., & Lan, J. (2021). SEAPP: A secure application management framework based on REST API access control in SDN-enabled cloud environment. *Journal of Parallel and Distributed Computing*, *147*, 108–123.

[27] Yasmin, J., Tian, Y., & Yang, J. (2020). A first look at the deprecation of RESTful APIs: An empirical study. In *2020 IEEE International Conference on Software Maintenance and Evolution (ICSME)*, 27 Sep.–3 Oct. 2020, Adelaide, SA, Australia (pp. 151–161). IEEE.

[28] Gokhale, S., Turcotte, A., & Tip, F. (2021). Automatic migration from synchronous to asynchronous JavaScript APIs. In *Proceedings of ACM Programming Languages*, *5*(OOPSLA), Chicago, IL, pp. 1–27.

[29] Parulkar, G. (2020). SDN fundamentals: Motivation, architecture, and benefits. *CSI Transactions on ICT*, *8*(1), 7–9.

[30] Abdou, A., Van Oorschot, P. C., & Wan, T. (2018). Comparative analysis of control plane security of SDN and conventional networks. *IEEE Communications Surveys & Tutorials*, *20*(4), 3542–3559.

[31] Benzekki, K., El Fergougui, A., & Elbelrhiti Elalaoui, A. (2016). Software-defined networking (SDN): A survey. *Security and Communication Networks*, *9*(18), 5803–5833.

[32] Hernandez-Valencia, E., Izzo, S., & Polonsky, B. (2015). How will NFV/SDN transform service provider opex? *IEEE Network*, *29*(3), 60–67.

[33] Henderickx, W. H., Hardwick, J. H., Filsfils, C. F., Tantsura, J. T., & Sivabalan, S. S. (2021). Path Computation Element Communication

Protocol (PCEP) Extensions for Segment Routing. *Collection of Restricted Reports in Transport Research, 2019, 4.*

[34] Singh, S. & Sharma, K. (2020) An evaluation of SDN facsimile, network monitoring system, measurement and its usance, 2020. *International Journal of Advanced Trends in Computer Applications, 7*(2), 25–36.

[35] Haleplidis, E., Pentikousis, K., Denazis, S., Salim, J. H., Meyer, D., & Koufopavlou, O. (2015). *Software-defined Networking (SDN): Layers and Architecture Terminology rfc7426.* RFC editor, p. 35.

[36] Scott-Hayward, S. & Arumugam, T. (2018). OFMTL-SEC: State-based security for software defined networks. In *2018 IEEE Conference on Network Function Virtualization and Software Defined Networks (NFV-SDN),* 27–29 Nov. 2018, Verona, Italy (pp. 1–7). IEEE.

[37] Anerousis, N., Chemouil, P., Lazar, A. A., Mihai, N., & Weinstein, S. B. (2021). The origin and evolution of open programmable networks and SDN. *IEEE Communications Surveys & Tutorials, 23*(3), 1956–1971.

[38] Matias, J., Garay, J., Toledo, N., Unzilla, J., & Jacob, E. (2015). Toward an SDN-enabled NFV architecture. *IEEE Communications Magazine, 53*(4), 187–193.

[39] Herrera, J. G. & Botero, J. F. (2016). Resource allocation in NFV: A comprehensive survey. *IEEE Transactions on Network and Service Management, 13*(3), 518–532.

[40] Kreutz, D., Ramos, F. M., Verissimo, P. E., Rothenberg, C. E., Azodolmolky, S., & Uhlig, S. (2014). Software-defined networking: A comprehensive survey. *Proceedings of the IEEE, 103*(1), 14–76.

[41] Shu, Z., Wan, J., Li, D., Lin, J., Vasilakos, A. V., & Imran, M. (2016). Security in software-defined networking: Threats and countermeasures. *Mobile Networks and Applications, 21*(5), 764–776.

[42] Mondal, A., Misra, S., & Maity, I. (2018). Buffer size evaluation of open-flow systems in software-defined networks. *IEEE Systems Journal, 13*(2), 1359–1366.

[43] Zhang, C., Sun, P., Hu, G., & Zhu, L. (2020). RETCAM: An efficient TCAM compression model for flow table of OpenFlow. *Journal of Communications and Networks, 22*(6), 484–492.

[44] Markoborodov, A., Skobtsova, Y., & Volkanov, D. (2020). Representation of the OpenFlow Switch Flow Table. In *2020 International Scientific and Technical Conference Modern Computer Network Technologies (MoNeTeC),* 27–29 Oct. 2020, Moscow, Russia (pp. 1–7). IEEE.

[45] Dong, L., Chen, L., He, B., & Wang, W. (2018). The research on designs of multiple flow tables in the openflow protocol. In *2018 27th International Conference on Computer Communication and Networks (ICCCN),* 30 July–2 Aug. 2018, Zhejiang, China (pp. 1–2). IEEE.

[46] Gamess, E., Tovar, D., & Cavadia, A. (2018). Design and implementation of a benchmarking tool for OpenFlow controllers. *International Journal of Computer Science and Information Technology*, *10*(11), 1–13.

[47] Panda, A., Samal, S. S., Turuk, A. K., Panda, A., & Venkatesh, V. C. (2019). Dynamic hard timeout based flow table management in openflow enabled SDN. In *2019 International Conference on Vision Towards Emerging Trends in Communication and Networking (ViTECoN)*, 30–31 Mar. 2019, Vellore, India (pp. 1–6). IEEE.

[48] Markoborodov, A., Skobtsova, Y., & Volkanov, D. (2020). Representation of the OpenFlow Switch Flow Table. In *2020 International Scientific and Technical Conference Modern Computer Network Technologies (MoNeTeC)*, October, Moscow, Russia (pp. 1–7). IEEE.

[49] Costa, L. C., Vieira, A. B., e Silva, E. D. B., Macedo, D. F., Vieira, L. F. M., Vieira, M. A. M., & da Rocha Miranda, M., Batista, G. F., Polizer, A. H., Gonçalves, A. V. G. S., Gomes, G., & Correia, L. H. A. (2021). OpenFlow data planes performance evaluation. *Performance Evaluation*, *147*, 102194.

[50] Li, J., Li, D., Yu, Y., Huang, Y., Zhu, J., & Geng, J. (2018). Towards full virtualization of SDN infrastructure. *Computer Networks*, *143*, 1–14.

[51] Jain, R. & Paul, S. (2013). Network virtualization and software defined networking for cloud computing: A survey. *IEEE Communications Magazine*, *51*(11), 24–31.

[52] Yazdinejad, A., Bohlooli, A., & Jamshidi, K. (2018). Efficient design and hardware implementation of the OpenFlow v1. 3 Switch on the Virtex-6 FPGA ML605. *The Journal of Supercomputing*, *74*(3), 1299–1320.

[53] Adeniji, O. D., Ayomıde, M. O., & Ajagbe, S. A. (2023). A model for network virtualization with OpenFlow protocol in software-defined network. In *Intelligent Communication Technologies and Virtual Mobile Networks* (pp. 723–733). Springer, Singapore.

[54] Amin, R., Reisslein, M., & Shah, N. (2018). Hybrid SDN networks: A survey of existing approaches. *IEEE Communications Surveys & Tutorials*, *20*(4), 3259–3306.

[55] Hamza, A., Gharakheili, H. H., Benson, T. A., & Sivaraman, V. (2019). Detecting volumetric attacks on lot devices via SDN-based monitoring of mud activity. In *Proceedings of the 2019 ACM Symposium on SDN Research*, 3–4 April 2019, San Jose, CA (pp. 36–48).

[56] Alvarez-Horcajo, J., Rojas, E., Martinez-Yelmo, I., Savi, M., & Lopez-Pajares, D. (2020). Hddp: Hybrid domain discovery protocol for heterogeneous devices in SDN. *IEEE Communications Letters*, *24*(8), 1655–1659.

[57] Salazar-Chacón, G. D. & Marrone, L. (2020). OpenSDN Southbound traffic characterization: Proof-of-concept virtualized SDN-infrastructure. In *2020 11th IEEE Annual Information Technology, Electronics and Mobile Communication Conference (IEMCON)*, 4–7 Nov. 2020, Vancouver, BC, Canada (pp. 0282–0287). IEEE.

[58] Deva Priya, I. & Silas, S. (2019). A survey on research challenges and applications in empowering the SDN-based Internet of Things. *Advances in Big Data and Cloud Computing, 750,* 157–167.

[59] Liu, Z., Ben-Basat, R., Einziger, G., Kassner, Y., Braverman, V., Friedman, R., & Sekar, V. (2019). Nitrosketch: Robust and general sketch-based monitoring in software switches. In *Proceedings of the ACM Special Interest Group on Data Communication*, 19–23 Aug. 2019, Beijing, China (pp. 334–350).

[60] Isyaku, B., Mohd Zahid, M. S., Bte Kamat, M., Abu Bakar, K., & Ghaleb, F. A. (2020). Software defined networking flow table management of open-flow switches performance and security challenges: A survey. *Future Internet, 12*(9), 147.

[61] Fang, V., Lvai, T., Han, S., Ratnasamy, S., Raghavan, B., & Sherry, J. (2018). Evaluating software switches: Hard or hopeless? *EECS Department, University of California, Berkeley, Tech. Rep. UCB/EECS-2018-136, 13,* 43.

[62] Singh, D., Ng, B., Lai, Y. C., Lin, Y. D., & Seah, W. K. (2019). Analytical modelling of software and hardware switches with internal buffer in software-defined networks. *Journal of Network and Computer Applications, 136,* 22–37.

[63] Kuźniar, M., Perešíni, P., Kostić, D., & Canini, M. (2018). Methodology, measurement and analysis of flow table update characteristics in hardware openflow switches. *Computer Networks, 136,* 22–36.

[64] Csikor, L., Szalay, M., Rétvári, G., Pongrácz, G., Pezaros, D. P., & Toka, L. (2020). Transition to SDN is HARMLESS: Hybrid architecture for migrating legacy ethernet switches to SDN. *IEEE/ACM Transactions on Networking, 28*(1), 275–288.

[65] Shalimov, A., Zuikov, D., Zimarina, D., Pashkov, V., & Smeliansky, R. (2013). Advanced study of SDN/OpenFlow controllers. In *Proceedings of the 9th Central & Eastern European Software Engineering Conference in Russia*, 24–25 Oct. 2013, Moscow, Russia (pp. 1–6).

[66] McKeown, N., Anderson, T., Balakrishnan, H., Parulkar, G., Peterson, L., Rexford, J., Shenker, S., and Turner, J. (2008). OpenFlow: Enabling innovation in campus networks. *ACM SIGCOMM Computer Communication Review, 38*(2), 69–74.

[67] Gaurav, A., Arya, V., & Santaniello, D. (2022). Analysis of machine learning based DDoS attack detection techniques in software defined network. *Cyber Security Insights Magazine (CSIM), 1*(1), 1–6.

[68] Plageras, A. P., Psannis, K. E., Stergiou, C., Wang, H., & Gupta, B. B. (2018). Efficient IoT-based sensor BIG Data collection–processing and analysis in smart buildings. *Future Generation Computer Systems, 82,* 349–357.

[69] Gupta, S. & Gupta, B. B. (2018). Security in wireless LAN (WLAN) and WiMAX systems. In *Computer and Cyber Security* (pp. 195–222). Auerbach Publications, Florida.

Chapter 5

SDN Controllers

The SDN controller is responsible for establishing and dismantling flows and paths in the network, making up the middle layer. The controller takes input about the capacity and demand of the networking device through which the traffic flows. The SDN controller manages two types of modules linked to network regulation and monitoring. The infrastructure layer's packet forwarding rules and the application layer's policies are both part of network control. The second is concerned with network monitoring and presents local and global network status.

5.1 Introduction

As we've already mentioned, the controller keeps track of the entire network, executes policy decisions, manages all of the SDN components that make up the network infrastructure, and provides northbound API access to applications [1–4]. When we stated that the controller executes policy decisions pertaining to routing, forwarding, redirecting, load balancing, and similar tasks, we meant both the controller itself and the applications that use it. Common application modules that are included with controllers include a learning switch, a router, a simple firewall, and a load balancer. These are actually SDN applications that are bundled with the SDN controller. In the previous chapters, we have discussed the SDN architecture and how it is different from that of a traditional network. In this chapter, we focus on the controller part specifically, which is actually programmed by the SDN developer.

The SDN controller is the entity responsible for network state management. In some cases, it requires a data repository to manage and even distribute this network state among other forwarding switches. These data repositories store data obtained by controlled network devices and related software, as well as data managed by SDN applications (for example, network state, some ephemeral configuration information, learnt topology, and control session data) [5]. The controller may have numerous, purpose-driven data management processes in various circumstances. Apart from managing and distributing network states, the SDN controller acts as a high-level data model that encapsulates the interactions between managed resources, policies, and other controller functions [6]. Yang modelling language has been used to develop these data models. The controller services are exposed to an application via a modern, generally RESTful (representational state transfer) application programming interface (API) [7, 8]. This simplifies the majority of the controller-to-application interface. This interface is best produced from the data model that represents the controller's services and features. The controller and its API are sometimes part of a development environment that creates the API code from the model. Moreover, a secure TCP connection is required between the controller and the attached entities.

5.2 SDN Controller Components

Generally, an SDN controller is composed of four basic components: a high-level language, a policy/rule update process, a network state collection process, and a network state synchronisation process. We discuss each of these components one by one in the following sections [9].

Next, a protocol that uses standards to offer application-driven network state on network devices is required to build an SDN controller. Further, a mechanism for discovering devices, topologies, and services; a path calculation system; and maybe other network-centric or resource-centric information services must be utilised to develop an SDN controller [10–12]. Figure 5.1 shows the SDN controller components.

5.2.1 A High-Level Language

The controller's primary role is to integrate application requirements into packet forwarding rules. This function specifies a communication

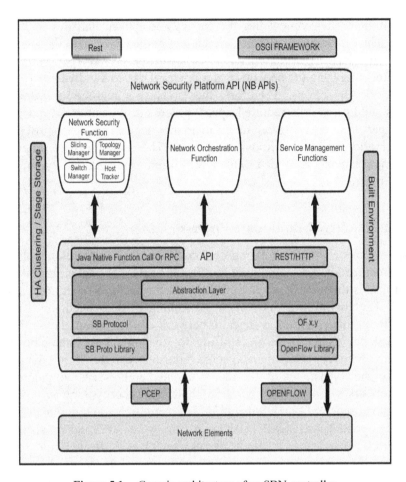

Figure 5.1.   Generic architecture of an SDN controller.

protocol, i.e., a programming language, between the control and application layers [13]. Following are some characteristics of the SDN controller's high-level language:

(a) The language should be able to convert network policies into packet forwarding behaviour. It should be able to mix policies from different network applications. Apart from that, it should also be able to resolve the issues caused by network applications.

(b) A network programming language should be able to provide the resources needed to check the network's status. The language's runtime environment has the capacity to gather statistics and data related to the network state, which it may then pass on to the application layer.

(c) Reconfiguring the network is not practical due to the diversity of network regulations. Therefore, the language's runtime environment should trigger the required update process of the networking device, apart from ensuring that other invariants, such as access control preservation and loop avoidance, are met. The common SDN programming languages needed to meet the current standards are Pyretic and Procera [14].

5.2.2 A Policy/Rule Update Process

The responsibility for creating packet forwarding rules rests with the SDN controller. Additionally, it outlines the rules for packet forwarding and instals them on the right switching hardware for efficient operation [15]. The forwarding rules in the switching devices need to be constantly modified due to changes in network configuration and dynamic control, for example, traffic shifting for dynamic load balancing and network recovery after an unexpected failure. Due to the SDN's dynamic nature, the consistency of the rules is updated and reserved to guarantee the network's appropriate operation, including security, loop avoidance, and the absence of black holes [13]. There are two ways in which rules can be updated consistently: strict consistency and eventual consistency. In strict consistency, an updated rule set or the original rule set is applied. This consistency is accomplished either at the packet-by-packet level of processing or at the level of each flow, where each packet of a flow is processed using either the original or the updated rule set. In eventual consistency, the earlier packets of the same flow are permitted to use the original rule set before or during the update procedure, and it ensures that, eventually, after the update procedure is complete, the subsequent packets use the updated rule set [16].

5.2.3 A Network State Collection Process

A global view of the complete network is subsequently built using information on the network status as indicated by traffic statistics, which include packet number, length time, data size, and bandwidth share. The application layer will use this data, or the network topology graph, to make further decisions as needed [17]. Each switching device in the network gathers and maintains statistics of local traffic in its onboard memory as part of the operation of network status collection, and the controller retrieves these data via a "pull" mode or a "push" mode [13].

5.2.4 A Network State Synchronization Process

Attributing control to a single centralised controller might result in a performance constraint, and hence, several controllers are deployed in P2P as backup or replication controllers to solve this. To ensure network functionality, all controllers should be able to create and maintain a global network view based on the network status collected by each individual controller [18]. In Ref. [19], the authors have used HyperFlow, which allows several controllers to share a global view of the network. These are the main components of any SDN controller that need to be considered while developing one. Now, we move a step ahead towards the current trends and implementation of SDN [13, 57].

The expansion of the data centre networking industry has also resulted in the introduction of a large number of new network pieces centred on the hypervisor switch/router/bridge design. This includes the network service virtualisation discussed later in the chapter. Network service virtualisation, also known as network functions virtualisation (NFV), will include even more of these components in the next-generation network architecture, highlighting the necessity for a controller to operate and manage these components.

5.3 VMWare

VMware has laid its foundation in the SDN and virtualisation domains by introducing NSX as the SDN network virtualisation and security platform that was created following VMware's acquisition of Nicira in 2012 [20]. VMware's NSX network virtualisation technology enables IT managers to virtualise network components without the need for manual intervention. They can manage networks at the hypervisor level with VMware NSX SDN technology, and they can provision, organise, and protect enterprise-scale networks with software [21]. NSX is important to VMware's strategy as it transitions virtualisation from servers to networks. Hypervisor-enabled network capabilities, dynamic virtual network management, enhanced

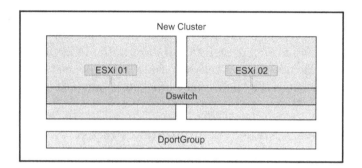

Figure 5.2.   VMware VSphere architecture.

network security, and robust automation are among the VMware NSX
SDN features [22].

NSX facilitates load balancing, logical switching, and micro segmentation that enhance the SDN platform's networking, operations, and security support for a company. VMware NSX is a hypervisor networking
solution for managing, automating, and delivering basic layer 4–7 (L4–
L7) services to virtual machine (VM) traffic [23]. NSX can provide data
flow between VMs within the hypervisor with switching, routing, rudi-
mentary load-balancing, and firewall functions. NSX needs non-VM traffic (handled by more than 70% of data centre servers) to be routed into the
virtual environment. Before discussing the NSX features and use cases,
one must first understand its components [24].

The architecture of VMware vSphere is fairly basic. In a cluster
referred to as "New Cluster," there are two ESXi hosts. A distributed virtual switch called "DSwitch," with a single port group named
"DPortGroup," is present on both hosts. ESXi is the bare metal hypervisor, as it does not need an OS to run. It directly runs on the system hardware. All of the VMs for NSX appliances are put into the "DSwitch,"
which is a distributed virtual switch. No traffic goes through the local
vSwitch0 anymore; all underlay traffic goes through the distributed virtual
switch [25, 26]. Figure 5.2 shows the architecture of VSphere.

Many tasks, ranging from management to packet forwarding, must be
carried out in order to enable SDN. We explain the NSX components in
the following section:

(a) **VMware NSX Manager:** The VMware NSX Manager integrates with the VMware vCenter Server, allowing you to manage the VMware NSX operations from within VMware vCenter. All VMware NSX operations and configurations are handled by VMware vCenter, which connects with the VMware NSX Manager via APIs to assign tasks to the relevant entity [27].

(b) **VMware NSX Controller:** Through the VMware NSX Controller, all virtual network provisioning and MAC address learning are managed. The VMware NSX Controller can be viewed as the SDN network's virtualised control plane.

(c) **VMware NSX Logical Distributed Router:** All packets passing via the virtualised SDN networks are forwarded and routed by the VMware NSX Logical Distributed Router (LDR) [28, 58]. It is responsible for providing the following functionalities:

- default gateway for all VMs,
- MAC address learning and flooding,
- routing of all data packets between separate virtual networks,
- integrating with VMware NSX Edge to move egress traffic outside of virtual networks,
- termination of a virtual tunnel endpoint (VTEP),
- employment and deployment of security policies,
- multi-tenancy.

The NSX LDR is an excellent tool for fine-grained virtual network segmentation. Multiple VMware NSX LDRs can be formed to support multi-tenancy or to create a completely different security zone to meet regulatory compliance with standards such as the Payment Card Industry Data Security Standard (PCI DSS). NSX LDR aids the network administrator in creating virtual switches that can be used as virtual extensible LAN (VXLAN) identifiers. These VXLAN identifiers can be used in the same way VLANs are used in physical networks [29]. Figure 5.3 shows the VMware LDR control and data planes.

The VMware NSX LDR is divided into two parts: the control plane and the data plane. The control plane is responsible for provisioning and managing network changes. Each VMware ESXi host also has an installed VMware NSX LDR to handle traffic forwarding and routing. Each VMware maintains a copy of NSX LDR operating in the

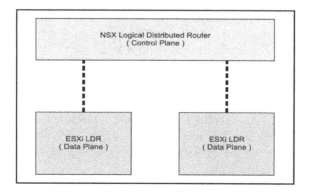

Figure 5.3.   VMware LDR control and data planes.

hypervisor. The VMware cluster has all of the gateway interfaces and IP addresses. This enables VMs to use their default gateway on the local hypervisor. There exist three types of MAC address learning methods: unicast, multicast, and hybrid [59].

(d) **VMware NSX Edge Gateway:** The bridge that connects the virtual networks to the outside world is the VMware NSX Edge Gateway. It serves as a virtual WAN router that can communicate with the actual networking hardware so that all internal virtual networks can access the WAN, the Internet, and any other networked physical resources. Centralised security policy enforcement between the real network and the virtualised networks is another capability of the VMware NSX Edge Gateway.

The LDR and NSX Edge Gateways have a full network of VXLAN tunnels. This allows any VMware ESXi host to interact directly using VXLAN tunnels when they have to perform switching or rerouting of traffic. The VMware NSX Edge Gateway removes the VXLAN header and directs traffic through its "Uplink" interface and into the Virtual Chassis Fabric if it needs to enter or leave the VMware NSX environment. When traffic enters or exits the VMware NSX environment, the VMware NSX Edge Gateway strips the VXLAN header and directs it through its Uplink interface into the Virtual Chassis Fabric. Figure 5.4 shows the architecture of VXLAN tunnels.

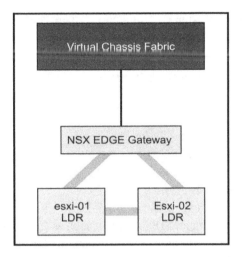

Figure 5.4. VXLAN tunnels.

5.4 CISCO Application Centric Infrastructure (ACI)

Cisco Application Centric Infrastructure (ACI) is a data-centre-focused SDN solution. Cisco ACI enables the definition of network infrastructure based on network policies, simplifying, optimising, and expediting the application deployment lifecycle. It is widely used in industries because it provides high software flexibility, efficient configuration, and hardware performance scalability. It also differs from other SDN technologies in terms of management, policy structure, and protocols. The hardware of ACI is the most recent generation of Cisco Nexus 9000 switches, and its software also includes the Data Centre Policy Engine, Additional Data Centre Pod, and Non-directly Attached Virtual and Physical Leaf Switches [30].

APIC is Cisco ACI's SDN controller. It develops the policies that define the network infrastructure of the data centre. ACI Fabric OS is used by Nexus 9000 switches to interface with APIC and build infrastructure based on policies. They can be either leaf (access) or spine (distribution) switches. Leaf switches connect all endpoints, including APICs, to the network. In the back-end, these leaf switches are linked together by spine switches. ACI can be installed using a variety of different models by utilising these components [31]. This encompasses on-premises, cloud-based (public, private, and hybrid clouds), and SD-WAN edge environments. Organisations can now leverage policy-based network management throughout their corporate WANs.

5.4.1 Characteristics and Advantages of ACI

In this section, we discuss the main features of ACI and how organisations benefit from these features [32]. Following are the characteristics:

(a) **Consistent infrastructure:** Cisco ACI encapsulates the underlying infrastructure's details. This simplifies the design and configuration of network environments.
(b) **Flexibility:** The whole network architecture of an enterprise is implemented as code using an SDN solution, such as Cisco ACI. This makes it simple to alter configurations to meet changing business requirements.
(c) **Hybrid environment:** Cisco ACI supports both on-premises and cloud-based infrastructure, allowing ACI environments to be deployed across numerous environments.
(d) **Orchestration and automation:** To construct network infrastructure based on network policies, Cisco ACI heavily relies on automation. This facilitates adjustments and boosts scalability.

Other than the above-mentioned features/advantages, SDN provides benefits such as container networking, orchestration, virtualisation, integration capabilities, and scalability. Customers may manage complexity, maximise business benefits, and deploy workloads in any place, small or large, on-premises or remotely, in private and public clouds, satellite data centres, and 5G-enabled telecom edges [33]. Table 5.1 lists some benefits rendered by the CISCO ACI controller

5.4.2 Components of CISCO ACI

Using a two-tier spine-leaf topology, the Cisco ACI fabric is composed of the APIC, ANP, and Cisco Nexus 9000 series switches [31, 34]. There are three main parts to the Cisco ACI architecture, which are discussed as follows:

1. **Application Policy Infrastructure Controller (APIC):** The APIC is regarded as the ACI architecture's brain. It is a centrally located software controller with centralised management, programmability (automation), rule enforcement, and network status monitoring features. It is responsible for fabric activation, switch firmware maintenance,

Table 5.1. Benefits of CISCO ACI.

S. No.	Benefit	Description
1.	Network operations acceleration	• Operational simplicity is achieved through common policy management and operation models for application, network, and security resources. • Network administration and visibility are centralised, with full automation and real-time network status monitoring. • Underlay and overlay networks are seamlessly integrated. • Northbound open APIs give DevOps teams flexibility and ecosystem partner integration. • A cloud-ready SDN solution. • Standardised management tool for both real and virtual environments. • Agile application deployment and automation of IT workflows.
2.	Integrated with multi-cloud securely	• Construct a business roadmap and offer disaster recovery. • With a zero-trust allow-list paradigm and novel features, such as policy enforcement, micro-segmentation, and analytics, there is inherent security. • Ability to maintain a uniform security posture across several clouds.
3.	Provide an exceptional application experience	• Any data centre and public cloud can benefit from a single policy and seamless connectivity • Through any hypervisor, any cloud, any workload and at any location, it can render a great application experience.

increasing and optimising performance, translating application policies into device-level instructions, integrating physical and virtual environments, and scalability [60].

Additionally, in contrast to SDN controllers, Cisco APIC does not directly alter the data flow. The leaf switches are configured to forward traffic in accordance with the stated policies, which are defined centrally. Furthermore, the APIC is entirely isolated from the data flow; thus, even if contact with the APIC is lost in a network, the fabric can still forward traffic. The needs for availability are thus consistently satisfied in ACI. In the ACI fabric, APIC is positioned between the ANP and the network infrastructure that supports ACI. They offer both a command-line interface (CLI) and a graphical user interface (GUI) that leverage this API to control the fabric. They expose a northbound API through XML and JSON.

In addition to a GUI and a CLI, it also supports REST APIs, Python APIs, and bash scripting. Additionally, the APIC offers a southbound open-source API that enables third-party network service providers to perform policy control over provided devices.

2. **Application Network Profile (ANP):** ANP, in contrast to APIC, is described as an aggregation of endpoint groups (EPGs), their connections, and the policies defining those connections. EPG is a logical collection of comparable endpoints that represents a service set or application tier and calls for a common set of policies. All application components and their interdependencies on the application fabric are logically represented by the ANP.

ANPs are primarily made to be logically modelled to match the way that applications are developed and delivered. Furthermore, the system manages connectivity, policy enforcement, and configuration rather than doing these tasks manually.

3. **CISCO ACI Fabric:** We can see that Cisco is growing its Nexus range with the recent addition of Cisco Nexus 9000 Series Switches for both traditional and Cisco ACI data centre installations to the family of Nexus switches. These switches control the virtual and physical network infrastructures by providing an application-aware switching fabric to be collaborated with an APIC. They are quite popular because they provide modular and fixed 1/10/40 gigabit Ethernet switch configurations. They are also designed to function in either the Cisco NX-OS mode or the Cisco ACI mode. Data centres may take full advantage of the Cisco ACI application policy-based services and infrastructure automation features in either mode because of the compatibility and consistency it provides with existing Cisco Nexus switches. These features make Cisco Nexus switches an essential part of the ACI architecture. Through a software upgrade, they offer customers investment protection and a simple migration to Cisco ACI.

As a result, these features of ACI make this technology suitable for switching in next-generation data centres and available to clients of all sizes.

5.5 VMware NSX vs. CISCO ACI

Now more than ever, businesses are adopting cloud-based solutions and networks that support software solutions, and an abundance of vendors are dominating the market with innovative takes on these technologies. Cisco and VMware are just two of the numerous market-leading companies that place an emphasis on SDN and infrastructure design [22]. The SDN solution proposed by VMware is NSX based on security software and virtual networking, while that proposed by CISCO is ACI. Both of these solutions have been discussed above.

The primary distinction between Cisco ACI and NSX is the availability of many device packages for the APIC controller and, in the case of Cisco ACI, the ability to conduct advanced network services, such as ACI L4–L7, by utilising the open SDK [35]. However, the advanced network services offered by VMware NSX from L4 to L7 are tightly controlled and run through a closed API.

ACI is an overlay architecture that treats physical and virtual networks as one unified entity, governed by a uniform set of policies centred on applications. On the other hand, to communicate with bare-metal apps and other network endpoints, NSX relies on network gateways, as it is a hypervisor overlay-based approach that is VMware-centric. Physical and virtual networks, L4–L7 services, and, eventually and probably, computation and storage may all be managed through a unified interface with ACI. ACI provides comprehensive visibility and troubleshooting capabilities, and it establishes a correlation between the network and application health statuses. NSX introduces a clean overlay network but lacks direct access to the actual network beneath it, leaving the correlation between the two (i.e., underlay and overlay networks) to other technologies. NSX only automates virtual networks; it does not yet offer any management of underlying physical devices.

Cisco ACI supports multi-hypervisor environments and provides open interfaces and APIs. APIC's (the SDN controller of ACI) open northbound and southbound APIs allow for seamless integration with existing management, orchestration, L4–L7 services, and physical and virtual devices [35]. This provides customers with total investment protection by allowing the integration of their existing IT systems into an ACI architecture. NSX restricts client options by delivering distinct products and features for vSphere and Linux-based hypervisors but no support for Microsoft Hyper-V. Table 5.2 shows a comparison between ACI and NSX.

Table 5.2.   Comparison between ACI and NSX.

Features	ACI	NSX
Automation	Full automation of physical as well as virtual devices is achieved through a single API.	Automation is restricted to virtual networks only. Physical network cannot be automated.
Support to legacy network	Legacy workloads can be connected directly to the fabric, while legacy hardware devices can be interfaced with the fabric using the multi-chassis LDAP protocol.	L2 gateways that run over ESXi can be used to support legacy networks, but they have poor performance and slower convergence.
Routing	Hardware implementation is utilised to perform routing at line rate for north–south and east–west bounds, irrespective of the workload assigned to the fabric.	Hypervisor is utilised for east–west bounds, but it puts the overhead of distributed logical router control for VM per IP address. Routing for north–south interfaces requires edge service router VMs to be deployed per IP address. Load balancing and redundancy can be achieved but with slow convergence.
Availability	Sub-second convergence can be achieved for link and node failures.	Sub-second convergence cannot be achieved.
Integration	Open SDK is utilised for L4–L4 service insertion, where partners can build a device package to represent their services to the APIC controller. It supports virtual and physical devices.	Closed API is utilised for L4–L7 service insertion.

5.6 Comparison of Other SDN Controllers

In this section, we discuss some major SDN controllers in a comparative way. Table 5.3 shows the comparative analysis of various SDN controllers.

Table 5.3. Comparative analysis of various SDN controllers.

Feature	GUI	Programming Language	Distributed Controller	OS support	Northbound API	Southbound API	East–westbound API	Modularity	Consistency	Multi-threading	License	Documentation
NOX [36]	Web based	C++	No	Linux	REST API	OpenFlow1.0	–	Low	No	Yes	GPL 3.0	Poor
POX [37]	GUI and CLI	Python	No	Linux, MacOS, Windows	REST API	OpenFlow 1.0	–	Low	No	No	Apache 2.0	Poor
RYU [38]	CLI	Python	No	Linux, MacOS	REST	OpenFlow 1.0–1.5	–	Fair	Yes	Yes	Apache 2.0	Good
BEACON [39]	CLI, web based	Java	No	Linux, MacOS, Windows	–	OpenFlow 1.0	–	Fair	No	Yes	GPL 3.0	Fair
ONOS [40]	CLI, web based	Java	Yes	Linux, MacOS, Windows	REST	OpenFlow 1.0	Raft	High	Yes	Yes	Apache 2.0	Good
Floodlight [41]	CLI, web based	Java	No	Linux, MacOS, Windows	REST, Java RPC, quantum	OpenFlow 1.0	–	Fair	Yes	Yes	Apache 2.0	Good
IRIS [42]	Web based	Java	No	Linux, MacOS, Windows	REST	OpenFlow 1.0–1.3	–	Fair	No	Yes	Apache 2.0	Fair
OpenDaylight [43]	CLI, web based	Java	Yes	Linux, MacOS, Windows	REST, NETCONF, XMPP	OpenFlow 1.0–1.3	Raft, Akka	High	Yes	Yes	EPL 1.0	Good
RunOS [44]	CLI, web based	C++	Yes	Linux	REST	OpenFlow 1.0–1.3	Maple	High	Yes	Yes	Apache 2.0	Fair

(*Continued*)

Table 5.3.   (*Continued*)

Feature	GUI	Programming Language	Distributed Controller	OS support	Northbound API	Southbound API	East–westbound API	Modularity	Consistency	Multi-threading	License	Documentation
HyperFlow [45]	–	C++	Yes	–	–	OpenFlow 1.0	Publish and subscribe	Fair	No	Yes	Proprietary	Fair
FlowVisor [46]	CLI, web based	C	No	Linux	JSON, RPC	OpenFlow 1.0	–	–	No	–	Proprietary	Fair
DISCO [47]	–	Java	Yes	–	REST	OpenFlow 1.0	AMQP	Good	No	–	Proprietary	Fair
Onix [48]	–	C++	Yes	–	ONIX API	OpenFlow 1.0, OVSDB	Zookeeper	Good	No	Yes	Proprietary	Fair
Microflow [49]	CLI, web based	C	No	Linux	Socket	OpenFlow 1.0–1.5	–	–	No	Yes	Apache 2.0	Fair
Open Contrail [50]	CLI, web based	C, C++, Python	No	Linux	REST	BGP, XMPP	–	High	Yes	Yes	Apache 2.0	Good
PANE [51]	CLI	Haskell	Yes	Linux, MacOS	PANE API	OpenFlow 1.0	Zookeeper	Fair	No	–	BSD 3.0	Fair
Maestro [52]	Web UI	JAVA	No	Linux MacOS, Windows	Ad hoc	OpenFlow 1.0	–	Fair	No	Yes	LGPL 2.1	Fair
NodeFlow [53]	CLI	Javascript	No	Node.js	JSON	OpenFlow 1.0	–	–	No	–	Cisco	Fair
POF Controller [54]	CLI, GUI	Java	No	Linux	–	OpenFlow 1.0	–	–	No	–	Apache 2.0	Fair
Ravel [55]	CLI	Python	No	Linux	–	OpenFlow 1.0	–	–	Yes	–	Apache 2.0	Fair
Rosemary [56]	CLI	C	No	Linux	Adhoc	OpenFlow 1.0–1.3, XMPP	–	Good	No	Yes	Proprietary	Fair

Exercises

Q.1. Discuss in detail the main components of a SDN controller.

Q.2. Explain the significance of the policy/rule update module in a SDN controller where the network dynamics change continuously.

Q.3. Elaborate on the difference between network state collection and network state synchronisation modules of a SDN controller.

Q.4. Discuss the architectural components of NSX, a SDN solution from VMware.

Q.5. Discuss the architectural components of ACI, a SDN solution from Cisco.

Q.6. How can ACI be integrated with multi-cloud computing, and what could be the challenges associated with it?

Q.7. Discuss in detail the difference between VMware NSX and Cisco ACI with respect to scalability and automation.

Q.8. Discuss Opendaylight, Ryu, POX, and HyperFlow SDN controllers.

References

[1] Karakus, M. & Durresi, A. (2017). A survey: Control plane scalability issues and approaches in software-defined networking (SDN). *Computer Networks*, *112*, 279–293.

[2] Lopes, F. A., Santos, M., Fidalgo, R., & Fernandes, S. (2015). A software engineering perspective on SDN programmability. *IEEE Communications Surveys & Tutorials*, *18*(2), 1255–1272.

[3] Nadeau, T. D. & Gray, K. (2013). *SDN: Software Defined Networks: An Authoritative Review of Network Programmability Technologies*. O'Reilly Media Inc., California.

[4] Schriegel, S., Kobzan, T., & Jasperneite, J. (2018). Investigation on a distributed SDN control plane architecture for heterogeneous time sensitive networks. In *2018 14th IEEE International Workshop on Factory Communication Systems (WFCS)*, June, Imperia, Italy (pp. 1–10). IEEE.

[5] Abdou, A., Van Oorschot, P. C., & Wan, T. (2018). Comparative analysis of control plane security of SDN and conventional networks. *IEEE Communications Surveys & Tutorials*, *20*(4), 3542–3559

[6] Benzekki, K., El Fergougui, A., & Elbelrhiti Elalaoui, A. (2016). Software-defined networking (SDN): A survey. *Security and Communication Networks*, *9*(18), 5803–5833.

[7] Medved, J., Varga, R., Tkacik, A., & Gray, K. (2014). Opendaylight: Towards a model-driven SDN controller architecture. In *Proceeding of IEEE International Symposium on a World of Wireless, Mobile and Multimedia Networks 2014*, 19 June 2014, Sydney, NSW, Australia (pp. 1–6). IEEE.

[8] Montoya-Munoz, A. I., Casas-Velasco, D. M., Estrada-Solano, F., Ordonez, A., & Rendon, O. M. C. (2017). A YANG model for a vertical SDN management plane. In *2017 IEEE Colombian Conference on Communications and Computing (COLCOM)*, 16–18 Aug. 2017, Cartagena, Colombia (pp. 1–6). IEEE.

[9] Klaedtke, F., Karame, G. O., Bifulco, R., & Cui, H. (2014). Access control for SDN controllers. In *Proceedings of the Third Workshop on Hot Topics in Software Defined Networking*, 22 Aug. 2014, Chicago, IL (pp. 219–220).

[10] Medved, J., Varga, R., Tkacik, A., & Gray, K. (2014). Opendaylight: Towards a model-driven SDN controller architecture. In *Proceeding of IEEE International Symposium on a World of Wireless, Mobile and Multimedia Networks 2014*, 19 June 2014, Sydney, NSW, Australia (pp. 1–6). IEEE.

[11] Bondkovskii, A., Keeney, J., van der Meer, S., & Weber, S. (2016). Qualitative comparison of open-source SDN controllers. In *NOMS 2016–2016 IEEE/IFIP Network Operations and Management Symposium*, 25–29 April 2016, Istanbul, Turkey (pp. 889–894). IEEE.

[12] Singh, S. & Jha, R. K. (2017). A survey on software defined networking: Architecture for next generation network. *Journal of Network and Systems Management, 25*(2), 321–374.

[13] Xia, W., Wen, Y., Foh, C. H., Niyato, D., & Xie, H. (2014). A survey on software-defined networking. *IEEE Communications Surveys & Tutorials, 17*(1), 27–51.

[14] Braun, W. & Menth, M. (2014). Software-defined networking using OpenFlow: Protocols, applications and architectural design choices. *Future Internet, 6*(2), 302–336.

[15] Wang, R., Butnariu, D., & Rexford, J. (2011). {OpenFlow-Based} server load balancing gone wild. In *Workshop on Hot Topics in Management of Internet, Cloud, and Enterprise Networks and Services (Hot-ICE'11)*. 29 March 2011, Boston.

[16] Kim, H. & Feamster, N. (2013). Improving network management with software defined networking. *IEEE Communications Magazine, 51*(2), 114–119.

[17] Raghavendra, R., Lobo, J., & Lee, K. W. (2012). Dynamic graph query primitives for SDN-based cloudnetwork management. In *Proceedings of the First Workshop on Hot Topics in Software Defined Networks*, 13 Aug. 2012, Helsinki, Finland (pp. 97–102).

[18] Fonseca, P., Bennesby, R., Mota, E., & Passito, A. (2012). A replication component for resilient OpenFlow-based networking. In *2012 IEEE*

Network Operations and Management Symposium, 16–20 April 2012, Maui, HI (pp. 933–939). IEEE.

[19] Tootoonchian, A. & Ganjali, Y. (2010). Hyperflow: A distributed control plane for openflow. In *Proceedings of the 2010 Internet Network Management Conference on Research on Enterprise Networking*, April (Vol. 3, pp. 10–5555).

[20] Kirkpatrick, K. (2013). Software-defined networking. *Communications of the ACM, 56*(9), 16–19.

[21] Thakurratan, R. S. (2017). *Learning VMware NSX*. Packt Publishing Ltd.

[22] Eriksson, J. & Hedlund, R. (2016). *Cisco ACI and VMware NSX, a Comparison between Software Defined Networks* (Dissertation).

[23] Thirupathi, V., Sandeep, C. H., Kumar, N., & Kumar, P. P. (2019). A comprehensive review on SDN architecture, applications and major benifits of SDN. *International Journal of Advanced Science and Technology, 28*(20), 607–614.

[24] VMware NSX Datasheet. Available at: https://www.vmware.com/content/dam/digitalmarketing/vmware/en/pdf/products/nsx/vmware-nsx-datasheet.pdf.

[25] Sosa, E. S. (2020). *Mastering VMware NSX for VSphere*. John Wiley & Sons, Hoboken, NJ.

[26] Sangha, T. & Wibowo, B. (2018). *VMware NSX Cookbook: Over 70 Recipes to Master the Network Virtualization Skills to Implement, Validate, Operate, Upgrade, and Automate VMware NSX for vSphere*. Packt Publishing Ltd., Birmingham, UK.

[27] Pettit, J., Pfaff, B., Stringer, J., Tu, C. C., Blanco, B., & Tessmer, A. (2018). Bringing platform harmony to VMware NSX. *ACM SIGOPS Operating Systems Review, 52*(1), 123–128.

[28] Keeriyattil, S. (2019). Microsegmentation and zero trust: Introduction. In *Zero Trust Networks with VMware NSX* (pp. 17–31). Apress, Berkeley, CA.

[29] Network, B. H. S. & Keeriyattil, S. Zero Trust Networks with VMware NSX.

[30] Cardona, R. (2020). *Learning the Cisco Application-Centric Infrastructure (ACI)*. Packt Publishing.

[31] Fordham, S. (2017). *Cisco ACI Cookbook*. Packt Publishing Ltd., Birmingham, UK.

[32] Tischer, R. & Gooley, J. (2016). *Programming and Automating Cisco Networks: A Guide to Network Programmability and Automation in the Data Center, Campus, and WAN*. Cisco Press, New Jersey.

[33] Dagenhardt, F., Moreno, J., & Dufresne, B. (2018). *Deploying ACI: The Complete Guide to Planning, Configuring, and Managing Application Centric Infrastructure*. Cisco, New Jersey.

[34] Lindstrom, P., Villars, R. L., & Marden, M. (2015). *Assessing the Business Value of SDN Datacenter Security Solutions*. International Data Corporation (IDC), Cisco, New Jersey.

[35] Abdullah, M. Z., Al-Awad, N. A., & Hussein, F. W. (2018). Performance comparison and evaluation of different software defined networks controllers. *International Journal of Computing and Network Technology*, 6(2).

[36] Gude, N., Koponen, T., Pettit, J., Pfaff, B., Casado, M., McKeown, N., & Shenker, S. (2008). Nox: Towards an operating system for networks. *ACM SIGCOMM Computer Communication Review*, 38(3), 105–110.

[37] POX Controller Manual Current Documentation [Online]. Available at: https://noxrepo.github.io/pox-doc/html/.

[38] Ryu SDN Framework Community. Ryu Controller. [Online]. Available at: https://osrg.github.io/ryu/index.html.

[39] Erickson, D. (2013). The beacon openflow controller. In *Proceedings of the Second ACM SIGCOMM Workshop*, 16 Aug. 2013, Hongkong, China (pp. 13–18).

[40] Berde, P., Gerola, M., Hart, J., Higuchi, Y., Kobayashi, M., Koide, T., Lantz, B., O'Connor, B., Radoslavov, P., Snow, W., & Parulkar, G. (2014). Onos: Towards an open, distributed SDN os. In *Proceedings of the Third Workshop on Hot Topics in Software Defined Networking (HotSDN'14)*, 22 Aug. 2014, Chicago, IL (pp. 1–6). ACM.

[41] Big Switch Networks. Project Floodlight [Online]. Available at: http://www.projectfloodlight.org/floodlight/.

[42] Lee, B., Park, S. H., Shin, J., & Yang, S. (2014). IRIS: The Openflow-based recursive SDN controller. In *16th International Conference on Advanced Communication Technology*, 16–19 Feb. 2014, Pyeongchang, Korea (South) (pp. 1227–1231). IEEE.

[43] OpenDaylight: A Linux foundation collaborative project [Online]. Available at: https://www.opendaylight.org/.

[44] GitHub. RunOS OpenFlow controller [Online]. Available at: https://github.com/ARCCN/runos.

[45] Tootoonchian, A. & Ganjali, Y. (2010). Hyperflow: A distributed control plane for openflow. In *Proceedings of the 2010 Internet Network Management Conference on Research on Enterprise Networking*, 27 April 2010, San Jose, CA (pp. 3–3).

[46] Sherwood R., Gibb, G., Yap, K., Appenzeller, G., Casado, M., Mckeown, N., & Parulkar, G. (2009). FlowVisor: A network virtualization layer. *Network*, 15, 1–132.

[47] Phemius, K., Bouet, M., & Leguay, J. (2014). DISCO: Distributed multidomain SDN controllers. In *IEEE/IFIP Network Operations and Management Symposium: Management in a Software Defined World*, 5–9 May 2014, Krakow, Poland.

[48] Koponen, T., Casado, M., Gude, N., Stribling. J., Poutievski, L., Zhu, M., Ramanathan, R., Iwata, Y., Inoue, H., Hama, T., & Shenker, S. (2010). ONIX: A distributed control platform for large-scale production networks.

In *USENIX Conference on Operating Systems Design and Implementation*, 4–6 Oct. 2010, Vancouver, BC, Canada (pp. 1–6).

[49] GitHub. MicroFlow: The light-weighted, lightning fast OpenFlow SDN controller [Online]. Available at: https://github.com/PanZhangg/Microflow.

[50] OpenContrail An open-source network virtualization platform for the cloud [Online]. Available at: http://www.opencontrail.org/.

[51] Ferguson, A. D., Guha, A., Liang, C., Fonseca, R., & Krishnamurthi, S. (2013). Participatory networking: An API for application control of SDNs. *ACM SIGCOMM Computer Communication Review*, *43*(4), 327–338.

[52] Cai, Z., Cox, A. & Ng, E. T. S. (2011). Maestro: A system for scalable OpenFlow control. Cs.Rice.Edu, p. 10 [Online]. Available at: http://www. cs.rice.edu/{~}eugeneng/papers/TR10-11.pdf.

[53] NODEFLOW: An openflow controller node style [Online]. Available at: http://garyberger.net/?p=537.

[54] Li, S., Daoyun, H., Wenjian, F., Shoujiang, M., Cen, C., Huibai, H., & Zuqing, Z. (2017). Protocol oblivious forwarding (POF): Software-defined networking with enhanced programmability. *IEEE Network*, *31*(2), 58–66.

[55] Wang, A., Mei, X., Croft, J., Caesar, M., & Godfrey, B. (2016). Ravel: A database-defined network. In *Proceedings of the Symposium on SDN Research*, 14–15 Mar. 2016, Santa Clara, CA (pp. 1–7).

[56] Shin, S., Yongjoo, S., Taekyung, L., Sangho, L., Jaewoong, C., Phillip, P., Vinod, Y., Jiseong, N., & Brent B. K. (2014). Rosemary: A robust, secure, and high performance network operating system Seungwon. In *Proceedings of the 2014 ACM SIGSAC Conference on Computer and Communications Security*, 3–7 Nov. 2014, Scottsdale, AZ (pp. 78–89).

[57] Al-Ayyoub, M., Nuseir, A., Alsmearat, K., Jararweh, Y., & Gupta, B. (2018). Deep learning for Arabic NLP: A survey. *Journal of Computational Science*, *26*, 522–531.

[58] Tewari, A. (2021) How does natural language processing apply to IoT? Insights2Techinfo, p. 1. Available at: https://insights2techinfo.com/how-does-natural-language-processing-apply-to-iot/.

[59] Deepak, K. J., Yamila, G.-M. E., Akshi, K., Brij, B. G., & Ketan, K. (2023). Knowledge-based Data Processing for Multilingual Natural Language Analysis. *ACM Transactions on Asian and Low-Resource Language Information Processing*. Just Accepted (February 2023). https://doi. org/10.1145/3583686.

[60] Gaurav, A., Gupta, B. B., Hsu, C. H., Castiglione, A., & Chui, K. T. (2021). Machine learning technique for fake news detection using text-based word vector representation. In *Computational Data and Social Networks: 10th International Conference, CSoNet 2021, Virtual Event,* November 15–17, 2021, Proceedings 10 (pp. 340–348). Springer International Publishing. California.

Chapter 6

The OpenFlow Switch

The foundation of software-defined networking (SDN) architecture is the OpenFlow (OF) protocol. The communication between an SDN controller and the network device/agent is defined by this protocol. This protocol was first created by Stanford University academics in 2008, and Google first implemented it in their backbone network in 2011–2012. The Open Networking Foundation (ONF) now oversees its administration. V1.5.1 is the most recent version in use in the sector. In the following sections, we discuss its basics and protocol structure.

6.1 Introduction to OpenFlow Protocol

OpenFlow was initially developed as a part of the Clean Slate Program at Stanford University. This initiative attempted to modify the network infrastructure that was slightly outdated and difficult to evolve. Additionally, the programme considered how this could be done. Martin Casado, a student at Stanford University, took the initiative in 2006 to lead a project on the management and protection of computer networks [1]. The goal of the project was to use a centralised controller to enable network administrators to easily define security control policies that were based on network flows and to apply these security policies to various network devices. This would allow for security control to be implemented over the entirety of network communication.

As a result of this project, professor Nick McKeown, who was also the director of the Clean Slate Program, and his team discovered that if the data forwarding and routing control modules of traditional network devices were separated, a centralised controller could be used to manage and configure various network devices through standard interfaces. As a result, network innovation and development would be facilitated by greater options for network resource design, management, and use. In 2008, they published a paper titled "OpenFlow: Enabling Innovation in Campus Networks," which introduced the ideas and application scenarios of OpenFlow in full for the first time, laying the groundwork for further development of the concept [1].

This team went on to present the SDN concept in 2009, based on OpenFlow, which received significant industry attention. The ONF, an organisation devoted to the promotion and implementation of SDN, was founded in 2011 in collaboration with Google, Facebook, Microsoft, and other businesses [2]. The ONF standardises OpenFlow and defines it as the first southbound standard communication interface in the SDN architecture between the control and forwarding layers [3].

OpenFlow is the default protocol that is utilised as the southbound connection between the SDN controller and the switch. The information obtained from the apps is collected by the SDN controller, which then turns it into flow entries. These flow entries are then sent to the switch through the OF. Monitoring switch and port statistics is another one of its potential applications inside network administration [4]. It allows the SDN concept to be implemented in both hardware and software. Scientists can use current hardware to create new protocols and study their performance, which is a significant element of OpenFlow. It is now included in commercially available routers and switches [5].

Now, we discuss the basic architecture of the OpenFlow 1.5.1 protocol. There are three main components associated with the OpenFlow architecture: switch, controller, and the OpenFlow protocol.

6.2 OpenFlow Switch

An OpenFlow Logical Switch is composed of multiple flow tables and a group table that handle packet lookups and forwarding, as well as multiple OpenFlow channels to an external controller. The switch communicates with the controller through the OpenFlow channels, and the controller manages the switch using this OpenFlow protocol [6, 7]. The controller can add, update, and eliminate flow entries in flow tables using the OpenFlow switch protocol. Each flow table in the switch has a collection of flow entries consisting of match fields, counters, and a set of instructions to be applied to matching packets [8]. Figure 6.1 shows the components of an OpenFlow switch.

Packet matching has been performed at the first flow table, and it continues at other flow tables in the pipeline. The first complete match in the flow table will be used for further processing of the packet. If a match is found in the flow table, the actions associated with the flow entry are implemented for the packet, while if a match is not discovered, then the action will be taken according to table-miss flow entry configuration [9]. The table-miss flow entry configuration can drop the packet, pass it to the OF controller, or pass it to the next flow table in the pipeline. The processes of packet forwarding, packet modification, and group table processing are all described by the actions that are included in instructions. Pipeline processing instructions send the packets to the following tables for processing [10]. When a flow entry's instruction set doesn't indicate a next table, table pipeline execution ends and the packet is changed or forwarded [11].

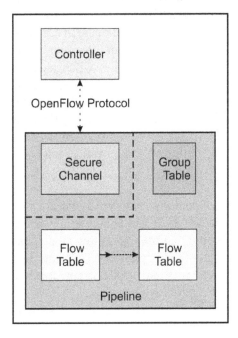

Figure 6.1.   Components of an OpenFlow switch.

A packet can be transmitted to a port. This port can be physical, logical, or reserved. We will discuss them later in this chapter. Actions that are connected with flow entries can also direct packets to a group, which defines additional processing if necessary. Groups define sets of operations for flooding as well as more sophisticated forwarding semantics, such as fast reroute and link aggregation or segregation. Switch designers are free to design the internal components as long as accurate match and instruction semantics are maintained [12, 13].

6.3 OpenFlow Ports

A port is essentially an interface where packets enter and exit the OpenFlow pipeline. A pipeline is nothing but a set of linked flow tables that are responsible for various actions to be taken on the packet. OpenFlow ports connect the OpenFlow processing module to the rest of the network.

OpenFlow switches are linked logically via their OpenFlow ports. A packet can be sent from one switch to another only via an output OpenFlow port on one switch and an ingress OpenFlow port on another [14]. A number of OpenFlow ports are made available for OpenFlow processing by an OpenFlow switch. Some network interfaces may be disabled for OpenFlow, and the OpenFlow switch may designate additional OpenFlow ports, as it is not necessary for a set of OpenFlow ports to be exactly the same as those provided by switch hardware [15]. An ingress port is used to receive OpenFlow packets and then forward them to the OpenFlow pipeline, which then forwards them to some output port. An OpenFlow port can be of three types: physical, logical, or reserved, which are discussed in the following [16, 17]:

1. **Physical ports:** OpenFlow physical ports are ports that have been defined by the switch itself and equate to a hardware interface of the switch. It is possible that the OpenFlow switch can be virtualised in some cases instead of using physical hardware. In such situations, an OpenFlow physical port may instead represent a virtual slice of the switch's associated hardware interface.
2. **Logical ports:** OpenFlow logical ports are switch-defined ports that don't exactly match a switch's hardware interface. Higher-level abstractions are achieved through logical ports that can also be built into the switch using methods other than OpenFlow. The only

distinction between physical and logical ports is that a logical port packet may have an extra pipeline field called Tunnel-ID, and when a packet delivered on a logical port is transmitted to the controller, both its logical and underlying physical ports are reported.

3. **Reserved ports:** Reserved ports are described by a particular specification. They outline general forwarding operations, including flooding and transmitting to the controller, using non-OpenFlow techniques such as "regular" switch processing. A switch is not required for all reserved ports. However, some require it [18]. Table 6.1 shows a list of reserved ports.

Table 6.1. List of reserved ports used in OpenFlow switch.

S. No.	Reserved Port Name	Port Description
1.	ALL	• It requires a switch. • It represents all the ports that the switch is capable of using to forward a particular packet. • It can only be utilised as an output port.
2.	CONTROLLER	• It also requires a switch. • It represents the OpenFlow controller with the control channel. • It can be used as an ingress as well as an output port.
3.	TABLE	• It also requires a switch and represents the commencement of the pipeline. • This port can only be used in an output action associated with a list of actions of the packet-out message. It sends the packet to the first flow table so that it can be processed through the normal OpenFlow pipeline.
4.	IN_PORT	• It also requires a switch. • It represents the packet ingress port and can be utilised as an output port if it sends the packet out of an ingress port.
5.	ANY	• It also requires a switch. • When no port is specified, this port will be used in OpenFlow requests. ANY port allows an OpenFlow instance to connect to any port or all ports. • It cannot be used either as an ingress port or an output port.

(Continued)

Table 6.1.   (*Continued*)

S. No.	Reserved Port Name	Port Description
6.	UNSET	• It also requires a switch. • A special value that indicates that the output port in the Action-Set has not been set. • It cannot be used either as an ingress port or an output port.
7.	LOCAL	• It may not require a switch. • A switch's local networking stack as well as its management stack can be represented by this port. • It can be used as an ingress as well as an output port.
8.	NORMAL	• It may not require a switch. • It represents forwarding via the switch's conventional non-OpenFlow pipeline. • It can only be used as the output port.
9.	FLOOD	• It may not require a switch. • It represents flooding, utilising the conventional, non-OpenFlow switch pipeline. • It can only be used as an output port; the actual result depends on the implementation.

OpenFlow-enabled switches do not support NORMAL and FLOOD ports. If OpenFlow switches are built in a hybrid way, then they may support both NORMAL and FLOOD ports. The OpenFlow switch can have ports added or removed at any time using the OpenFlow Configuration Protocol. The port state can also be changed by utilising the underlying port mechanism. Flow table content can never be changed due to port addition, modification, and removal [19]. In fact, flow table entries having references to the removal or change of port numbers need not be removed or modified. Packets that are referenced to the removed ports are dropped. Any flow entries or group entries that are still referencing a port number after it has been deleted and then utilised for a different physical or logical port may be effectively re-targeted to the new port, sometimes with unfavourable outcomes. Therefore, it is up to the controller to remove any flow entries or group entries that refer to a deleted port, if necessary.

Packets transmitted to logical ports seldom return to the same OpenFlow switch; instead, they are either consumed by the logical port or forwarded across a physical port. Logical ports can be used to integrate a network service or complex processing into the OpenFlow switch [20]. The use of logical ports for packet recirculation is optional, and OpenFlow supports several methods of port recirculation. The most basic kind of recirculation occurs when a packet sent out on a logical port returns to the switch via the same logical port. This type of recirculation can be used for loopback or unidirectional processing. Another type of recirculation happens between a port pair in which a packet forwarded from one logical port reverts back to the switch from another logical port of the pair [21]. When using port recirculation, a switch should defend itself from packet infinite loops. This technique is implementation dependent and is not covered by the specification. For example, the switch might attach an intrinsic recirculation count to each packet, which is incremented with each recirculation, and delete packets when the counter exceeds a switch-defined threshold.

6.4 OpenFlow Tables

The core of any OpenFlow switch is the OpenFlow table. A flow table consists of flow entries, and each flow entry is associated with header fields, counters, and actions. The header fields are needed to determine if an incoming packet matches the corresponding flow entry. If a match is found, the packet is assigned to this flow [22, 48]. The counters are used to track flow-specific statistics, such as the number of packets forwarded or lost for this flow. The action fields specify what the switch should perform if a matching packet is received. Figure 6.2 shows the basic structure of a flow table in OpenFlow V1.0 [23, 24, 49].

Flow entry 0		Flow entry 1			Flow entry i		Flow entry n	
Header	Ingress port: 014 Output port: 1016 192.16.4.27	Header	Ingress port: 0** Output port: * 204.*.*.*		Header	Ingress port: 20 Output port: 765 192.45.78.16	Header	Ingress port: 987 Output port: 23* 196.*.*.*
Counter	Field value	Counter	Field value		Counter	Field value	Counter	Field value
Action	Field value	Action	Field value		Action	Field value	Action	Field value

Figure 6.2. OpenFlow V1.0 flow table.

(a) **Pipeline processing:** OpenFlow-based switches can be divided into two categories: pure OpenFlow switches and hybrid OpenFlow switches. OpenFlow-only switches can only perform OpenFlow operations. In this type of switch, every packet is processed via the OpenFlow pipeline and cannot be handled in any other way [18, 25]. On the contrary, the other OpenFlow-enabled hybrid switch supports both types of operations, i.e., OpenFlow operations and normal Ethernet switch operations.

Ethernet operations include L2 switching, L3 routing, VLAN operations, QoS, and access control mechanisms [26]. There should be some classification mechanism that classifies the traffic outside of OpenFlow and routes the traffic toward the normal or OpenFlow pipeline accordingly [11]. This classification is not specified in the current version of OpenFlow, i.e., V1.5.1. Figure 6.3 shows the pipeline processing of an OpenFlow switch.

Each OpenFlow logical switch has one or more flow tables integrated into its OpenFlow pipeline.

These flow tables have a number of flow entries defining actions, headers, and counters. The processing of the OpenFlow pipeline stipulates how packets engage with those flow tables. An OpenFlow switch must

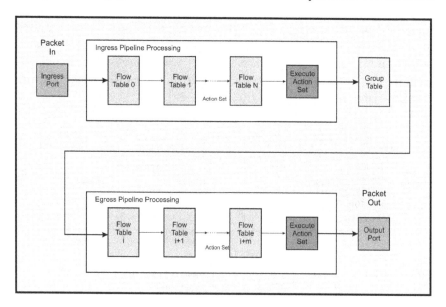

Figure 6.3.   Pipeline processing of OpenFlow switch.

have at least one ingress flow table and may have additional flow tables as an option [27]. Pipeline processing is significantly streamlined when an OpenFlow switch has only one flow table. The traversal order of the flow tables is predefined by the developer, starting from zero.

Pipeline processing is carried out in two stages: ingress and egress processing. Ingress processing at the first flow table is where pipeline processing always begins; the packet must first be compared to the flow entries of flow table 0 [28]. Depending on how the match in the first table turns out, further ingress flow tables might be employed. The OpenFlow switch may carry out egress processing in the context of an output port if the result of ingress processing is to transfer the packet to that port. Egress processing is always an option for OpenFlow processing. It might be the case that an OpenFlow switch does not support any egress processing. In this case, if no first egress table is specified, then the packet must get processed by the output, and most probably, it gets out of the pipeline processing through the output port [29, 30]. If an egress table is given, then the packet must match the flow entries, and action would be taken according to the matched entry. Figures 6.4 and 6.5 show the flowcharts of ingress and egress processing in an OpenFlow switch, respectively.

When a packet is processed by the flow table, it must be matched to one of the flow entries. If a flow entry is detected, the instruction set contained within it is executed. These instructions can explicitly route the packet to a different flow table through the Goto-Table instruction, where the same operation is repeated. A flow entry could only route a packet to a flow table number greater than its own, implying that pipeline processing can only continue forward and not backward [31]. The GoTo-table instruction is not present in the last flow table of the pipeline processing. If the matched flow entry does not route the packet to the next flow table, then it implies that it is the last flow table of the pipeline processing. Now, the packet will get processed according to the instruction set associated with this last flow table and be forwarded.

A table miss occurs when a packet does not match a flow entry in a flow table. The response to a table miss is determined by the table configuration [32]. The table-miss flow entry in the flow table can describe how to process unmatched packets, including dropping, passing, or delivering them to controllers via packet-in messages.

The OpenFlow pipeline is a switch abstraction over the switch hardware. In some scenarios, OpenFlow switches are virtualised on hardware to allow multiple instances or hybrid switches. Sometimes, even when the

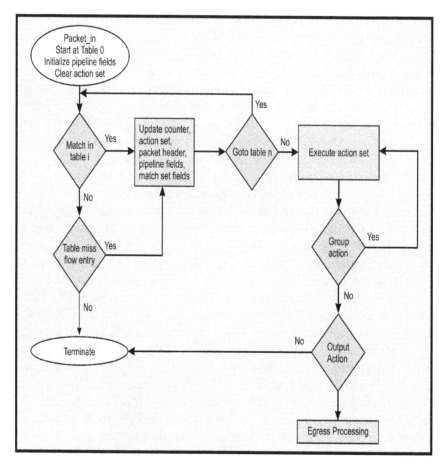

Figure 6.4.   Flowchart of ingress processing in an OpenFlow switch.

switch is not built on virtualization, then also mapping of hardware to OpenFlow pipeline would be difficult. For example, if a flow table can process only Ethernet packets, then non-Ethernet packets must be mapped onto the Ethernet packets [33, 34]. In this direction, the OpenFlow pipeline requires consistent mapping to hardware and consistent behaviour from the OpenFlow pipeline. Table 6.2 shows some consistencies that need to be checked while processing a packet in an OpenFlow pipeline.

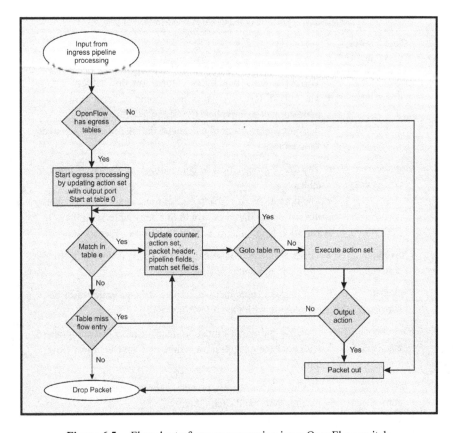

Figure 6.5.   Flowchart of egress processing in an OpenFlow switch.

(a) **Flow tables and flow entries:** The main components of a flow entry
   are described [18, 35] in Figure 6.6:

   - **Match fields:** Match fields contain the fields that are to be
     matched with the incoming OpenFlow packets. They include
     packet headers, ingress ports, and other pipeline fields, such as
     metadata, that are specified by the previous table.
   - **Priority:** matching the flow entry's precedence.
   - **Counters:** Counters get updated when the packets are matched.
   - **Instructions:** Instructions are to change the pipeline processing or
     action set.
   - **Timeouts:** Timeout is the maximum time taken by the switch to
     expire the flow.

Table 6.2.   Types of consistencies used in OpenFlow.

S. No.	Consistency Type	Description
1.	Table consistency	• The packet must match in all OpenFlow flow tables. • The only difference in matching should be because of flow table content and explicit OpenFlow processing. • Packet headers cannot be changed during processing between flow tables.
2.	Group consistency	• The use of groups must be compatible with the use of flow tables. • The operations of a group bucket must apply to the packet in the same way that they would in a flow table, with the sole variation being due to explicit OpenFlow processing.
3.	Flow entry consistency	• There should be consistency between the actions of a flow entry and the matched flow entry.
4.	Packet-in consistency	• The packets contained within packet-in messages must be compatible with OpenFlow flow tables.
5.	Packet out consistency	• A packet-out request must produce a packet that complies with both the packet-in procedure and the OpenFlow flow tables.
6.	Port consistency	• The ingress and egress processes for an OpenFlow packet must be consistent with each other.

Match Fields	Priority	Counters	Instructions	Timeouts	Cookie	Flags

Figure 6.6.   Main components of a flow entry in a OpenFlow table.

- **Cookie:** This is the controller-selected data not visible to the admin. It filters flow entries caused by flow statistics, flow modification, and flow deletion requests. These values are not used for packet processing.
- **Flags:** Flows change the ways flows can be managed.

Match fields and priority together are the two fields that are used to identify a flow table entry uniquely. The table-miss flow entry is the flow entry that wildcards all fields and has priority equal to 0.

(b) **Packet matching:** The flow table is checked to see if a matching flow entry exists when a packet enters the OpenFlow switch via an input port (or, in some situations, from the controller) [36]. For matching against flow entries, the arriving packet's match fields include the following:

1. Input port
2. VLAN ID
3. VLAN priority
4. Ethernet source address
5. Ethernet destination address
6. Ethernet frame type
7. IP source address
8. IP destination address
9. IP protocol
10. IP type of service (ToS) bits
11. TCP/UDP source port
12. TCP/UDP destination port.

These 12 basic tuples have been used in OpenFlow since the inception of OpenFlow V1.0. However, some of these fields are optional. By outlining three distinct categories of compliance in its V.1.0 conformance-testing procedure, the ONF has clarified this misunderstanding. The three levels are layer-one conformance, which supports all 12 match fields, layer-two conformance, which only supports layer-two header field matching, and layer-three conformance, which only supports layer-three header field matching.

The switch begins by carrying out a table lookup in the first flow table, and depending on the processing pipeline, it may carry out table lookups in additional flow tables as well.

From the packet, packet pipeline fields and packet header fields are extracted. Depending on the kind of packet, different protocol header fields, such as Ethernet source addresses or IPv4 destination addresses, are commonly used for table lookups. Matches can be made against the ingress port, the metadata field, and other pipeline fields, in addition to the packet headers. Information can be passed across tables in a switch using metadata. If actions taken in a previous table using the Apply-Actions command affected the packet headers or pipeline fields, those changes are represented in the packet header fields and pipeline fields, which represent the packet in its current state.

When a flow entry and a packet are a match, it means that all of the flow entry's match fields correspond to the header fields and pipeline fields. Any value that coincides with the unmasked bits in the match fields of the incoming packet will be considered a match if the flow entry's match fields are wildcarded using a bit mask. The packet is compared to flow entries in the flow table, and only the highest-priority flow entry matching the packet is chosen. The counters associated with the chosen flow entry must be updated, and the instruction set in the chosen flow entry must be implemented. If more than one matching flow entry has the same highest priority, the identified flow entry is explicitly undefined. Only when a controller writer never sets the OFPFF_CHECK_OVERLAP bit on flow mod messages and inserts overlapping entries may this situation occur [37].

Every flow table must have a table-miss flow entry. The table-miss flow entry specifies how to process mismatched packets in the flow table, such as sending them to the controller, dropping them, or sending them to a following table. The table-miss flow entry can be recognised by its match and its priority; more specifically, it omits all of the match fields and uses wildcards for all of the match fields. It also has the lowest priority (0). A table-miss flow entry may not be as capable as an ordinary flow entry. Sending packets to the controller via the CONTROLLER reserved port and deleting packets via the Clear-Actions instruction are the bare minimum functionality requirements for the table-miss flow entry [37].

By default, packets that cannot be matched by flow entries are rejected if the table-miss flow entry does not exist. This default behaviour can be changed through a switch's configuration, for instance, through the OpenFlow configuration protocol. If the flow table allows it, a flow entry with the lowest priority (0) and a match that does not wildcard all match fields may be utilised; nonetheless, this is not a table-miss flow entry. Utilising such a flow entry would only make sense if a table-miss flow entry was not utilised; otherwise, they would overlap, making matching impossible. The controller shouldn't produce non-table-miss flow entries with the lowest priority (0) because of this [38].

6.5 Instructions and Actions

The packets that match a specific flow entry are processed according to the instructions contained in that entry. As a result of these instructions, modifications are made to the packet, action set, and/or pipeline. A switch does not need to support all types of instructions but only some *required instructions*. A controller can support some instructions optionally after enquiring the switch, which are called *optional instructions*. Examples of required instructions are *Clear_Actions*, *Write_Actions*, and *Goto_Table*. Examples of optional instructions are *Apply_Actions*, *Write_Metadata*, and *Stat_Trigger,* Each flow entry can only have one of each type of instruction in its associated instruction set. The order in which the actions are executed is specific, e.g., *Apply_Actions, Clear_Actions, Write_Actions, Write_Metadata, Stat_Trigger,* and *Goto_Table*. The only restrictions are that *Clear_Actions* must be executed before *Write_Actions* and *Apply_Actions* must be executed before *Write_Metadata* [37, 39].

Each packet has its own set of actions. By default, this set is null. With a *Write_Action* or *Clear_Action* command linked to a matching flow entry, the action set can be updated. When a flow entry's instruction set does not contain a Goto-Table instruction, pipeline processing ceases, and the packet's action set is executed. The action set for egress processing has one restriction: neither the output action nor the group action can be added to it. When a group action and an output action are both provided in an action set, the group action takes priority and the output action is discarded [39].

The action set for ingress processing gets initialised empty, but the action set for egress processing gets initialised at the beginning of the egress process with an output action for the current output port. If neither an output nor a group action is given in an action set, the packet is dropped. The packet is lost if no group action is supplied and the output action refers to a non-existent port. Ingress and egress process the output action in different ways. The packet must begin egress processing on the port specified by the output action or group action included in the ingress action set. When the egress action set has an output action, the packet must leave egress processing, be processed by the port, and, in the majority of circumstances, be sent out of the switch.

6.6 Counters

Counters are kept for each flow table, flow entry, port, queue, group, group bucket, metre, and metre band. Software-implemented OpenFlow-compliant counters can be maintained by polling hardware counters with more constrained ranges. Reference count, packet lookups, and packet matches are some of the counters maintained for a per-flow table. Received packets, received bytes, and duration are some of the counters maintained for a per-flow entry [50, 51]. Received packets, transmitted packets, received bytes, and transmitted bytes are some of the examples of counters that are maintained for a per-port number. A switch need not support all counters. Even if the object has no influence on the packet or if the packet is ultimately deleted or forwarded to the controller, packet-related counters for an OpenFlow object must count every packet using that object.

6.7 Group Table

A group table consists of multiple entries where OpenFlow is capable of representing additional ways of forwarding. Figure 6.7 shows the main components of a group flow entry in an OpenFlow table.

A group entry may include zero or more buckets, with the exception of an *indirect group*, which always contains a single bucket. A bucket normally has an output action that transmits the packet to a port, along with actions

Group Identifier	Group Types	Counters	Action Buckets
An unsigned 32-bit integer that uniquely identifies the group on the OpenFlow switch.	Group semantics determination.	Updated after a packet has been processed by a group.	A sorted list of action buckets, with each action bucket containing a collection of executable actions and related parameters.

Figure 6.7.   Main components of a group flow entry in a OpenFlow Group table.

that change the payload. If the switch allows group chaining, a group action that calls another group may likewise be included in a bucket.

6.8 Metre Table

A metre table is made up of metre entries that define per-flow metres. By utilising per-flow metres, OpenFlow may implement rate-limiting, a simple QoS operation that restricts a collection of flows to a specified bandwidth. A metre keeps tabs on the rate of the allotted packets and allows for rate limiting. The flow entries are directly connected to the metres. Any flow entry can specify a metre action in a list of actions if the switch supports it. The same flow table may have different flow entries that use different metres, the same metre, or no metres at all.

6.9 Evolution of OpenFlow

In practice, the term SDN was not coined until a year after OpenFlow first appeared on the market in 2008, but the existence and acceptance of OpenFlow by academic communities and networking companies signalled a major change in networking that we are still witnessing today. Despite the fact that the word SDN was used in the academic community as early as 2009, it did not have a significant influence on the larger networking market until 2011. The original concept of OpenFlow was published in 2008. By 2011, OpenFlow had gained enough traction that ownership of the standard was transferred to the ONF. Deutsche Telekom, Facebook, Google, Microsoft, Verizon, and Yahoo! founded the ONF in 2011 [40]. In its current incarnation, it oversees the OpenFlow specification and consists of several working groups.

The OpenFlow protocol has changed over the course of ONF's standardisation process, from version 1.0 with only 12 fixed match fields and a single flow table to the most recent version with numerous tables, over 41 matching fields, and an assortment of new functionalities. Capability and scalability have been significantly increased with every version released [41].

In this section, we discuss the different versions of OpenFlow and what features are added to each version to make it better than the previous one. Table 6.3 shows the evolution of the OpenFlow protocol, with a description of each version proposed so far.

Table 6.3.　Evolution and development of OpenFlow.

OpenFlow Version	Added Feature	Description
OpenFlow 1.1 [42]	Multiple flow tables	• Unlike in V1.0, it supports table chaining to forward packets for subsequent matching to other flow tables through the GoTo instruction, resulting in increased flexibility. • It significantly increases the complexity of the matching logic and the degree and type of packet alterations that might take place.
	Groups	• This is a refinement of the *FLOOD* option, where it supports features such as multicast. • A group table has group entries, where each flow entry has a varied number of action buckets. • It enables applying an action set to a group of flows instantly, and it would take time to apply action to every single flow.
	MPLS and VLAN support	• Supporting multiple levels of VLAN tags requires extensive support for popping and pushing tags; after this, MPLS [43] tagging is quite obvious to be supported. • A large complexity overhead when multiple tags are encountered.
	Virtual ports	• Unlike in V1.0, where an output port is directly mapped to the physical port, V1.1categorised ports into classes, namely standard ports and reserved virtual ports.
	Controller connection failure	• Connection loss between controller and switch is a serious issue, which was resolved in V1.0 by the introduction of an emergency flow cache. However, this cache was not included in V1.1. Instead, two modes had been introduced: fail secure mode and fail standalone mode. • If connection gets lost between switch and controller, switch enters any of these two modes. • In the fail secure mode, the switch continues to work normally like a V1.1 switch, but all controller-bound messages are dropped. • In the fail standalone mode, the switch additionally stops OpenFlow pipeline processing and operates in its native switch or router mode.

Table 6.3.   *(Continued)*

OpenFlow Version	Added Feature	Description
OpenFlow 1.2 [44]	IPv6 support	• Unlike static matching in V1.1, it supports matching on IPv6 source address, destination address, protocol number, traffic class, ICMPv6 type, ICMPv6 code, IPv6 neighbour discovery header fields, and IPv6 flow labels, via OpenFlow Extensible Match (OXM).
	Extensible matches	• OXM descriptors have been added to V.1.2 to allow for general and extensible packet matching. • OXM specifies a collection of type–length–value (TLV) pairings that can describe or define almost any of the header fields required for matching by an OpenFlow switch.
	Experimenter extensions	• The OPENFLOW BASIC match class has the ability to match any combination of header fields by allowing multiple match classes. • The EXPERIMENTER match class is defined, allowing for matching on fields in the packet payload and offering an almost unlimited horizon for new flow configurations. • It allows EXPERIMENTER extensions through dedicated fields and code points assigned by ONF.
	Multiple controllers	• The switch can be configured to connect with multiple controllers at the same time. The switch has to make sure that it only sends a message to a controller when that controller sends it a command. • A controller may act in three modes: slave, equal, and master to the switch. In slave mode, the controller can only request data from the switch, i.e., there are no modifications in the configuration of the switch. • In equal mode, the controller has full flexibility to alter the configuration of the switch. • In master mode too, the controller can change the configuration of the switch but can force one switch to be the master and other switches to be slaves.

(Continued)

Table 6.3.   (*Continued*)

OpenFlow Version	Added Feature	Description
OpenFlow 1.3 [45]	Table miss support	• A separate flow entry for table miss has been described in the flow table, just as a normal flow entry is described. • The matching language represented by the flow tables, entries, and related instructions and actions is given more flexibility by this feature.
	Metre per flow	• A metre is a switch element used to measure and control the packet/byte rate. • When a packet/byte rate reaches a threshold value, the metre will trigger its metre band associated with the threshold. • A metre may have multiple metre bands, and this metre band is called a rate limiter. • When a packet is processed by a band, it means it has reached the maximum bandwidth, and this packet will have to perform some action, such as dropping.
	Per connection event filtering	• Introduction of multiple controllers in the previous version leads to improved load balancing and fault tolerance. This does not dictate how to dampen asynchronous switch-to-controller messages that a controller does not want to receive. • Due to this feature, the controller can filter out specific reason codes that it does not want to receive.
	Auxiliary connections	• It adds another level of parallelism by permitting numerous connections per communication channel, resulting in increased throughput.
	Cookies	• Messages containing new packets that are forwarded to the controller are augmented with a cookie field holding a policy identification. This expedites the controller's message processing compared to if it had to search its full database. • This cookie enables the switch to cache the flow entry referenced by this cookie and bypass the complete packet-matching logic, resulting in a performance boost.
	Provider Backbone Bridging (PBB) tagging	• Using MAC-in-MAC encapsulation, PBB enables complete domain separation between the user-layer-two domain and the provider domain.
	Per flow QoS	• Meters are associated with flow entries, not queues or ports, allowing granular control over QoS. • Multiple flow entries can all point to the same metre.

Table 6.3. (*Continued*)

OpenFlow Version	Added Feature	Description
	Capability negotiation	• Requests can span multiple messages.
OpenFlow 1.4 [46]	Bundles	• OpenFlow 1.4.0 introduces the bundles mechanism to "bundle" a group of OpenFlow messages as a single operation, enabling the quasi-atomic application of related changes and better synchronisation of changes across a sequence of switches.
	Optical ports	• Optical ports are responsible for configuring and monitoring the transmission and reception frequencies and the power of a laser. • The inclusion of optical port compatibility facilitates the use of SDN in systems employing fibre channels, such as Fiber Channel over Ethernet (FCoE).
	Synchronized table	• Supports flow table monitoring by offering synchronisation in a multi-controller system. • Sends an update to a controller whenever another controller makes a change to a given set of flow table entries.
	Extended experimenter extension API	• Can easily add ports, tables, queues, instructions, actions, etc.
	Flow entries deletion	• When a metre is erased from a switch, all flow entries utilising that metre are eliminated, and the switch notifies the relevant controller.
	Improved extensibility	• Utilises TLV encodings to provide flexibility to switches so that new features can be added easily in the future.
OpenFlow 1.5 [47]	Egress tables	• Actions should be performed upon leaving a port (packet encapsulation or decapsulation, tunnels).
	Packet type	• This version is able to handle non-Ethernet packets, i.e., IP packets.
	TCP flags matching	• Syn, Ack, and Fin may be used to detect the beginning and end of a TCP connection.
OpenFlow 1.5.1	Bugs	• This version is able to detect and fix bugs.

Exercises

Q.1.   Discuss the OpenFlow switch architecture and its components. Also, discuss why OpenFlow is so popular as a southbound interface when we talk about the SDN paradigm.

Q.2.   Elaborate on OpenFlow ports, and what are the different types of ports included in OF 1.5.1?

Q.3.   Discuss how logical ports can be utilised to obtain abstraction.

Q.4.   Discuss how pipeline processing is introduced in OF 1.5.1 and why it was not included in the previous versions of OF.

Q.5.   State the difference between ingress and egress pipeline processing, and discuss why it was not included in the previous version.

Q.6.   Discuss how a packet is processed in the ingress and egress pipelines with a flowchart.

Q.7.   Discuss the significance of the GoTo instruction in an OpenFlow switch with a suitable example.

Q.8.   Elaborate on why consistency is important in an OpenFlow switch, and explain the different types of consistencies that need to be checked while processing a packet.

Q.9.   Discuss the flow table entry format and its different fields.

Q.10.   Elaborate on why wildcard entries are used for packet matching in SDN networking with an example.

Q.11.   Explain the significance of group tables and compare their performance with a single flow table.

Q.12.   Discuss how rate limiting is implemented in SDN networking.

Q.13.   Discuss the advantages as well as the challenges of including multiple controllers in OpenFlow 1.2.

Q.14.   Discuss the benefits and complexity of including table-miss flow entry and cookies in OpenFlow 1.3.

Q.15.   Discuss the optical ports in OpenFlow 1.4.

Q.16.   Elaborate on the important features of OpenFlow 1.5 and 1.5.1.

References

[1] McKeown, N., Anderson, T., Balakrishnan, H., Parulkar, G., Peterson, L., Rexford, J., Shenker, S., & Turner, J. (2008). OpenFlow: Enabling innovation in campus networks. *ACM SIGCOMM Computer Communication Review, 38*(2), 69–74.

[2] Al-Somaidai, M. B. & Yahya, E. B. (2014). Survey of software components to emulate OpenFlow protocol as an SDN implementation. *American Journal of Software Engineering and Applications, 3*(6), 74–82.

[3] McGeer, R. (2012). A safe, efficient update protocol for OpenFlow networks. In *Proceedings of the First Workshop on Hot Topics in Software Defined Networks*, 13 Aug. 2012, Helsinki, Finland (pp. 61–66).

[4] Shalimov, A., Zuikov, D., Zimarina, D., Pashkov, V., & Smeliansky, R. (2013). Advanced study of SDN/OpenFlow controllers. In *Proceedings of the 9th Central & Eastern European Software Engineering Conference in Russia*, 24–25 Oct. 2013, Moscow, Russia (pp. 1–6).

[5] Braun, W. & Menth, M. (2014). Software-defined networking using OpenFlow: Protocols, applications and architectural design choices. *Future Internet, 6*(2), 302–336.

[6] Bianco, A., Birke, R., Giraudo, L., & Palacin, M. (2010). Openflow switching: Data plane performance. In *2010 IEEE International Conference on Communications*, 23–27 May 2010, Cape Town, South Africa (pp. 1–5). IEEE.

[7] Kuzniar, M., Peresini, P., Canini, M., Venzano, D., & Kostic, D. (2012). A soft way for openflow switch interoperability testing. In *Proceedings of the 8th International Conference on Emerging Networking Experiments and Technologies*, 10–13 Dec. 2012, Nice, France (pp. 265–276).

[8] Vaughan-Nichols, S. J. (2011). OpenFlow: The next generation of the network? *Computer, 44*(08), 13–15.

[9] Jouet, S., Cziva, R., & Pezaros, D. P. (2015). Arbitrary packet matching in OpenFlow. In *2015 IEEE 16th International Conference on High Performance Switching and Routing (HPSR)*, 1–4 July 2015, Budapest, Hungary (pp. 1–6). IEEE.

[10] Bianchi, G., Bonola, M., Capone, A., & Cascone, C. (2014). Openstate: Programming platform-independent stateful openflow applications inside the switch. *ACM SIGCOMM Computer Communication Review, 44*(2), 44–51.

[11] Nguyen, X. N., Saucez, D., Barakat, C., & Turletti, T. (2015). Rules placement problem in OpenFlow networks: A survey. *IEEE Communications Surveys & Tutorials, 18*(2), 1273–1286.

[12] Rotsos, C., Sarrar, N., Uhlig, S., Sherwood, R., & Moore, A. W. (2012). OFLOPS: An open framework for OpenFlow switch evaluation. In *International Conference on Passive and Active Network Measurement*, March (pp. 85–95). Springer, Berlin, Heidelberg.

[13] Isyaku, B., Mohd Zahid, M. S., Bte Kamat, M., Abu Bakar, K., & Ghaleb, F. A. (2020). Software defined networking flow table management of openflow switches performance and security challenges: A survey. *Future Internet, 12*(9), 147.

[14] Wazirali, R., Ahmad, R., & Alhiyari, S. (2021). SDN-openflow topology discovery: An overview of performance issues. *Applied Sciences, 11*(15), 6999.

[15] Isyaku, B., Mohd Zahid, M. S., Bte Kamat, M., Abu Bakar, K., & Ghaleb, F. A. (2020). Software defined networking flow table management of open-flow switches performance and security challenges: A survey. *Future Internet, 12*(9), 147.

[16] Niang, B. (2018). Software Defined Networking (SDN) for universal access. In *Emerging Technologies for Developing Countries: Second EAI International Conference (AFRICATEK 2018)*, 29–30 May 2018, Cotonou, Benin (Vol. 260, p. 133). Springer.

[17] Nantoume, A., Kone, B., Kora, A. D., & Niang, B. (2018). Software defined networking (SDN) for universal access. In *International Conference on Emerging Technologies for Developing Countries*, May (pp. 133–144). Springer, Cham.

[18] Found, O. N. (2020). Specification, OpenFlow Switch. "Version 1.5.1 (Protocol version 0x06)." Open Networking Foundation (2015), Cited in pp. ix and 22.

[19] Das, R. K., Jha, M., & Harizan, S. (2022). Performance Appraisal of 6LoWPAN and OpenFlow in SDN Enabled Edge-Based IoT Network. In *Advanced Computational Paradigms and Hybrid Intelligent Computing* (pp. 21–29). Springer, Singapore.

[20] Luo, Y., Cascon, P., Murray, E., & Ortega, J. (2009). Accelerating OpenFlow switching with network processors. In *Proceedings of the 5th ACM/IEEE Symposium on Architectures for Networking and Communications Systems*, 19–20 Oct. 2009, Princeton, NJ (pp. 70–71).

[21] Sedar, R., Borokhovich, M., Chiesa, M., Antichi, G., & Schmid, S. (2018). Supporting emerging applications with low-latency failover in P4. In *Proceedings of the 2018 Workshop on Networking for Emerging Applications and Technologies*, 20 Aug. 2018, Budapest, Hungary (pp. 52–57).

[22] Yang, T., Liu, A. X., Shen, Y., Fu, Q., Li, D., & Li, X. (2018). Fast open-flow table lookup with fast update. In *IEEE INFOCOM 2018-IEEE Conference on Computer Communications*, 16–19 April 2018, Honolulu, HI (pp. 2636–2644). IEEE.

[23] Qiao, S., Hu, C., Guan, X., & Zou, J. (2016). Taming the flow table over-flow in openflow switch. In *Proceedings of the 2016 ACM SIGCOMM Conference*, August (pp. 591–592).

[24] Li, H., Huang, T., Yang, T., Li, W., & Zhang, G. (2019). A fast flow table engine for open vswitch with high performance on both lookups and updates. In *Proceedings of the ACM SIGCOMM 2019 Conference Posters and Demos*, 19–23 Aug. 2019, Beijing, China (pp. 125–127).

[25] Krishna, H., van Adrichem, N. L., & Kuipers, F. A. (2016). Providing band-width guarantees with OpenFlow. In *2016 Symposium on Communications and Vehicular Technologies (SCVT)*, 22 Nov. 2016, Belgium (pp. 1–6). IEEE.

[26] Wang, W., Hu, Y., Que, X., & Gong, X. (2012). Autonomicity design in openflow based software defined networking. In *2012 IEEE Globecom Workshops*, 3–7 Dec. 2012, Anaheim, CA (pp. 818–823). IEEE.

[27] Bosshart, P., Gibb, G., Kim, H. S., Varghese, G., McKeown, N., Izzard, M., Mujica, F., & Horowitz, M. (2013). Forwarding metamorphosis: Fast programmable match-action processing in hardware for SDN. *ACM SIGCOMM Computer Communication Review*, 43(4), 99–110.

[28] Li, Y., Zhang, D., Taheri, J., & Li, K. (2018). SDN components and OpenFlow. In *Big Data and Software Defined Networks*, 1st edn (pp. 49–67). IET Digital Library, London.

[29] Congdon, P. T., Mohapatra, P., Farrens, M., & Akella, V. (2013). Simultaneously reducing latency and power consumption in openflow switches. *IEEE/ACM Transactions on Networking*, 22(3), 1007–1020.

[30] da Costa Cordeiro, W. L., Marques, J. A., & Gaspary, L. P. (2017). Data plane programmability beyond openflow: Opportunities and challenges for network and service operations and management. *Journal of Network and Systems Management*, 25(4), 784–818.

[31] Lara, A., Kolasani, A., & Ramamurthy, B. (2013). Network innovation using openflow: A survey. *IEEE Communications Surveys & Tutorials*, 16(1), 493–512.

[32] Zarek, A., Ganjali, Y., & Lie, D. (2012). *Openflow Timeouts Demystified*. University of Toronto, Toronto, Ontario, Canada.

[33] Panda, A., Samal, S. S., Turuk, A. K., Panda, A., & Venkatesh, V. C. (2019). Dynamic hard timeout based flow table management in openflow enabled SDN. In *2019 International Conference on Vision Towards Emerging Trends in Communication and Networking (ViTECoN)*, 30–31 March 2019, Vellore, India (pp. 1–6). IEEE.

[34] Kuźniar, M., Perešíni, P., Kostić, D., & Canini, M. (2018). Methodology, measurement and analysis of flow table update characteristics in hardware openflow switches. *Computer Networks*, 136, 22–36.

[35] Hu, F., Hao, Q., & Bao, K. (2014). A survey on software-defined network and openflow: From concept to implementation. *IEEE Communications Surveys & Tutorials*, 16(4), 2181–2206.

[36] Goransson, P., Black, C., & Culver, T. (2016). *Software Defined Networks: A Comprehensive Approach*. Morgan Kaufmann, Burlington, Massachusetts, United States.

[37] Found, O. N. (2015). Specification, OpenFlow Switch. "Version 1.5.1 (Protocol version 0x06)." Open Networking Foundation.

[38] Yang, J., Hu, C., Zheng, P., Wang, R., Zhang, P., & Guan, X. (2016). Rethinking the design of openflow switch counters. In *Proceedings of the 2016 ACM SIGCOMM Conference*, 22–26 Aug. 2016, Florianopolis, Brazil (pp. 589–590).

[39] Goransson, P., Black, C., & Culver, T. (2016). *Software Defined Networks: A Comprehensive Approach.* Morgan Kaufmann, Burlington, Massachusetts, United States.

[40] Kirkpatrick, K. (2013). Software-defined networking. *Communications of the ACM, 56*(9), 16–19.

[41] Tourrilhes, J., Sharma, P., Banerjee, S., & Pettit, J. (2014). The evolution of SDN and OpenFlow: A standards perspective. *IEEE Computer Society, 47*(11), 22–29.

[42] OpenFlow switch specification, Version 1.1.0 (wire protocol 0x02). Open Networking Foundation; February 28, 2011. Retrieved from Pfaff Ben, Bob Lantz, & Bea Heller. "Openflow switch specification, version 1.3.0." Open Networking Foundation 42 (2012).

[43] Davie, B., Doolan, P., & Rekhter, Y. (1998). *Switching in IP Networks.* Morgan Kaufmann, San Francisco, CA.

[44] OpenFlow switch specification, Version 1.2.0 (wire protocol 0x03). Open Networking Foundation; December 5, 2011. Retrieved from. OpenFlow Consortium, "OpenFlow Switch Specification Version 1.3.0 (Wire Protocol 0x04)." The OpenFlow Consortium (2012).

[45] OpenFlow switch specification, Version 1.3.0 (wire protocol 0x04). Open Networking Foundation; June 25, 2012. Retrieved from Pfaff Ben, Bob Lantz, & Bea Heller. "Openflow switch specification, version 1.3.0." Open Networking Foundation 42 (2012).

[46] Specification, O. S. 1.4. 0 (Wire Protocol 0x05). October 14, 2013. ONF TS-012. [HTML]. Available at: https://www.opennetworking.org/images/stories/downloads/sdn-resources/onf-specifications/openflow/openflow-spec-v1.4.0.pdf.

[47] Found, O. N. (2015). Specification, OpenFlow Switch. "Version 1.5. 1 (Protocol version 0x06)." Open Networkig Foundation (2015).

[48] Mishra, A., Gupta, N., & Gupta, B. B. (2021). Defense mechanisms against DDoS attack based on entropy in SDN-cloud using POX controller. *Telecommunication Systems, 77,* 47–62

[49] Khan, A. & Colace, F. (2021). Knowledge graph: Applications with ML and AI and open-source database links in 2022. Insights2Techinfo. Available at: https://insights2techinfo.com/knowledge-graph-applications-with-ml-and-ai-and-open-source-database-links-in-2022/.

[50] Almomani, A., Gupta, B. B., Atawneh, S., Meulenberg, A., & Almomani, E. (2013). A survey of phishing email filtering techniques. *IEEE Communications Surveys & Tutorials, 15*(4), 2070–2090.

[51] Al-Smadi, M., Qawasmeh, O., Al-Ayyoub, M., Jararweh, Y., & Gupta, B. (2018). Deep Recurrent neural network vs. support vector machine for aspect-based sentiment analysis of Arabic hotels' reviews. *Journal of Computational Science, 27,* 386–393.

Chapter 7

SDN Application Plane

In the previous chapter, we discussed the preliminaries of networking and its related concepts, the architectural modelling of the SDN framework, and its components. We have discussed the SDN controller and various SDN controllers offered by Big Tech giants. In this chapter, we discuss the SDN application plane and how it plays an important role in an SDN environment.

7.1 Introduction

Network intelligence and state are now built into network devices and disseminated throughout the infrastructure. Decisions can only be made based on local information, which frequently leads to suboptimal global resource distribution. Employing network-wide policies can improve resource distribution efficiency, but all connected devices must be configured. This causes extensive delays and increased costs, and it can also lead to discrepancies, security breaches, or non-compliance with rules [1]. Additionally, in order to connect hosts over variable distances, link speeds, and topologies, vast discrete sets of protocols are utilised. The majority of these protocols are often developed separately from one another, without the use of any abstraction layer. This results in ever-increasing complexity, and as a direct consequence, static networks exist inside an otherwise dynamic environment [2].

Despite being heterogeneous, static, and complex, network devices communicate with each other and try to utilise the resources over the Internet efficiently. Most of the services are provided to the users with the best-effort approach. This is due to the fact that the application layer does not have any provisions that can inform the service about the appropriate time for data transfer [3]. SDN is an emerging technology that opens up the control layer and makes it directly programmable. This opens the door to simplifying the networking process. Networks that are enabled by SDN offer an automated abstraction layer between applications and the network, which, as a result, reduces the operational complexity within complex and heterogeneous environments [4].

The application layer [5, 6] is the layer that defines all of the attributes, services, and rules. In order to react, applications require information about network appliances and topology. These applications can develop end-to-end functionalities and make decisions depending on network changes. Applications have the ability to change the behaviour of the network in a dynamic manner whenever the network topology, feature requirements, or policy requirements are adjusted. Application programming interfaces (APIs) are what make it possible for all of the SDN layers to communicate with one another.

According to the ONF, the rise of cloud services and the corresponding hike in network capacity and constant shifting traffic pattern within a data centre which needs to be managed at a granular level, necessitate a new network paradigm, such as SDN [7]. SDN is defined by the ONF as a new network paradigm in which the network can be programmed directly and the control and forwarding planes are segregated. One of the most distinguishing features of SDN is that intelligence is embedded in the SDN controller in a centralised way. Besides, SDN architectures support a set of APIs that enable the implementation of common network services tailored to meet business objectives [8]. SDN is now being addressed by various SDOs in addition to the ONF. For example, the Internet Engineering Task Force (IETF) has established the Software-Defined Networking Research Group (SDNRG) to focus on this topic. The ONF and the SDNRG have both proposed quite different SDN architectures. First, we discuss the architecture proposed by the SDNRG [9].

7.1.1 SDNRG Architecture

The architecture proposed by the SDNRG has five components: forwarding plane, control plane, operational plane, management plane, and application plane. The forwarding plane, which is also known as the data plane, is responsible for handling or forwarding data packets on the data path. Second, the control plane is in charge of making decisions on how every packet is treated, i.e., whether it should be forwarded to the output port or to the controller. It is the responsibility of this layer only to push such decisions to the underlying network devices. The operation plane handles the operational state of the network. The management plane manages the configuration and maintains the network devices [10]. The application plane is the layer where network functionalities, such as firewalls, routers, and load balancers reside. Apart from these five planes, the SDNRG also defines two abstraction layers: the device and resource abstraction layer and network service abstraction layer. The first abstracts the forwarding and operational planes of network devices and exposes them to the control and management planes via the control plane southbound interface and the management plane southbound interface, respectively [11]. The second abstraction layer exposes the control and management planes to the application plane via a northbound interface. Service abstractions are provided by the Network Services Abstraction Layer (NSAL) for usage by applications and other services. In the concept of "abstraction layers," it introduced some core SDN ideas. The NSAL is the first. Between the SDN controllers and the higher-level applications and network services, this layer "sits." It serves as these controllers' API. It also introduced additional abstraction layers, such as the Device and Resource Abstraction Layer (DRAL), the Control Abstraction Layer (CAL), and the Management Abstraction Layer (MAL) [11]. Each of these levels or APIs offers the higher layers a standard method of informing the layer or layers below them of the requirements they have.

On the other hand, the architecture proposed by the ONF, which consists of three layers, has been discussed in the previous chapters.

Figure 7.1 shows the architecture proposed by the SDNRG with different abstraction layers.

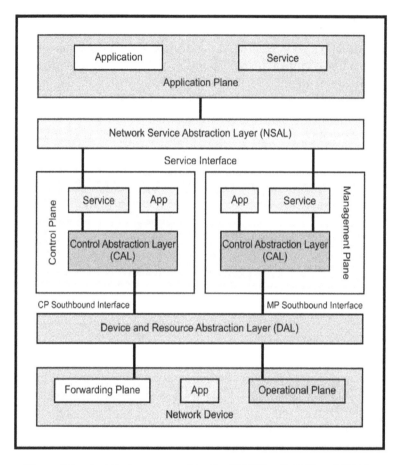

Figure 7.1.   Architecture proposed by the SDNRG with DAL and NSAL.

7.2 Network Service Abstraction Layer

RFC 7426 specifies a network services abstraction layer as a layer that provides service abstractions that can be used by applications and services between the control and application planes. This layer offers an abstract view of network resources that conceals the underlying data plane devices' details. This layer could enable a generalised view of control plane operations, allowing applications to be built that could run on a variety of controller network operating systems. This layer is somewhat similar to virtual machines that run multiple applications simultaneously, irrespective of the underlying hardware. The network abstraction layer could be perceived as a component of the northbound interface whose functionality can be embedded in the control or application layer [12]. A wide range of applications can be run on the application layer, some of which are firewalls and load balancers.

A variety of network applications could be used with SDN. Multiple lists and even different main categories of SDN-based network applications have been produced by several published SDN surveys. Figure 7.1 shows some major categories of SDN applications. A user is given the ability to interact with SDN applications and configure their parameters through the use of the user interface. Applications must support user interaction. Again, there are two different interfaces that could be used. A user who is physically located in the same physical space as the SDN application server (which may or may not also include the control plane) has access to the keyboard and display of the server. The degree of detail about the lower levels of the model that is visible to the upper levels is referred to as abstraction in the context of the debate. More details are represented by less abstraction, and vice versa. A process known as an abstraction layer converts a high-level request into the low-level commands needed to fulfil the request [13]. One such mechanism is an API. It protects software at a higher degree of abstraction from the implementation specifics of a lower level of abstraction. A network abstraction is responsible for representing the fundamental attributes or characteristics of network elements (such as switches, connections, ports, and flows) so that network applications can be fully programmed for the intended functionality without having to write the code for the same set of functions again and again.

7.2.1 Abstractions in SDN

In the above section, we discussed abstraction and what it really means in the context of SDN. Now, we discuss the different types of abstractions that exist in SDN.

SDN emphasises the importance of abstractions in networking and considers that the network control plane requires three abstractions [14–16]:

1. **Forwarding abstraction:** It is a flexible forwarding paradigm that abstracts forwarding hardware and is critical for moving beyond vendor-specific solutions. By masking the intricacies of the

underlying switching technology, the forwarding abstraction enables control software to determine data plane forwarding behaviour. The forwarding function of the data plane is supported by this abstraction. The forwarding hardware is abstracted away, allowing for flexibility and vendor independence.

2. **Abstractions of state distribution:** The control programme should not be required to deal with a variety of distributed states and should operate from a network perspective. In addition, as seen in Figure 7.1, the network operating system can generate a network view by inter- acting with forwarding elements. In the context of distributed control- lers, this concept appears. A cooperative group of distributed controllers keeps track of the network's condition and routes through it. The dispersed state of the entire network may be represented by partitioned data sets, with controller instances sharing routing infor- mation, or by a replicated data set, in which case the controllers would have to work together to maintain a consistent understanding of the overall network.

3. **Specification abstraction:** It translates the controls specified in the abstract view into a global-view configuration. Even when several col- laborating controllers are utilised, the distribution abstraction gives a comprehensive picture of the network as if there were a single central controller. The global network may then be seen coherently. This view offers precisely the right amount of granularity for the application to be able to express goals, such as routing or security policies, without supplying the information required to actually carry out the goals.

7.2.2 Scenarios Describing Abstractions in SDN

A cornerstone of computer science is the concept of abstraction levels. It is a fundamental tenet of achieving efficiency through layered, modular scaling. Network operators programme each network device one at a time through proprietary APIs. SDN solutions and agnostic forwarding abstrac- tions, such as OpenFlow, are essentially building blocks, not panaceas [17]. What OpenFlow does provide is a vendor-agnostic low-level network instruction set that is likely to be flexible enough to serve as a foundation abstraction as it matures. We can create controllers and apps that regulate forwarding and/or collect vital information about the state of your network using a consistent set of primitives. This is how abstractions in SDN work. Now, we discuss some scenarios that explore abstractions in SDN.

7.2.2.1 *OpenFlow*

An OpenFlow switch keeps a forwarding table with a list of prioritised rules. Each rule contains a pattern that specifies a set of packets and actions that describe packet transformations. When a packet reaches a switch, the switch looks for a rule whose pattern corresponds to the headers of the packet and executes the related actions [18]. While if no rules match, the switch encloses the packet in an OpenFlow message and transmits it to the controllers, if more than one rule matches, the switch applies the actions of the highest priority rule. The controllers have two options: They can handle the packet directly or they can send messages to the switch telling it to add or remove rules from its forwarding table. Hardware limitations set a table's maximum size; however, most switches have room for at least a few thousand rules. Every rule has related counters that maintain fundamental information, including the quantity and aggregate size of all packets processed by that rule, in order to provide traffic monitoring. Using OpenFlow messages, controllers can access these counters. In order to perform traffic engineering applications, they can also configure the physical ports on a switch by establishing queues that rate-limit traffic or ensure a minimum bandwidth [19]. OpenFlow provides hardware abstraction for all these processes. The OpenFlow specification outlines a minimum set of features that switches must have in addition to a communication interface that controllers can use to interact with switches. These features include directions for adding and removing forwarding rules as well as alerts for flows, topology, and traffic statistics.

7.2.2.2 *Updates*

It is generally acceptable in conventional networks for configuration modifications to be eventually consistent. For example, if the network configuration is revised as a result of a link failure, a packet may traverse a switch twice: once in the original state and once in the revised state. This can result in behaviours such as forwarding loops or the loss of packets. However, because the majority of networks only provide best-effort delivery, momentary failures during the transition may be acceptable as long as the network finally converges to the new state [17, 20, 21]. However, gradual, regular updates are not always enough in SDN. Sometimes, more frequent updates are required. For instance, in addition to managing forwarding rules, an SDN controller may also manage filtering rules. These rules may be essential for providing invariants, such as access control or isolation between the traffic of tenants that share the network. If configuration updates are sent to switches in a way that is only eventually consistent, these invariants can easily be broken while the network is in a state of transition. When compared to conventional networks, the requirement for regular configuration upgrades that provide good consistency is a substantial shift. Consider the scenario of a load balancer where the network is initially set up to route incoming requests to a number of replica back-end servers. Additional servers will eventually go online. The controller then creates a new configuration that distributes the workload among the additional servers in an even manner [22]. The network is intended to always send incoming traffic to one of the back-end servers while maintaining connection affinity — all packets in a connection should be forwarded to the same server. The starting and end configurations in this scenario are simple to compute, but transitioning between them while retaining the necessary invariants is hard. Because the controller lacks the capacity to atomically change the state of the whole network, packets crossing the network must be handled by old, new, or even intermediate configurations having a mix of forwarding rules from both configurations.

Consistent update abstractions make it possible for a controller to bring the forwarding state of an entire network up to date while also guaranteeing that a packet will never go over a path that is in the process of switching between two different states. The abstractions themselves are simple to explain; the controller software identifies the version of the state that is being pushed into the network, and the update subsystem ensures that every packet moving through the network "sees" only a consistent version of the state. The state update subsystem of the controller can offer several consistency models to the application, which is an additional level of abstraction beyond versioning [23].

For any SDN controller, updates are a basic abstraction. However, despite some promising first results, many questions remain unanswered. The apparent issue is efficiency: The update mechanisms demand a lot of rule space and control messages to accomplish transitions. In large networks, the costs can be enormous. However, optimisation techniques with a holistic investigation should be adopted to deal with the issues related to efficiency.

7.2.2.3 *Modular Structure*

Processes in operating systems allow for resource sharing between several users on a single machine. Memory, locks, file descriptors, and sockets are only some of the system resources that are tied to each process's thread of execution [17, 24]. All process communication must occur through these well-defined interfaces in order to function properly within the operating system. Although "network operating systems" and SDN controllers have been contrasted, existing controllers lack abstractions similar to processes. It is challenging to create programmes using a modular approach since the majority of controllers grant applications unrestricted access to the forwarding tables on every switch in the network. This is problematic because modularisation should come naturally to network programming. Routing, broadcast, monitoring, and access control are key building elements used to construct SDN systems [25]. However, because most SDN controllers lack modularity, programmers must reimplement these core services from scratch in each new application rather than merely using pre-existing libraries.

Consider the scenario where a video-conferencing application receives low-latency service from the network and a backup application is granted the ability to route traffic along various distinct channels as long as there is adequate bandwidth. The programmer needs to take both functions into account at the same time in order to guarantee that the service-level prerequisites of each application are satisfied. This issue is brought about by the fact that enabling programmes to directly change low-level network state makes it practically hard to design SDN applications in a modular fashion.

Changing the programming interface that SDN applications make use of is one method to make those applications more flexible. SDN programmers could utilise a high-level language that compiles to OpenFlow rather than explicitly maintaining low-level forwarding rules on switches. Programmers should be able to independently create and test modules using such a language without being concerned about unforeseen interactions. A module could even be switched out for another one that has the same functionality by a programmer.

In certain contexts, programmers have the responsibility of ensuring that the merged programmes will not cause any kind of conflict with one another. Utilising an abstraction that enables many applications to run concurrently while still limiting each to its own "slice" of the network is one way to ensure that isolation is maintained. This is the other way to maintain modularity in SDN applications. FlowVisor serves as a hypervisor that sits between the controller and the switches. It scrutinises every event and control message to make certain that the programme and the traffic it generates are contained within their own section of the network.

When different modules' behaviours are combined, there is a possibility of conflict arising. If, for instance, one module uses up all of the available bandwidth on a link, then other modules won't be able to use that link anymore. The PANE controller [26] gives administrators of networks the ability to establish module-specific access control policies and quotas for network resources. PANE takes advantage of this approach in order to deliver an API to end-host programmes that enable them to make requests for network resources. For instance, a video-conferencing application can be easily adapted to use the PANE API to reserve bandwidth for a high-quality video session. This can be done in a number of different ways. PANE makes certain that its request for bandwidth does not go over the limits that have been established by the administrator and that it does not deprive other applications of resources.

The technology behind SDN relies heavily on abstractions that can break down complicated programmes into more manageable parts. Without them, programmers are required to write programmes in a technique known as monolithic programming, which involves simultaneously constructing, testing, and thinking about the potential relationships between each component of the programme.

7.2.2.4 *Virtualisation*

SDN separates the network management software from the actual forwarding components. The forwarding logic is not, however, separated from the underlying physical network topology. This implies that any time the topology changes, a software that uses shortest-path routing must update its whole topology representation. Some SDN controllers now offer primitives for creating applications in terms of virtual network elements in order to solve this problem [27]. There are other possibilities to improve the scalability and fault tolerance of SDN systems by decoupling programmes from topology.

Consider the scenario of a data centre where it is commonly desired to let different tenants impose their own regulations on the hardware connected to a common physical network. However, since Ethernet and IP have overlapping addresses and services, it is difficult to ensure that traffic generated by one tenant is separated from that of other tenants [28]. Using virtual switches, each tenant can be given a configurable virtual network without interfering with other tenants.

It is a common practice to establish access control by encoding data, such as MAC or IP addresses, into configurations. Sadly, this means that security can be compromised by topology changes, such as a host migrating from one location to another [29]. If, instead, access control lists are configured in terms of a virtual switch that is connected to each host, then the policy does not change regardless of whether or not the topology does. By isolating the forwarding logic of applications from the unique physical topologies on which they run, virtualisation can make applications more portable and scalable.

VMware's Network Virtualisation Platform (NSX) is the most well-known example of a virtual network abstraction for SDN [30, 31]. Similar abstractions are supported by the Pyretic controller. These controllers reveal to programmers the same underlying structure at the virtual and physical levels, for example, a graph reflecting the network topology allows programmes designed for the physical network to be utilised at the virtual level and vice versa. The programmer must establish a mapping between the elements of the logical and physical networks in order to define the virtual network. A large arbitrary topology can be made to appear like a big switch by mapping all of the physical network's switches onto the single virtual switch and concealing all of the internal links.

Although virtualisation abstractions are straightforward in theory, putting them into practice can be a real challenge. Platforms such as NSX use a controller hypervisor to translate logical events and control signals into their physical counterparts. Most platforms stamp incoming packets with a tag (such as a VLAN tag or an MPLS label) that directly associates them with one or more virtual networks, simplifying the accounting required to execute virtualisation. Modern SDN controllers rely heavily on virtualisation abstractions. Bifurcation programmes from the physical architecture streamlines applications and allows multiple programmes to share the network without interfering.

Despite the fact that numerous commercial controllers currently allow virtualisation, there are many unanswered questions. The level of detail that should be presented at the logical level is one issue [32]. Current SDN virtualisation systems use the same programming interface at the logical and physical levels, omitting resources such as link capacities, queues, and local switch capacities. Another issue is figuring out how to mix virtualisation with other abstractions, such as continuous updates. Because both abstractions are usually implemented through tagging schemes, realising this combination directly is not always possible. Finally, present platforms do not allow nested virtualisation efficiently. There are no fundamental concerns semantically; however, there are practical implications of establishing nested virtualisation utilising hypervisors [33].

7.3 Traffic Engineering

Traffic engineering (TE), an essential network function, focuses on the monitoring, analysis, and management of network traffic flows in order to optimise resource usage and quality-of-service (QoS) standards compliance. SDNs have many advantages over traditional networks when it comes to supporting TE because of their distinguishing characteristics. These characteristics include the isolation of control and forwarding, global centralised control, and programmability of network behaviour [34].

IP-based traffic engineering, in general, provides a solution to the issue of multipath traffic load balancing by improving the efficiency of the IP routing algorithm in order to prevent network congestion. In Ref. [35], researchers have proposed an algorithm to adjust the routing calculation based on the link weights of an open-source shortest path (OSPF). This mechanism would render multiple shortest routing paths for traffic load balance. There are many such mechanisms proposed by researchers [36, 37]. IP-based TE technology has two obvious drawbacks: First, traffic cannot be segmented in a random proportion when OSPF link weights are utilised to control routing of a network, making it impossible to fully utilise network resources; and second, when links fail or the link weights of the network topology change, the OSPF protocol takes some time to congregate to a fresh network topology, potentially causing network congestion, packet losses, delays, outages, and routing loops. To overcome these shortcomings, instead of using IP headers to forward network packets, researchers came up with a different technique called Multi-Protocol Label Switching (MPLS) [37]. Data centre networks have stringent demands for high link-bandwidth utilisation, green energy savings, and high reliability, but it is challenging to meet these standards due to MPLS's complex protocol mechanism, resulting in a large performance overhead.

To sum up, traditional networks have a tight coupling between control management and data forwarding because the entire network is controlled by distributed devices, making it impossible to achieve fine-grained control of traffic management and making it challenging to enhance the network's flexibility and scalability [38, 39]. Therefore, SDN is a great solution to these problems related to traffic engineering. The following are properties of SDN which are helpful for resolving present network traffic engineering issues:

- **Traffic measurement:** The ability to build scalable global measurement jobs in SDN in a flexible manner is a great feature that helps in resolving issues related to traffic engineering. These jobs can collect real-time information regarding the status of the network, and the controller can monitor and analyse traffic centrally [40].
- The OpenFlow switch incorporates numerous stream table pipelines, which results in improved flexibility and productivity in flow management.
- **Organising and managing the flow of traffic:** The requirements of the traffic application can be evaluated globally, which allows for the possibility of flexible and granular traffic scheduling [41].

However, despite the fact that SDN offers a significant amount of assistance for traffic engineering, it still has numerous issues that need to be resolved. There are no studies available at this time that would indicate that the conventional network TE approach can be fully compatible with the SDN [41]. Another issue is that traditional IP networks and SDNs will continue to coexist for a considerable amount of time, and there has been very little study done on the topic of TE technology for hybrid IP/SDN networks [42]. Because of this, the development of TE technologies that are based on SDN is of utmost importance for the further use of SDN.

A number of different applications for TE have been suggested, such as ElasticTree [43], Hedera [44], OpenFlow-based server load balancing [45], Plug-n-Serve [46] and Aster*x [47], In-packet Bloom filter [48], SIMPLE [49], QNOX [50], QoS framework [51], QoS for SDN [52], ALTO [53], ViAggre SDN [54], ProCel [55], FlowQoS [56], and Middlepipes [57]. In addition to these, new recommendations also include approaches for flow control, fault tolerance, topology updating, and traffic characterisation [58], as well as the optimisation of rule placement and the use of MAC as a universal label for effective routing in data centres. Most applications are primarily concerned with engineering traffic in order to reduce power consumption, increase overall network usage, provide improved load balancing, and use other general traffic optimisation approaches.

One of the earliest TE applications that was envisioned for use with SDN was load balancing. Scalability is the most important issue related to this application. The positioning of network services within the network is also made simpler by SDN load balancing [59]. The load-balancing service can take the proper steps every time a new server is deployed to evenly distribute the traffic across the available servers, taking into account both the network demand and the corresponding host's available processing capability. This makes managing the network easier and gives network operators more flexibility.

Data centre networks aim to eliminate or reduce the impact of bottlenecks on the performance of the computing services they provide. For traffic patterns that place strain on the network, a linear bisection bandwidth can be implemented through the investigation of path variety in a data centre layout [60]. To maximise aggregated network use with little scheduling overhead, a method such as this has been proposed for use in an SDN environment. Another intriguing application for large-scale service providers is traffic optimisation, which is used in situations when dynamic scale-out is necessary.

7.3.1 Traffic Measurement and Management

The study of traffic measurement is an essential component of research on TE. This section discusses related technologies from the perspective of the following three aspects: a universal framework for flow measurement, traffic analysis and prediction technologies, and technologies for designing network parameters and monitoring.

7.3.1.1 *Measurement of Network Parameters*

Network parameters are a group of indicators that show the state of the network at the moment. Effective network management is a requirement for reasonable network parameter design. Consequently, one of the main tasks of network measurement is the creation of network parameters. We believe that the three primary categories of SDN network measurement metrics are those related to network topology, network traffic, and network performance.

The number of network nodes, link bandwidths, connection setups, and port statuses are all examples of network topology parameters. The SDN controller actively identifies the current network topology using the Link Layer Discovery Protocol (LLDP) [61], in accordance with the OpenFlow specification, and keeps global topology data.

The total number of data packets, the number of bytes per second, and so on are all examples of network traffic characteristics that describe how many or how quickly network packets move through a piece of networking hardware or a network port. Network traffic characteristics are viewed as a crucial foundation for identifying the present network status and analysing user activity in a network. There are two distinct types of network traffic in a software-defined networking environment: control traffic and data traffic. Two types of data flows can be distinguished in SDN: control traffic, which travels between the SDN controller and switches, and data traffic, which travels only between the switches themselves. Gathering statistics on the number and size of packets traversing each switch port, as well as the end-to-end traffic matrix of the entire network, which reflects the flow between any two nodes in the network, is necessary for identifying flow characteristics. Many solutions for measuring network parameters have been proposed by researchers [62–65].

Latency, bandwidth usage, throughput rates, packet loss, etc., are just a few of the many metrics used to measure a network's performance. In order to measure several aspects of a network's performance, Van Adrichem *et al.* [66] proposed a network monitoring module called OpenNetMon. OpenNetMon provides continuous monitoring of network performance metrics, such as throughput, packet loss, and latency. To start, it uses an adjustable frequency to only poll the last switch in the forwarding chain to determine the throughput. The counter will yield the total number of packets (N) for each flow during the sampling interval (T), and the throughput of the forwarding path may be calculated as the number of packets divided by the sampling interval, i.e., N/S. Second, when it calculates packet loss rates, it first obtains counter statistics by querying the first and last switches on the forwarding path. Next, the increment of the last counter is subtracted from the increment of the first counter in a measurement cycle. Finally, the result is divided by the time, which gives the packet loss rate of this forwarding path. Third, OpenNetMon sends probe messages to the data layers of the forwarding path, and once these messages have traversed all nodes in the path, they are returned to the controller, where the communication delays can be derived by calculating time differences.

7.3.1.2 *Generic Framework for Traffic Measurement*

There are two common ways to gauge traffic on a network: actively and passively. Passive measurement merely watches traffic going via SDN switches, while active measurement generates additional detecting traffic. Many SDN performance measures use standard IP network traffic monitoring methods based on packet sampling, in which SDN switches randomly crawl local packets to acquire traffic statistics. Cisco's NetFlow [67] is a well-known technology for packet sampling and analysis. NetFlow uses five tuples to identify flows, and a switch stores cache record information for each flow. When a flow arrives, NetFlow compares the flow's head with the information stored in a local cache record. If they match, the package count is updated; otherwise, a new item is added to the cache record for this new flow. Other flow sampling solutions include sFlow [68] and JFlow [69]. In large-scale networks, all of the above measurement methods place a significant burden on the SDN central controller. As a result, they are unsuitable for SDN applications.

To efficiently support a wide range of SDN measurement tasks and applications, a comprehensive SDN measurement framework must be designed. Traffic data collection and aggregation are two critical components of traffic measurement that require hardware support at the data layer, such as the TCAM. However, the hardware resources of SDN switches are frequently constrained. Furthermore, network applications have numerous concurrent flow monitoring task requirements, rather than enabling only one measurement activity at a time. As a result, how to deploy hardware resources in a reasonable manner to enable accurate and effective flow measurement is equally critical. Accordingly, Moshref *et al.* [70] proposed DREAM, an adaptive management architecture for hardware resources that may effectively strike a balance between measurement accuracy and resource costs.

7.3.1.3 *Analysis and Prediction of Traffic*

Network measurement includes traffic analysis and prediction, which has as one of its objectives identifying abnormal network traffic and examining potential network eventualities, such as network congestion. Analysis and prediction can offer better data for managing and scheduling network traffic. However, there is yet another significant item, which is to determine whether the network's present status is accurate, including any issues with routing loops or current network equipment configurations. There are many solutions that have been proposed for the analysis and prediction of SDN traffic [71, 72].

The process of data forwarding in networks is dependent on a wide variety of network equipment that perform a variety of functions. This process is complex and prone to possible configuration issues, software bugs, and other issues, which may cause a variety of network mistakes, such as routing loops. The SDN makes it easier to use network applications; however, owing to the complexity of the programme itself, it is still challenging to eliminate the possibility of making errors. In light of this, accurate status identification and validation constitute a significant research task for the SDN's field of traffic measurement. In this domain also, many solutions have been proposed [73–75].

7.3.2 Traffic Management and Scheduling

The availability of a network is one of the primary focuses of network management, along with performance optimisation. One of the most significant ways to improve the QoS of the network is to schedule network traffic in a reasonable manner. In general, there are several paths between the source and destination nodes in an SDN, which provide potential for traffic scheduling. With the help of the aforementioned network measurement technologies, the SDN controller is able to keep track of how each path is currently being used, allowing us to create a traffic scheduling algorithm that can proactively plan data forwarding paths to best suit the needs of the users [103]. In this section, we cover the technologies that are used for traffic management in SDN from the following perspectives: QoS-guaranteed scheduling, traffic load balancing, traffic management for hybrid IP/SDN networks, and energy-saving scheduling.

7.3.2.1 *Scheduling for QoS Guarantee*

Many types of real-time commercial traffic, including audio data and instant messages, are highly susceptible to transmission delays and packet losses. So, one of the most pressing challenges in traffic management is the fair allocation of network resources to guarantee service quality for commercial operations. Due to SDN's open control interface, a variety of traffic scheduling algorithms can be implemented within a network to meet the QoS requirements for a wide range of applications. Many scheduling algorithms [76–78] have been proposed by researchers in SDN.

7.3.2.2 *Traffic Load Balancing*

There are two distinct kinds of network traffic in SDN: data layer traffic and control layer traffic. The primary benefit of load balancing in a SDN, in comparison to traditional networks, is that calculations for forwarding decisions are centralised rather than distributed. This allows for the consideration of multiple optional link utilisation rates and flow characteristics in a more comprehensive manner, which in turn allows for improved load-balancing strategy planning. Packet-level, rather than flow-level, traffic partitioning is a straightforward approach. Even though it considerably enhances the efficiency of load balancing, this technique worsens the TCP send window reordering problem, which in turn causes the send window to be shrunk when it needn't be [79]. To deal with this issue, many improvised equivalency multipath routing technology (ECMP) schemes have been proposed [80–82]. ECMP, which is based on a hash algorithm, is an efficient approach for load balancing. Many other solutions have also been proposed for traffic load balancing in SDN [83–85].

7.3.2.3 *Traffic Management for Hybrid Networks* (*IP and SDN*)

TE technologies that are based on SDN provide excellent solutions for the optimisation of networks. However, because the transition from traditional networks to SDN takes a considerable amount of time, a hybrid network that combines IP and SDN has emerged. As a result of the fact that not every node in a hybrid IP/SDN network possesses the capabilities of an SDN switch, we are only able to gain an accurate view of the network in part. It is more difficult to control traffic on a hybrid IP/SDN network as compared to a network that only uses SDN. As a result, the difficulty lies in the question of how to control traffic in the hybrid IP/SDN network.

In Ref. [86], the authors describe a traffic management architecture that is well suited for hybrid IP/SDN networks. In particular, they make an effort to make use of the centralised controller in order to achieve high network usage while simultaneously lowering the number of lost packets and delays. In the first step, we formulate optimisation issues for the SDN controllers in the context of partial deployment for use in TE. To address this issue, the fully polynomial time approximation scheme (FPTAS) was developed. Experiments show that improvements in performance are possible in an IP/SDN hybrid network setting by employing these strategies.

Energy-saving scheduling is discussed in the following section on data centre networking.

7.4 Data Centre Networking

Applications have evolved to provide organisations with more pertinent and timely information. As a result, these apps have become increasingly dispersed and are accessed from an increasing number of places by a larger number of users throughout a firm and its supply chain. This evolution places a great strain on the network, which must adapt to meet these demands. Enterprises have tens of thousands of apps operating in their data centres, which have been developed over the years and face a variety of network difficulties. The early days of networking were also the simplest. Traditionally, data centre applications were hosted on mainframes or minicomputers and accessed by a small group of authorised users via terminals wired directly to the servers. With the proliferation of apps and the evolution of their underlying architectures, IT infrastructures have turned to virtualisation [87]. The first of its kind, server virtualisation was created to address problems such as resource allocation and application accessibility. After virtualising their networks, businesses will discover that they have isolated resources that need to communicate with each other. This will depend on a variety of aspects, including the location of the resources, whether they are local or remote, and whether or not they are connected to an SDN [88].

The term "data centre" can refer to anything from a modest server room to a massive cloud data centre. Large data centres have been quick to adopt SDN because of the promise it holds for making better use of scarce network resources in the face of ever-shifting traffic patterns, software, end users, and even application service providers. Because of SDN's advantages, we anticipate that eventually even less-active and

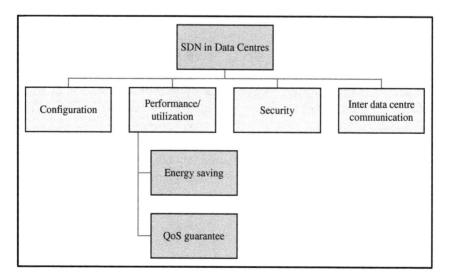

Figure 7.2.   Classification of SDN functionalities in a data centre.

smaller data centres will implement it. SDN and network virtualisation are sometimes used interchangeably. Although related, they are distinct concepts. Network virtualisation encapsulates a real network's functions to create one or more virtual networks. The goal could be to provide a simplified representation of the underlying resources or to enable regulated access to those resources among untrusted clients. Network virtualisation can be implemented via SDN. SDN might also be applied to a virtualised network. SDN can be applied to a data centre in the categories of configuration, performance/utilisation, security, and inter-data-centre communication. Figure 7.2 shows the classification of SDN functionalities in data centre networking.

7.4.1 Network Monitoring and Configuration

In data centre networking (DCN), the configuration of devices, such as switches, routers, and middleboxes, which are physical as well as increasingly virtualised nowadays, plays an important role. More than a thousand individual switches might make up a cloud-scale DCN, and they might all have somewhat varied capabilities and features [87, 104]. Operators are given a high-level, abstracted picture of the network through network management tools. The tools translate complex operator commands into simpler interfaces offered by specific hardware or software components [89, 105].

The integration of SDN into a suite of network management tools allows for granular control over how network resources are divided up among applications and users by providing a centralised, unified view of network resources and a single point for monitoring and configuration. There is no requirement for a network to consist of nodes that are statically configured according to broad assumptions about traffic volumes and types and that can only respond slowly to sudden shifts in demand. With the help of SDN-based technologies, the network administrator can define a consistent policy that is then automatically deployed and policed [89]. It is possible for the policy to be intricate and dynamic. A cloud data centre's policy, for instance, may constantly need updating when new tenants are added, older tenants leave, or service requirements are modified.

It's not easy to provide a holistic view of all available network resources. It's not just the many types of network nodes (switches, routers, and middleboxes) that need to be accounted for; even nodes that perform the same function may have varying levels of functionalities, for example, switches may have different-sized CAM tables or switches supporting different OpenFlow versions [90]. Researchers have addressed some of these problems, and they have utilised a software-defined approach in order to conceal the underlying complexity with intelligent algorithms.

When a network is configured, it is important to keep an eye on the operation of the devices to ensure their correct working. Applying SDN has benefits in this area as well, such as dynamically modifying the amount of switch resources (CPUs and CAM tables) needed for monitoring in an OpenFlow network so as to strike a balance between resource utilisation and the accuracy of measurements. It is possible to change both the granularity and frequency of the information being collected depending on the requirements. For example, in a congested area, it may be acceptable to reduce the amount of detail that is being monitored in order to prioritise allowing data packets to pass through [91]. On the other hand, in order to positively detect a denial-of-service attack, additional in-depth monitoring could be required in particular areas of the network. In contrast to the conventional practice of devoting a predetermined number of resources to network monitoring, SDN makes it possible to maintain this level of flexibility.

7.4.2 Performance/Utilisation of Resources in Data Centre

A slight boost in performance (higher throughput, lower latency) at the larger data centres can be converted into a competitive advantage. Performance can be enhanced by the employment of methods including virtual-machine (VM) consolidation, layer 4–7 load balancing, and traffic splitting and engineering on the network.

Moving two communicating VMs closer to one another within a data centre can help minimise latency by shortening the distance between them. Since, fewer links and intermediate devices are required to transfer the traffic between VMs, this also results in s reduction in the overall utilisation of the network. First and foremost, the function of SDN is to guarantee that data packets will continue to be delivered to a VM after the latter has been moved, making the relocation undetectable to both the VM itself and the communicating partners. This ensures that TCP connections will not be broken. Second, SDN can be utilised to reserve or assign network resources in order to support a fast VM migration over the DCN. The advantages that moving a VM has must offset the disadvantages of the migration process, which consumes resources, such as network bandwidth, CPU time, and storage space.

Layer 4 load balancing has typically been implemented using specialised hardware appliances, while virtual appliances have lately become available from manufacturers. The distribution of client flows over a number of data centre servers offering a shared service specified by a TCP port number is known as layer 4 load balancing. Duet [92] is an SDN-based software and hardware load balancer. The majority of the work required for load balancing is offloaded to DCN switches, which allows for underutilised resources in switches that are already installed in the data centre network to be utilised. This naturally scales with the data centre while incurring the least amount of additional cost. The primary purpose of Duet's software load balancing is to provide fault tolerance.

Traffic splitting utilises redundant network paths within a network. Redundant pathways are part of a network architecture, allowing for device or link failure. Since this redundancy in the network incurs significant investment, the objective is to utilise the resources during normal network operation, enhancing the overall network's resource utilisation. While basic traffic splitting may work in some cases, an SDN-based solution may offer additional benefits. Planck [93] expands upon earlier efforts to keep tabs on data centre switches by delivering a programme that can reroute congested flows in a matter of milliseconds.

7.4.2.1 *Energy Saving in Data Centres*

The amount of energy consumed grows in proportion to the size and number of data centres. This has prompted researchers and the industry to control and reduce data centre energy use. Initially, the focus was on consolidating VMs in order to power down servers during off-peak hours; however, researchers' attention has shifted to the network, which consumes a major amount of a data centre's total power consumption. The network of a data centre, in particular, is typically designed to be able to keep up with peak demand. This means that there should be ample amounts of bandwidth available to prevent bottlenecks anywhere in the network. Additionally, there should be redundant links and devices to reduce the likelihood of the network becoming partitioned as a result of a failure. These requirements impose an initial equipment cost as well as an ongoing expense because all linkages and devices must be powered constantly, even though the network functions at a fraction of its maximum capacity most of the time.

By enabling flows to be routed (or rerouted) across a fraction of the switches and links in a DCN, SDN can aid in the goal of lowering energy consumption. Inactive nodes, such as switches and links, can be turned off or placed in an energy-saving standby mode until they are needed again, potentially during high-demand times. Energy-aware traffic engineering (ETE) provides a straightforward method [94] for turning off inter-switch connectivity when traffic patterns indicate that it is not needed, i.e., at night. For more advanced research, the energy profile of the switches is taken into account, and when given the option, the more power-hungry devices are turned off first [95]. First, SDN makes these methods possible by providing a broad perspective of the entire network and making it possible to collect information on the types and quantities of flows currently active in the system. Second, to reduce packet loss and latency spikes, all switches can be reconfigured via the control plane to release unused devices and links before being powered off.

7.4.2.2 *QoS in Data Centre Networking*

QoS refers to the practice of providing certain types of traffic with preferential treatment over others, typically in the form of guaranteed latency, bandwidth, and/or packet loss. Congestion hotspots in a data centre can be reduced in two ways: first, by providing more bandwidth than is currently being used, and second, by employing TE to ensure that all users are making fair use of available bandwidth or by tilting the scales in favour of certain users or regular processes [96]. Congestion has several sources, but a lack of bandwidth is just one of them. Packets' latency can also be affected by other aspects, such as the amount of time it takes for switches and routers to process incoming packets and the number of operations performed on each packet. Additionally, traffic profiles shift in a cloud data centre because tenants enter and exit, scale their consumption up and down, and alter the applications they are using. This kind of scenario is too dynamic to be accommodated by standard TE methods.

The QoS that is provided by SDN is able to flexibly handle varying service granularity for distinct flows, in addition to policies that are always changing. SDN can be utilised to dynamically reroute flows away from a congestion hotspot while nonetheless guaranteeing the required level of service. Modifying apps to ask for in-advance guarantees for their traffic is one method by which QoS has been implemented for data centres utilising SDN [97].

7.4.3 Security for Data Centres

The use of SDN can improve a network's security in many different ways. In the context of a DCN, an SDN can be used to implement a security policy, either in place of or, more often, in addition to conventional security mechanisms, such as VLANs and firewalls. An SDN-based solution should dynamically adjust the behaviour of the network so that it is consistent with any new security policies that are implemented. If the security policy is too intricate and nuanced to be implemented in its entirety using static mechanisms or on devices with limited resources, then SDN can facilitate a means to dynamically reconfigure either or both. Self-service provisioning in the cloud, where tenants create and migrate virtual machines and virtual networks, add and configure virtual security devices, and define their own security rules for their virtual clouds, is made easier using SDN in a cloud data centre [98]. Validating and merging these sub-policies and making sure that the result doesn't go against the supplier's super-policy is a difficult task that SDN can help with, for example, SDN can translate the high-level policies to low-level policies as per the device configuration and validate the successful implementation through active packet probing [99].

7.4.4 Inter-Data-Centre Communication

Data centre owners frequently maintain multiple data centres to serve a specific purpose, such as redundancy, disaster recovery, or the placement of services in close proximity to specific customer demographics to minimise latency or Internet backbone bandwidth utilisation [100, 106]. The same logic applies to tenants of data centres who may operate across many data centres from different providers. If a data centre operator is also a wide area network (WAN) provider, there is a chance of exchanging reliability for reduced costs by utilising lesser bandwidth lines that are run at high utilisation. In the event of a connection loss, prompt response is essential to minimise temporary congestion. SDN has been utilised to achieve this goal with minimal additional overhead.

Operators in cloud multi-data centres can offer their tenants the freedom to set up, alter the scale as needed, and shut down virtual links between their networks located in separate data centres using the operators' already physical links [101]. SDN offers the means for self-service adjustments to virtual links, including the ability to specify characteristics such as bandwidth needs and QoS choices. Here, SDN shines because it allows for the fine-grained automation of the configuration of network connections across data centres, which is essential when those connections must handle the traffic of various tenants while still meeting performance guarantees [102].

Exercises

Q.1.   Compare the SDN architectures proposed by ONF and SDNRG.

Q.2.   Discuss the network service abstraction layer that forms an interface between the control and application planes.

Q.3.   Discuss the device and resource abstraction layer interfaced between the control and data planes.

Q.4.   Discuss the control abstraction layer and management abstraction layer of the SDNRG model in detail.

Q.5.   Discuss how abstractions benefit the configuration update mechanism and virtualisation of SDN networking.

Q.6.   How is traffic engineering in traditional networking different from that in SDN networking?

Q.7.   What are the aspects of traffic measurement and management that need to be considered for a SDN network?

Q.8. In SDN networking, why is a generic framework for traffic measurement essential when, at the data plane, there exist numerous devices from different vendors?

Q.9. What factors must be taken care of for maintaining the QoS in SDN?

Q.10. Discuss why proposing traffic engineering solutions for hybrid network (IP/SDN) is more beneficial than proposing solely for SDN.

Q.11. How can SDN functionalities be classified in a data centre environment?

Q.12. How can SDN help with data centre network monitoring and configuration?

Q.13. How can SDN help increase resource utilisation in a data centre?

Q.14. How can SDN contribute to ensuring security and energy savings in a data centre network?

References

[1] Ahmad, I., Namal, S., Ylianttila, M., & Gurtov, A. (2015). Security in software defined networks: A survey. *IEEE Communications Surveys & Tutorials*, *17*(4), 2317–2346.

[2] Semong, T., Maupong, T., Anokye, S., Kehulakae, K., Dimakatso, S., Boipelo, G., & Sarefo, S. (2020). Intelligent load balancing techniques in software defined networks: A survey. *Electronics*, *9*(7), 1091.

[3] Al-Somaidai, M. B. & Yahya, E. B. (2014). Survey of software components to emulate OpenFlow protocol as an SDN implementation. *American Journal of Software Engineering and Applications*, *3*(6), 74–82.

[4] Braun, W. & Menth, M. (2014). Software-defined networking using OpenFlow: Protocols, applications and architectural design choices. *Future Internet*, *6*(2), 302–336.

[5] Abdou, A., Van Oorschot, P. C., & Wan, T. (2018). Comparative analysis of control plane security of SDN and conventional networks. *IEEE Communications Surveys & Tutorials*, *20*(4), 3542–3559

[6] Benzekki, K., El Fergougui, A., & Elbelrhiti Elalaoui, A. (2016). Software-defined networking (SDN): A survey. *Security and Communication Networks*, *9*(18), 5803–5833.

[7] Dhamecha, K., & Trivedi, B. (2013). SDN issues — A survey. *International Journal of Computer Applications*, *73*(18), 30–35.

[8] Xia, W., Wen, Y., Foh, C. H., Niyato, D., & Xie, H. (2014). A survey on software-defined networking. *IEEE Communications Surveys & Tutorials*, *17*(1), 27–51.

[9] Haleplidis, E., Denazis, S., Pentikousis, K., Salim, J. H., Meyer, D., & Koufopavlou, O. (2014, August). Software-defined networking (SDN): Layers and architecture terminology. *Internet Engineering Task Force, Internet Draft*, RFC 7426.

[10] Meyer, D. (2013). The software-defined-networking research group. *IEEE Internet Computing*, *17*(6), 84–87.

[11] Mendiola, A., Astorga, J., Jacob, E., & Higuero, M. (2016). A survey on the contributions of software-defined networking to traffic engineering. *IEEE Communications Surveys & Tutorials*, *19*(2), 918–953.

[12] Gringeri, S., Bitar, N., & Xia, T. J. (2013). Extending software defined network principles to include optical transport. *IEEE Communications Magazine*, *51*(3), 32–40.

[13] Hoang, D. B. & Pham, M. (2015). On software-defined networking and the design of SDN controllers. In *2015 6th International Conference on the Network of the Future (NOF)*, 30 Sep.–2 Oct. 2015, Montreal, Canada (pp. 1–3). IEEE.

[14] Lin, P., Bi, J., Hu, H., Feng, T., & Jiang, X. (2011). A quick survey on selected approaches for preparing programmable networks. In *Proceedings of the 7th Asian Internet Engineering Conference*, 9–11 Nov. 2011, Bangkok, Thailand (pp. 160–163).

[15] Sieber, C., Blenk, A., Hock, D., Scheib, M., Höhn, T., Köhler, S., & Kellerer, W. (2015). Network configuration with quality of service abstractions for SDN and legacy networks. In *2015 IFIP/IEEE International Symposium on Integrated Network Management (IM)*, 11–15 May 2015, Ottawa, ON, Canada (pp. 1135–1136). IEEE.

[16] Riggio, R., Marina, M. K., Schulz-Zander, J., Kuklinski, S., & Rasheed, T. (2015). Programming abstractions for software-defined wireless networks. *IEEE Transactions on Network and Service Management*, *12*(2), 146–162.

[17] Casado, M., Foster, N., & Guha, A. (2014). Abstractions for software-defined networks. *Communications of the ACM*, *57*(10), 86–95.

[18] McKeown, N., Anderson, T., Balakrishnan, H., Parulkar, G., Peterson, L., Rexford, J., Shenker, S., & Turner, J. (2008). OpenFlow: Enabling innovation in campus networks. *SIGCOMM CCR*, *38*(2), 69–74.

[19] Parniewicz, D., Doriguzzi Corin, R., Ogrodowczyk, L., Rashidi Fard, M., Matias, J., Gerola, M., Fuentes, V., Toseef, U., Zaalouk, A., Belter, B., Jacob, E., & Pentikousis, K. (2014). Design and implementation of an OpenFlow hardware abstraction layer. In *Proceedings of the 2014 ACM SIGCOMM Workshop on Distributed Cloud Computing*, 18 Aug. 2014, Chicago, IL (pp. 71–76).

[20] Reitblatt, M., Foster, N., Rexford, J., & Walker, D. (2011). Consistent updates for software-defined networks: Change you can believe in! In *Proceedings of the 10th ACM Workshop on Hot Topics in Networks*, 14–15 Nov. 2011, Cambridge, MA (pp. 1–6).

[21] Nguyen, T. D., Chiesa, M., & Canini, M. (2017). Decentralized consistent updates in SDN. In *Proceedings of the Symposium on SDN Research*, 3–4 April 2017. Santa Clara, CA (pp. 21–33).

[22] Liu, W., Bobba, R. B., Mohan, S., & Campbell, R. H. (2015). Inter-flow consistency: A novel SDN update abstraction for supporting inter-flow constraints. In *2015 IEEE Conference on Communications and Network Security (CNS)*, 28–30 Sept. 2015, Florence, Italy (pp. 469–478). IEEE.

[23] Canini, M., Kuznetsov, P., Levin, D., & Schmid, S. (2015). A distributed and robust SDN control plane for transactional network updates. In *2015 IEEE Conference on Computer Communications (INFOCOM)*, 26 April–1 May 2015, Hong Kong, P.R. China (pp. 190–198). IEEE.

[24] Zaballa, E. O., Franco, D., Jacob, E., Higuero, M., & Berger, M. S. (2021). Automation of Modular and Programmable Control and Data Plane SDN Networks. In *2021 17th International Conference on Network and Service Management (CNSM)*, 25–29 Oct. 2021, Izmir, Turkey (pp. 375–379). IEEE.

[25] Gude, N., Koponen, T., Pettit, J., Pfaff, B., Casado, M., McKeown, N., & Shenker, S. (2008). NOX: Towards an operating system for networks. *ACM SIGCOMM CCR*, *38*(3), 105–110.

[26] Ferguson, A. D., Arjun, G., Chen, L., Rodrigo, F., & Shriram, K. (2013), Participatory networking: An API for application control of SDNs. *ACM SIGCOMM Computer Communication Review*, *43*(4), 327–338.

[27] Jain, R. & Paul, S. (2013). Network virtualization and software defined networking for cloud computing: A survey. *IEEE Communications Magazine*, *51*(11), 24–31.

[28] Blenk, A., Basta, A., Reisslein, M., & Kellerer, W. (2015). Survey on network virtualization hypervisors for software defined networking. *IEEE Communications Surveys & Tutorials*, *18*(1), 655–685.

[29] Li, J., Li, D., Yu, Y., Huang, Y., Zhu, J., & Geng, J. (2018). Towards full virtualization of SDN infrastructure. *Computer Networks*, *143*, 1–14.

[30] Martín, C., Teemu, K., Rajiv, R., & Scott, S. (2010). Virtualizing the network forwarding plane. In *Proceedings of the Workshop on Programmable Routers for Extensible Services of Tomorrow (PRESTO'10)* (pp. 1–6). Association for Computing Machinery, New York, NY, USA, Article 8. https://doi.org/10.1145/1921151.1921162.

[31] Teemu, K., Keith, A., Peter, B., Martin, C., Anupam, C., Bryan, F., Igor, G., Jesse, G., Paul, I., Ethan, J., Andrew, L., Romain, L., Shih-Hao, L., Amar, P., Justin, P., Ben, P., Rajiv, R., Scott, S., Alan, S., Jeremy, S., Pankaj, T., Dan, W., Alexander, Y., Ronghua, Z. (2014), Network virtualization in multi-tenant datacenters. In *The Proceedings of 11th USENIX Symposium on Networked Systems Design and Implementation (NSDI 14)*, 2–4 April 2014, Seattle, WA (pp. 203–216).

[32] Brief, O. S. (2014). OpenFlow-enabled SDN and network functions virtualization. *Open Network Foundation, 17*, 1–12.

[33] Pinheiro, B., Cerqueira, E., & Abelem, A. (2016). NVP: A network virtualization proxy for software defined networking. *International Journal of Computers Communications & Control, 11*(5), 697–707.

[34] Shu, Z., Wan, J., Lin, J., Wang, S., Li, D., Rho, S., & Yang, C. (2016). Traffic engineering in software-defined networking: Measurement and management. *IEEE Access, 4*, 3246–3256.

[35] Fortz, B. & Thorup, M. (2000). Internet traffic engineering by optimizing OSPF weights. In *Proceedings of 19th Annual Joint Conference of the IEEE Computer and Communications Societies INFOCOM*, Vol. 2, Tel Aviv, Israel (pp. 519–528).

[36] Chen, M., Wang, J., Lin, K., Wu, D., Wan, J., Peng, L., & Youn, C.-H. (2016, September). Multipath planning based transmissions for IoT multimedia sensing. In *Proceedings of the IEEE IWCMC*, Paphos, Cyprus (pp. 1–10).

[37] Swallow, G. (2000, December). MPLS advantages for traffic engineering. *IEEE Communications Magazine, 37*(12), 54–57.

[38] Li, Y. & Chen, M. (2015). Software-defined network function virtualization: A survey. *IEEE Access, 3*, 2542–2553.

[39] Liu, J., Li, Y., Chen, M., Dong, W., & Jin, D. (2015). Software-defined Internet of Things for smart urban sensing. *IEEE Communications Magazine, 53*(8), 55–63.

[40] Chen, M., Qian, Y., Mao, S., Tang, W., & Yang, X. Software-defined mobile networks security. *Mobile Networks and Applications. 21*, 729–743.

[41] Akyildiz, I. F., Lee, A., Wang, P., Luo, M., & Chou, W. (2014). A roadmap for traffic engineering in SDN-OpenFlow networks. *Computer Networks, 71*, 1–30.

[42] Agarwal, S., Kodialam, M., & Lakshman, T. V. (2013). Traffic engineering in software defined networks. In *Proceedings of the IEEE INFOCOM*, 14–19 April 2013, Turin, Italy (pp. 2211–2219).

[43] Heller, B., Seetharaman, S., Mahadevan, P., Yiakoumis, Y., Sharma, P., Banerjee, S., & McKeown, N. (2010). ElasticTree: Saving energy in data center networks. In *Proceedings of the 7th USENIX Conference on Networked Systems Design and Implementation, Series NSDI'10*, USENIX Association, Berkeley, CA, USA (pp. 249–264).

[44] Al-Fares, M., Radhakrishnan, S., Raghavan, B., Huang, N., & Vahdat, A. (2010). Hedera: Dynamic flow scheduling for data center networks. In *Proceedings of the 7th USENIX Conference on Networked Systems Design and Implementation, Series NSDI'*, USENIX Association, Berkeley, CA, USA (pp. 89–92).

[45] Wang, R., Butnariu, D., & Rexford, J. (2011). OpenFlow-based server load balancing gone wild. In *Proceedings of the 11th USENIX Conference on Hot Topics in Management of Internet, Cloud, and Enterprise Networks and Services, Series (Hot-ICE'11)*, USENIX Association, Berkeley, CA, USA (pp. 1–12).

[46] Handigol, N., Seetharaman, S., Flajslik, M., McKeown, N., & Johari, R. (2009). Plug-n-Serve: Load-balancing web traffic using Seetharaman, S., Flajslik, M., McKeown, N., & Johari, R. (2009). Plug-n-Serve: Load-balancing web traffic using OpenFlow. *ACM Sigcomm Demo*, 4(5), 6.

[47] Handigol, N., Seetharaman, S., Flajslik, M., Gember, A., McKeown, N., Parulkar, G., Akella, A., Feamster, N., Clark, R., Krishnamurthy, A., Brajkovic, V., & Anderson, T. (2009). Aster*x: Load-Balancing Web Traffic over Wide-Area Networks. Open Networking Summit Demo (2011).

[48] Macapuna, C., Rothenberg, C., & Magalhaes, M. (2010). In-packet bloom filter based data center networking with distributed OpenFlow controllers. In *2010 IEEE GLOBECOM Workshops (GC Wkshps)*, 6–10 Dec. 2010, Miami, FL (pp. 584–588). IEEE.

[49] Qazi, Z. A., Tu, C.-C., Chiang, L., Miao, R., Sekar, V., & Yu, M. (2013). SIMPLE-fying middlebox policy enforcement using SDN. In *Proceedings of the Conference on Applications, Technologies, Architectures, and Protocols for Computer Communications, Series (SIGCOMM'13)*, New York, NY, USA. ACM.

[50] Jeong, K., Kim, J., & Kim, Y.-T. (2012). QoS-aware network operating system for software defined networking with generalized OpenFlows. In *Network Operations and Management Symposium (NOMS)*, 16–20 April 2012, Maui, HI (pp. 1167–1174). IEEE.

[51] Kim, W., Sharma, P., Lee, J., Banerjee, S., Tourrilhes, J., Lee, S.-J., & Yalagandula, P. (2010). Automated and scalable QoS control for network convergence. In *Proceedings of the 2010 Internet Network Management Conference on Research on Enterprise Networking, Series (INM/WREN'10)*, Berkeley, CA (pp. 1–1). USENIX Association.

[52] Sharma, S., Staessens, D., Colle, D., Palma, D., Figueiredo, J. G. R., Morris, D., Pickavet, M., & Demeester, P. (2014). Implementing quality of service for the software defined networking enabled future internet. In *Third European Workshop on Software Defined Networks*, 1–3 Sep. 2014, Budapest, Hungary (pp. 49–54).

[53] Scharf, M., Gurbani, V., Voith, T., Stein, M., Roome, W., Soprovich, G., & Hilt, V. (2013). Dynamic VPN optimization by ALTO guidance. In *2013 Second European Workshop on Software Defined Networks (EWSDN)*, 10–11 Oct. 2013, Berlin, Germany (pp. 13–18).

[54] Skoldstrom, P. & Sanchez, B. C. (2013). Virtual aggregation using SDN. In *2013 Second European Workshop on Software Defined Networks*, 10–11 Oct. 2013, Berlin, Germany (pp. 56–61).

[55] Nagaraj, K. & Kattl, S. (2014). ProCel: Smart traffic handling for a scalable software epc. In *Proceedings of the Third Workshop on Hot Topics in Software Defined Networking, ser. HotSDN'14* (pp. 43–48). ACM. New York, NY, USA.

[56] Seddiki, M. S., Shahbaz, M., Donovan, S., Grover, S., Park, M., Feamster, N., & Song, Y.-Q. (2014). FlowQoS: QoS for the rest of us. In *Proceedings of the Third Workshop on Hot Topics in Software Defined Networking, ser. HotSDN '14* (pp. 207–208). ACM. New York, NY, USA.

[57] Jamjoom, H., Williams, D., & Sharma, U. (2014). Don't call them middleboxes, call them middlepipes. In *Proceedings of the Third Workshop on Hot Topics in Software Defined Networking, ser. HotSDN '14* (pp. 19–24). ACM. New York, NY, USA.

[58] Akyildiz, I. F., Lee, A., Wang, P., Luo, M., & Chou, W. (2014, October). A roadmap for traffic engineering in SDN-OpenFlow networks. *Computer Networks, 71*, 1–30.

[59] Handigol, N., Seetharaman, S., Flajslik, M., McKeown, N., & Johari, R. (2009). Plug-n-Serve: Load-balancing web traffic using OpenFlow. *ACM Sigcomm Demo, 4*(5), 6.

[60] Voellmy, A., Wang, J., Yang, Y. R., Ford, B., & Hudak, P. (2013). Maple: Simplifying SDN programming using algorithmic policies. In *Proceedings of the ACM SIGCOMM 2013 Conference on SIGCOMM, ser. SIGCOMM'13*, New York (pp. 87–98). ACM.

[61] Huang, W.-Y., Chou, T.-Y., Hu, J.-W., & Liu, T.-L. (2014). Automatical end to end topology discovery and flow viewer on SDN. In *Proceedings of 28th International Conference on Advanced Information Networking and Application Workshops (WAINA)*, 13–16 May 2014, Victoria, BC, Canada (pp. 910–915).

[62] Yuan, L., Chuah, C. N., & Mohapatra, P. (2011). ProgME: Towards programmable network measurement. *IEEE/ACM Transactions on Networking, 19*(1), 115–128.

[63] Tootoonchian, A., Ghobadi, M., & Ganjali, Y. (2010). OpenTM: Traffic matrix estimator for OpenFlow networks. In *Passive and Active Measurement*, April (pp. 201–210). Springer. Berlin, Germany.

[64] Malboubi, M., Wang, L., Chuah, C.-N., & Sharma, P. (2014), Intelligent SDN based traffic (de) aggregation and measurement paradigm (iSTAMP). In *Proceedings of IEEE Conference on Computer and Communications (INFOCOM)*, 27 April–2 May 2014, Toronto, Canada (pp. 934–942).

[65] Hu, Z. & Luo, J. (2015). Cracking network monitoring in DCNs with SDN. In *Proceedings of IEEE Conference on Computer and Communications*, 26 April–May 2015, Hong Kong, China (pp. 199–207).

[66] van Adrichem, N. L. M., Doerr, C., & Kuipers, F. A. (2014). OpenNetMon: Network monitoring in OpenFlow software-defined networks. In *Proceedings of IEEE/IFIP Network Operations and Management Symposium*, 5–9 May 2014, Krakow, Poland (pp. 1–8).

[67] (2004). NetFlow [Online]. Available at: http://www.cisco.com/c/en/us/products/ios-nx-os-software/ios-netflow/index.html.

[68] (2004). sFlow [Online]. Available at: http://www.sflow.org/sFlowOverview.pdf.

[69] Myers, A. C. (1999). JFlow: Practical mostly-static information flow control. In *Proceedings of the 26th ACM SIGPLAN-SIGACT Symposium on Principles of Programming Languages*, San Antonio, TX (pp. 228–241).

[70] Moshref, M., Yu, M., Govindan, R., & Vahdat, A. (2015). DREAM: Dynamic resource allocation for software-defined measurement. *ACM SIGCOMM Computer and Communications Review*, *44*(4), 419–430.

[71] Mehdi, S. A., Khalid, J., & Khayam, S. A. (2011). Revisiting traffic anomaly detection using software defined networking. In *Proceedings of the 5th Symposium on Recent Advances in Intrusion Detection*, September, Menlo Park, CA (pp. 161–180).

[72] Zuo, Q., Chen, M., Wang, X., & Liu, B. (2015). Online traffic anomaly detection method for SDN. *Journal of Xidian University*, *42*(1), 155–160 (in Chinese).

[73] Mai, H., Khurshid, A., Agarwal, R., Caesar, M., Godfrey, P. B., & King, S. T. (2011). Debugging the data plane with anteater. *ACM SIGCOMM Computer and Communications Review*, *41*(4), 290–301.

[74] Canini, M., Venzano, D., Perešíni, P., Kostić, D., & Rexford, J. (2012). A NICE way to test OpenFlow applications. In *Proceedings of the 9th USENIX Symposium on Network System Design Implementation (NSDI)*, 25–27 April 2012, San Jose, CA (pp. 127–140).

[75] Khurshid, A., Zou, X., Zhou, W., Caesar, M., & Godfrey, P. (2013). VeriFlow: Verifying network-wide invariants in real time. In *Proceedings of the 10th USENIX Symposium on Network System Design Implementation (NSDI)*, 13 Aug. 2012, Helsinki, Finland (pp. 15–27).

[76] Yan, J., Zhang, H., Shuai, Q., Liu, B., & Guo, X. (2015). HiQoS: An SDN-based multipath QoS solution. *China Communications*, *12*(5), 123–133.

[77] Egilmez, H. E., Dane, S. T., Bagci, K. T., & Tekalp, A. M. (2012). OpenQoS: An OpenFlow controller design for multimedia delivery with end-to-end quality of service over software-defined networks. In *Proceedings of the Signal and Information Processing Association Annual Summit and Conference*, 3–6 Dec. 2012, Hollywood, CA (pp. 1–8).

[78] Ongaro, F., Cerqueira, E., Foschini, L., Corradi, A., & Gerla, M. (2015). Enhancing the quality level support for real-time multimedia applications in software-defined networks. In *Proceedings of the International*

Conference on Computer, Network and Communications, 16–19 Feb. 2015, Garden Grove, CA (pp. 505–509).

[79] Chiesa, M., Kindler, G., & Schapira, M. (2014). Traffic engineering with equalcost-multipath: An algorithmic perspective. *Proceedings of the IEEE INFOCOM*, April/May, 1590–1598.

[80] Han, G., Dong, Y., Guo, H., Shu, L., & Wu, D. (2015). Cross-layer optimized routing in wireless sensor networks with duty cycle and energy harvesting. *Wireless Communications and Mobile Computing*, *15*(16), 1957–1981.

[81] Chen, M., Leung, V. C. M., Mao, S., & Yuan, Y. (2007). Directional geographical routing for real-time video communications in wireless sensor networks. *Computer Communications*, *30*(17), 3368–3383.

[82] Chen, M., Leung, V. C. M., Mao, S., & Li, M. (2008). Cross-layer and path priority scheduling based real-time video communications over wireless sensor networks. In *Proceedings of the 67th IEEE Vehicular Technology Conference (VTC)*, May, Singapore (pp. 2873–2877).

[83] Al-Fares, M., Radhakrishnan, S., Raghavan, B., Huang, N., & Vahdat, A. (2010). Hedera: Dynamic flow scheduling for data center networks. In *Proceedings of the Network System Design Implementation Symposium (NSDI)*, USENIX Association, 28–30 April 2010, USA (pp. 89–92).

[84] Curtis, A. R., Kim, W., & Yalagandula, P. (2011). Mahout: Low-overhead datacenter traffic management using end-host-based elephant detection. In *Proceedings of the IEEE INFOCOMM*, 10–15 April 2011, Shanghai, China (pp. 1629–1637).

[85] Benson, T., Anand, A., Akella, A., & Zhang, M. (2011). MicroTE: Fine grained traffic engineering for data centers. In *Proceedings of the 7th International Conference on Software Engineering and New Technologies*, 6–9 Dec. 2011, Tokyo, Japan (pp. 1–12).

[86] Agarwal, S., Kodialam, M., & Lakshman, T. V. (2013). Traffic engineering in software defined networks. In *Proceedings of the IEEE INFOCOM*, 14–19 April 2013, Turin, Italy (pp. 2211–2219).

[87] Sherwin, J. & Sreenan, C. J. (2021). Software-defined networking for data centre network management: A survey.

[88] Kreutz, D., Ramos, F. M. V., Verissimo, P. E., Rothenberg, C. E., Azodolmolky, S., & Uhlig, S. (2014). Softwaredefined networking: A comprehensive survey. *Proceedings of the IEEE*, *103*(1), 14–76, Art no. 6994333. Doi: 10.1109/JPROC.2014.2371999.

[89] Hyojoon, K. & Feamster, N. (2013). Improving network management with software defined networking. *Communications Magazine, IEEE*, *51*(2), 114–119. Doi:10.1109/MCOM.2013.6461195.

[90] Moshref, M., Yu, M., Govindan, R., & Vahdat, A. (2014). DREAM: Dynamic resource allocation for softwaredefined measurement. In *SIGCOMM 2014 — Proceedings of the 2014 ACM Conference on Special*

Interest Group on Data Communication (pp. 419–430). Doi:10.1145/2619239. 2626291.

[91]   Foster, N., McKeown, N., Rexford, J., Parulkar, G., Peterson, L., & Sunay, O. (2020). Using deep programmability to put network owners in control. *SIGCOMM Computer Communication Review, 50*(4), 82–88. Doi: 10.1145/3431832.3431842.

[92]   Gandhi, R., Hongqiang, H., Liu, Y., Charlie, H., Guohan, L., Jitendra, P., Lihua, Y., & Ming, Z. (2014). Duet: Cloud scale load balancing with hardware and software. In *SIGCOMM 2014 — Proceedings of the 2014 ACM Conference on Special Interest Group on Data Communication* (pp. 27–38). Doi: 10.1145/2619239.2626317.

[93]   Rasley, J., Stephens, B., Dixon, C., Rozner, E., Felter, W., Agarwal, K., Carter, J., & Fonseca. R. (2014). Planck: Millisecond-scale monitoring and control for commodity networks. In *SIGCOMM 2014 — Proceedings of the 2014 ACM Conference on Special Interest Group on Data Communication* (pp. 407– 418). Doi:10.1145/2619239.2626310.

[94]   Ba, J., Wang, Y., Zhong, X., Feng, S., Qiu, X., & Guo, S. (2018). An SDN energy saving method based on topology switch and rerouting. In *NOMS 2018 — 2018 IEEE/IFIP Network Operations and Management Symposium*, 23–27 April 2018 (pp. 1–5). Doi:10.1109/NOMS.2018.8406202.

[95]   Tran Manh, N., Nguyen Huu, T., Ngo Quynh, T., Hoang Trung, H., & Covaci, S. (2015). Energy-aware routing based on power profile of devices in data center networks using SDN. In *Electrical Engineering/Electronics, Computer, Telecommunications and Information Technology (ECTI-CON), 2015 12th International Conference*, 24–27 June 2015 (pp. 1–6). Doi: 10.1109/ECTICon.2015.7207042.

[96]   Hu, S., Kai, C., Haitao, W., Wei, B., Chang, L., Hao, W., Hongze, Z., & Chuanxiong, G. (2015). Explicit path control in commodity data centers: Design and applications. In *Presented at the Proceedings of the 12th USENIX Conference on Networked Systems Design and Implementation*, Oakland, CA.

[97]   Ferguson, A. D., Guha, A., Liang, C., Fonseca, R., & Krishnamurthi, S. (2013). Participatory networking: An API for application control of SDNs. In *SIGCOMM 2013 — Proceedings of the ACM SIGCOMM 2013 Conference on Applications, Technologies, Architectures, and Protocols for Computer Communication* (pp. 327–338). Doi: 10.1145/2486001.2486003.

[98]   Arora, D., Benson, T., & Rexford, J. (2014). ProActive routing in scalable data centers with PARIS. In *DCC 2014 — Proceedings of the ACM SIGCOMM 2014 Workshop on Distributed Cloud Computing* (pp. 5–10). Doi: 10.1145/2627566.2627571.

[99]   Cohen, R., Barabash, K., Rochwerger, B., Schour, L., Crisan, D., Birke, R., Minkenberg, C., Gusat, M., Recio, R., & Jain, V. (2013). An intent-based approach for network virtualization. In *Proceedings of the 2013 IFIP/IEEE*

International Symposium on Integrated Network Management, IM 2013 Ghent, Belgium (pp. 42–50).

[100] Zheng, J., Xu, H., Chen, G., & Dai, H. (2016, March). Minimizing transient congestion during network update in data centers. In *Proceedings — International Conference on Network Protocols (ICNP)* (pp. 1–10). doi:10.1109/ICNP.2015.33.

[101] Baucke, S., Ben Ali, R., Kempf, J., Mishra, R., Ferioli, F., & Carossino, A. (2013). Cloud Atlas: A software defined networking abstraction for cloud to WAN virtual networking. In *Cloud Computing (CLOUD), 2013 IEEE Sixth International Conference*, 28 June–3 July 2013 (pp. 895–902). doi:10.1109/CLOUD.2013.44.

[102] Liu, J., Li, Y., & Jin, D. (2014). SDN-based live VM migration across datacenters. In *Presented at the Proceedings of the 2014 ACM conference on SIGCOMM*, Chicago, IL (pp. 583–584).

[103] Nie, X., Peng, J., Wu, Y., Gupta, B. B., & Abd El-Latif, A. A. (2022). Real-time traffic speed estimation for smart cities with spatial temporal data: A gated graph attention network approach. *Big Data Research, 28,* 100313.

[104] Chui, K. T., Gupta, B. B., Chi, H. R., & Zhao, M. (2023). Convolutional neural network and deep one-class support vector machine with imbalanced dataset for anomaly network traffic detection. In *International Conference on Cyber Security, Privacy and Networking (ICSPN 2022),* February (pp. 248–256). Springer International Publishing, Cham.

[105] Chui, K. T., Kochhar, T. S., Chhabra, A., Singh, S. K., Singh, D., Peraković, D., Almomani, A., & Arya, V. (2022). Traffic accident prevention in low visibility conditions using vanets cloud environment. *International Journal of Cloud Applications and Computing (IJCAC), 12*(1), 1–21.

[106] Mishra, A., Gupta, B. B., Hsu, C. H., & Chui, K. T. (2021). The early detection of malicious communication with DNS traffic through the use of simple features. In *2021 IEEE 10th Global Conference on Consumer Electronics (GCCE),* 12–15 Oct. 2021, Kyoto, Japan (pp. 291–293). IEEE.

Chapter 8

Network Function Virtualisation

Advancements in the Internet of Things (IoT) and in information and communication technology (ICT) and a growing demand for more quality-oriented advanced services have led to the development of network function virtualisation (NFV). It enables businesses to design, provide, and ease into significantly more advanced services and operations. In the previous chapter, we studied SDN and its related concepts. In this chapter, we study about NFV, virtualisation, and how it can be integrated with SDN.

8.1 Introduction

Product development in the telecommunications business has followed strict protocols for protocol adherence, stability, and quality. However, hardware development standards resulted in delayed development, extended product cycles, and dependence on proprietary hardware. At the SDN OpenFlow World Congress in October 2012, a working group on network function virtualisation produced a white paper on OpenFlow and SDN. This report from the European Telecommunications Standards Institute (ETSI) group kicked off the trend towards network function virtualisation. In this white paper, they have addressed the major issues and challenges faced by the network operators in operating the network, especially the introduction of new proprietary hardware into the legacy infrastructure, to provide better and more advanced services to end consumers [1]. Following are the challenges that they had addressed:

- adaptations to design for the newly introduced networking device;
- addressing cost of deployment and physical restriction;
- addressing equipment complexity in the new proprietary hardware;
- resuming the cycle before the returns on capital expenditures and investments have been completely realised;
- expertise required to manage and operate new proprietary gear and software;
- addressing the equipment's short lifecycle, causing them to become outdated quickly.

The group suggested using NFV to address these issues and boost productivity by "maximising standard IT virtualization technology to strengthen many network equipment types onto industry standard high-volume servers, switches, and storage, which could be located in Datacentres, Network Nodes, and in the end user premises."[1].

The top seven telecom companies in the world formed the Internet specification group (ISG) under the independent standardisation organisation known as the ETSI in order to achieve this goal and define a set of specifications that would enable a transition from the traditional vendor- and network-centric approach to an NFV-based network. This group formally began working in early 2013, with the goal of creating specifications and an architectural framework that can support the virtualised execution of network tasks performed by vendor-supplied specialised hardware devices [2–4]. This group considered the following three main key factors for this project:

1. **Dynamic operations:** granular control over the functional parameters of network functions as well as network state monitoring.
2. **Flexibility:** scalable and automated network function deployment.
3. **Decoupling:** complete segregation of hardware and software.

Now, we discuss the basic architecture of ETSI NFV in a detailed way.

8.1.1 ETSI NFV Framework

Heterogeneous and proprietary networking devices have rendered network operation, management, and service deployment very cumbersome tasks. NFV was developed to take virtualisation a step ahead to benefit the IT industry. Through the use of NFV, network services are decoupled from their corresponding proprietary hardware appliances [1]. This makes it possible for the services to instead execute within virtual machines (VMs) as software. Standard computation, storage, and network function resources can be virtualised by administrators and installed on COTS hardware, such as the ×86 servers. As a result, NFV enables numerous virtualised network functions (VNFs) to run on a single server and scale to utilise the remaining free resources. This infrastructure virtualisation often leads to efficient use of the resources available with a data centre. NFV may virtualise the control and data planes both outside and inside the data centre.

It is easier to comprehend why this strategy has attracted the attention of businesses looking for more automated and agile ways to build and manage widely dispersed network infrastructure and resources when one has a basic understanding of the various components of an NFV architecture [5].

VNFs, NFV infrastructure (NFVI), and NFV management and orchestration (MANO) are the main elements of an NFV architecture. This architectural framework, also known as the ETSI NFV framework, serves as the foundation for the standardisation and development of NFV [6–9]. Figure 8.1 presents an overview of ETSI NFV. The framework broadly includes resource allocation, data flow between VNFs, and management of VNFs. ISG divided the complete framework into three main layers: infrastructure layer, virtualised functions layer, and management layer. Figure 8.2 shows the architectural components of the NFV framework. However, these layers have been documented with more formal names. Following are the details:

(a) **NFVI layer:** This component serves as the primary support for the entire architectural structure. This block brings together the various components necessary for virtualisation, including the software that enables it, the hardware needed to host VMs, and the resources that can be virtualised [10]. The NVFI is built on low-cost, standardised ×86 computer hardware and software, which enable both the physical and virtual network layers. This software includes hypervisors, VMs, and virtual infrastructure administrators.

It provides the physical resources, such as computation, storage, and network, as well as the software that is used to deploy and manage VNFs [11]. The NFVI serves as the virtualisation layer that sits atop the hardware and abstracts its resources so that they can be logically segregated and distributed to enable VNFs. This layer is independent of the geographic location of the physical resources.

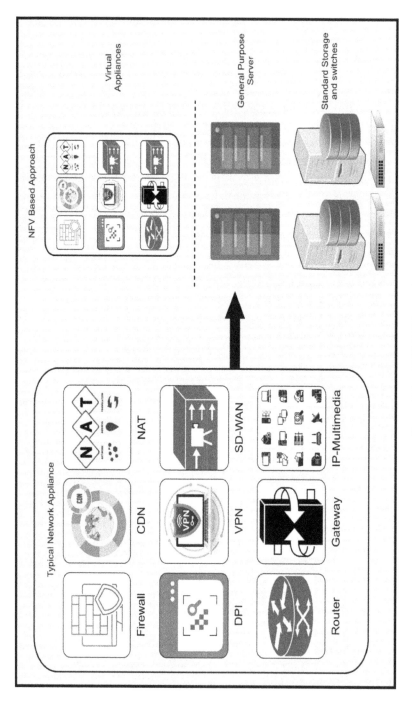

Figure 8.1.   ETSI NFV overview.

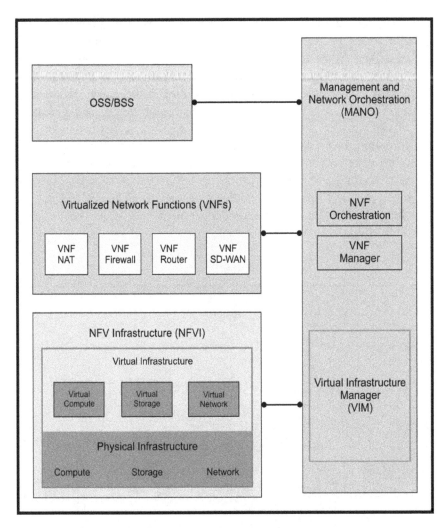

Figure 8.2.   Architectural components of ETSI NFV framework.

(b) **VNF layer:** The VNF block makes use of the VMs that are provided by the NFVI and then expands on top of them by adding the software responsible for implementing the VNFs. A VNF encompasses services such as routers, switches, software-defined wide area networks (SD-WANs), and firewalls, and an increasing number of other network services are now accessible as software from manufacturers such as Cisco, Juniper Networks, and Palo Alto Networks [11, 12].

VNFs are deployed on-demand through the NFV framework, which eliminates the deployment latencies inherent in traditional network hardware. Additionally, when VNFs are remotely deployed, there is no longer a need for on-site technical capabilities to be present. In hybrid and multi-cloud systems, VNFs offer the agility required to predict or adapt to dynamic network performance or growth demands.

(c) **MANO layer:** The design defines MANO as a distinct block that communicates with both the NFVI and VNF blocks. The management of all resources in the infrastructure layer is entrusted by the framework to the MANO layer, which also oversees resource creation and deletion as well as resource allocation to VNFs [11, 13]. Figure 8.3 shows NFV orchestration and management. MANO is composed of three additional modules.

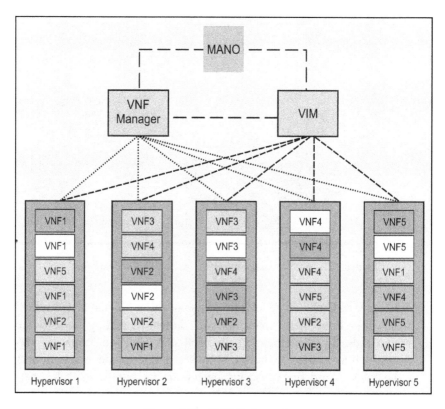

Figure 8.3.   NFV Orchestration.

- **NFV orchestrator:** It manages the VNF onboarding process, life-cycle management, global resource allocation and management, and validation and authorisation of NFVI resource requests [14].
- **VNF manager:** It manages the lifespan of VNF instances, acting as a coordinator and adaptor for NFVI and event reporting.
- **Virtual infrastructure manager:** It exercises command and management over the computing, storage, and network resources of the NFVI.

There is no specialised or proprietary hardware built to run these virtual network functions. A general-purpose hardware device with generic hardware resources, such as a processor (CPU), storage, memory, and network interfaces, can be utilised to operate these VNFs. Utilising commercially available hardware is one way to achieve this goal. However, this can be made possible through commercial off-the-shelf (COTS) devices. It is not necessary for it to be a single COTS device; rather, it can be an integrated hardware solution that offers any combination of the necessary hardware resources to run VNFs [15]. Technologies related to virtualisation can be utilised to share the hardware among several different VNFs. This NFVI can leverage commercial COTS hardware as a common pool of resources and carve off subsets of these resources to create "virtualised" computing, storage, and network pools that can be allocated as needed by the VNFs.

A VNF vendor will provide provisions for the minimum requirement of resources for the VNFs to be implemented. However, the vendor cannot provision the requirements for the specific hardware for VNF implementation. The resource request made by a VNF can be satisfied by the virtualisation layer, which makes use of the physical hardware. The VNF does not have any visibility into this process, nor is it aware of the presence of any other VNFs that may have been sharing the same physical hardware with it. Today's network architecture management, in contrast, is vendor-specific and has few controls and data points released by vendors. Only with vendor cooperation is it feasible to add additional requirements or improve management capabilities. It is feasible to handle the networking entities on a more granular level with NFV. As a result, the NFV design would be incomplete without specifying the methodology to control, automate, coordinate, and connect these layers and functional blocks in a flexible, modular, and automated manner.

This requirement has made researchers add another block called MANO that manages and interfaces with the NFVI and VNF layers.

The MANO block is in charge of controlling the layers and is designed to have complete insight into them. It is fully aware of their utilisation, operational status, and usage statistics. Additionally, MANO has an interface with the operational support system (OSS) and the billing support system (BSS) to collect usage statistics [16].

Now, we discuss service chaining in traditional networks and where NFVs fit in this technology.

8.2 Service Chaining

Service chaining is defined as the sequence of service functions a packet must go through in the network. The idea of chaining multiple services together is not exactly ground-breaking; however, recent developments in technologies such as software-defined networking (SDN) and NFV, which make it possible to chain services in a dynamic fashion, are largely responsible for the rise in popularity of this practice [17]. Network service chaining, also known as service function chaining (SFC), is a capability that makes use of SDN capabilities to create a chain of connected network services, such as L4–L7 services, including firewalls, network address translation (NAT), and intrusion protection.

First, we discuss static service chaining and dynamic service chaining.

8.2.1 Static Service Chaining

The traditional method of service chaining involves implementing network functions using hardware middleboxes, and these boxes are all physically connected to one another. Middleboxes are utilised by network operators with the aim of improving network performance or enhancing network security [17, 18]. Some examples of middleboxes include NAT, web proxies, firewalls, and load balancers.

These middleboxes are designed to support a wide range of applications. Sometimes, though only a few services are required, a complete pipeline of services must be implemented to get the traffic pass through [21, 61]. It implies the fact that every service in the pipeline must have enough computing and storage resources to manage the traffic, even though the service only has to let the traffic go through without processing it. There are many limitations to static service-based chaining [19]:

(a) We have already mentioned that all the services in the pipelines must have enough computing and storage resources, irrespective of whether they are required for processing or not. In static service chaining, middleboxes tend to be built with full capacity.

(b) Scalability is another issue where, if required, scaling up the capacity of the service to process the increasing traffic is not possible.

(c) There is no service provisioning at the granular level, i.e., how each service is applicable to every traffic flow.

(d) The most important factor is the high capital and operational expenditure for introducing new hardware into the existing Internet infrastructure. If an operator wants to introduce some new application, he first identifies whether an existing service chain can cater to this new application. If yes, then good, and if no, then he has to set up an entirely service chaining.

(e) Inconsistency in configuration is another major issue related to this approach, as there is manual intervention and physical connection between the devices.

In Figure 8.4, we can see that if subscriber 1 wants to play an online game on his mobile, then he might be requiring only a graphics optimisation service, i.e., a video optimisation and firewalling service. He may not require other services; however, this network traffic has to pass through the entire pipeline, resulting in inefficient utilisation of resources. To overcome these issues, dynamic service chaining came into existence.

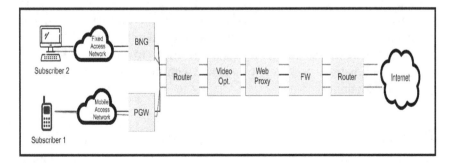

Figure 8.4. Static service chaining.

8.2.2 Dynamic Service Chaining

SDN and NFV enable dynamic service chaining by substituting VMs for conventional middleboxes [22, 62]. The traffic in dynamic service chaining merely has to be directed through appropriate network functions in accordance with predetermined flow criteria. An SDN controller, due to its ability to create a global view of the network, introduces dynamicity in the network [23, 63]. This is called a software controller service chain. This dynamicity allows a network operator to introduce new service chains by merely changing the policy in the SDN controller. The SDN controller is embedded with intelligence to forward traffic to a specific network function according to its label; for example, traffic for a VLAN or MAC address is forwarded according to its service chain [24, 64]. The most important advantage of dynamic service chaining is that a single service function can be used simultaneously in multiple service chains, resulting in efficient utilisation of resources. Following are the other advantages [25, 26]:

- SDN–NFV-based SFC induces more flexibility into the network, where the SDN controller has to programme the existing service functions into a chain for a new user by defining a policy.
- It definitely cuts capital and operational costs by allowing the network operator to define the service chain by choosing from the existing service functions. Moreover, a test environment for new software can be easily created using this technique, allowing the network operator to revert the network back to its original state if required. Next, capital expenses can be cut down through traffic optimisation and hardware cost reduction. Traffic optimisation is in terms of intelligently diverting traffic towards the required service functions and thus investing only in the frequently used service functions. Lastly, there is no denying the fact that technologies such as service chaining and NFV alleviate the need for investing in vendor-specific hardware [27, 28].
- Service functions need not be designed with full capacity, unlike static service chaining.

Conversely, SDN and NFV allow an operator to reduce the amount of time it takes to bring a new service to market by replacing physical devices with VMs. New service chains can be built with a simple change in policy associated with a flow since the centralised controller in SDN has a global view of the network [29]. Deep packet inspection is currently used by a dedicated classification device to classify traffic as it enters network gateways. The traffic is then intelligently redirected to the necessary services based on the service identifier. The actual identifier can be programmed directly into the switch flow tables or derived from a field in the traffic, such as the network service header (NSH), virtual local area network (VLAN), or source MAC address (SMAC) [30, 31]. This enables more efficient use of network and computation resources, as traffic only goes via required services. Thus, the provider is no longer required to continuously overprovision the network.

8.3 Issues in Implementing Service Chaining in NFV

Connecting numerous VNFs is a critical issue in NFV implementation. This is known as "service chaining." For VNFs hosted within a single cloud, this entails configuring the data centre network so that traffic flows across multiple VMs in accordance with the tenant's regulations. Similarly, tenants would like their rules to handle traffic for VNFs situated in multiple cloud data centres. This, however, necessitates elastic network links across clouds that can be built on demand [32, 33]. As WAN link capacities are extremely limited and expensive, VNF installation is frequently confined to a subset of available clouds.

Problems within service chains have become indicative of NFV's issues. The number and variety of functions in a service chain are severely limited by deployment constraints. This results in either sticking with old, physical network function providers or creating more silos, which is unfortunate because the aim of NFV was to remove these two obstacles [34]. Unfortunately, this may result in higher expenses as the operator switches from a model with fixed physical infrastructure to one with software-based dynamic infrastructure. Following are the three physical limitations for implementing service chaining in NFV:

1. **Scalability in a heterogeneous environment:** The reality of the physical infrastructure must be taken into account from a deployment viewpoint while scaling services. Unfortunately, operators may have three or four vendors offering various services in a heterogeneous solution environment. One vendor might offer parental control, another antivirus, another optimisation, etc., in an example of all-IP

traffic management [35]. They inevitably need several physical components and are unlikely to operate smoothly or work on the front end. Each box increases total traffic management latency, which will lead to a low quality of experience (QoE).

For GiLAN services, the time spent on the mobility path is currently between 5 and 10 ms. This means that when deploying multiple services, if the user-plane traffic has to move between different physical COTS hardware, this delay will automatically increase, which can lead to poor QoE. Not only does poor QoE result in low network speed test ratings, but it also adds to customer attrition.

2. **Signalling metadata and control plane:** The transfer of metadata from the classifier and head-end to the lightweight directory access protocol (LDAP) store is frequently a fundamental prerequisite for carrying out a particular function on the service chain. This is common when the function is policy based and used by the signalling store to provide a subscriber-specific service [36]. This begins with policy reference and network identification, but it can expand rapidly.

There are several methods for accomplishing this, beginning with network service headers (NSHs). There is incompatibility between functionalities and the number of metadata that must be managed due to the multitude of equipment and protocols from multiple suppliers. All of this can result in considerable inefficiencies, particularly when the network needs to transmit every packet [37]. As a result, all suppliers must agree on the basic rules of the service chain, and information should be cached so that modifications can be conveyed. Vendors must make this crucial design modification.

3. **Multi-tenancy and switching rules:** In projects such as Open vSwitch, operators have made major efforts to establish chaining rules and their scalability. There is opportunity for improvement in open source to handle both the volume of rules and the updates required to those rules [38]. This may lead to a monolithic service chain with no multi-tenancy, a simplified switching framework, or fewer functions in the chain.

Following are the three strategies that vendors can adopt to deal with these issues:

1. **Smart scaling:** Increased flexibility in the construction of VNF components would improve mapping onto physical hardware in the case of virtual GiLAN, allowing all components to be on a single physical

COTS blade and lowering latency for data transfer. A blade system with 40 cores, for instance, might have eight cores designated as hypervisors and the remaining 32 divided into four, eight, or sixteen cores. Operators can better plan for hardware planning and failovers by using more consistent sizes [39]. A broader selection of off-the-shelf components can also be advantageous to carriers.

2. **Cooperative control and signalling:** Working groups can be quite important in this area. The popular technique used most often today is NSH; however, it is not suitable for all situations and can greatly overload the payload. Standardisation and interoperability can both be important. First off, vendor lock-in has negatively impacted the options available to network providers in the case of NSH, where each domain player and switching provider has their own flavour [40, 41].

    The second issue is the demand for innovative thought leadership when it comes to expanding and improving data communication between functions. The work being done in this area by the industry with vector packet processing (VPP) could be a step in the right direction.

3. **Multi-tenancy and switching rules:** Certain operator groups collaborate and employ internal orchestration within each function. This is contrary to logic. As part of mobile data traffic management, packets and payloads will be dissected for application-level analysis into individual VNF components. This applies to traffic management operations, such as transport optimisation and switching to parental controls. For the sake of enforcing the policy rules, this results in packet, flow, and session data reconstruction at various stages. At best, this is wasteful, involves complex switching, and involves extra hops; at worst, it increases latency, results in subpar QoE, and causes subscriber attrition.

8.4 Open-Source Projects on NFV

There are several related standardisation entities (standard organisations), such as the IETF, IRTF, ETSI, Broadband Forum (BB-Forum), Alliance for Telecommunications Industry Solutions (ATIS) (which is also in collaboration with industry organisations, such as the Global System for Mobile Communications (GSMA), Metro Ethernet Forum (MEF), and Tele Management Forum (TMF)), under which specific NFV research groups conduct various research activities to contribute to various architectures [43, 44]. The IRTF focuses primarily on long-term research issues pertaining to the Internet, whereas the IETF works in parallel with the IRTF but focuses largely on short-term issues pertaining to the Internet and supports engineering and uniform standards for the Internet. The NFV Research Group (NFVRG) is one of the IRTF research groups that focuses on NFV-related issues [45]. This research group was chartered in 2015 and concluded its work in 2018. The IETF Service Function Chaining Working Organization (IETF-SFC-WG) is another group that is dedicated to NFV SFC and performing standardisation activities for alternative service delivery methods, operations, and management. The NFV architecture and reference framework NFV-MANO are primary areas of interest for the ETSI NFV-ISG. In order to develop new business models and needs for enabling the adoption of NFV technology, the ATIS NFV forum focuses on advancing industry solutions [46]. The BB Forum is an organisation that brings together a number of TNOs, corporations, vendors, and organisations that provide broadband network solutions.

There are various active NFV projects at the moment, including OpenNFV, Opensource MANO (OSM), OPEN BATON, Kubernetes, and others, as shown in Table 8.1.

Table 8.1.   List of some major NFV projects.

Project Name	Conducting Organization	Description
ZOOM [48]	TM Forum	• Focuses on VNFM, VIM, NFVO, and OSS/BSS. • Enables agile service automation and control in a NFV environment.
OPNFV [49]	Linux Foundation	• Focuses on VIM and NFVI. • In order to speed up the implementation of NFV in future networks, it is important to facilitate testing and integration of NFV and to do so on an open-source platform.
OpenNFV [30]	Hewlett-Packard	• Focuses on VNFM, VIM, NFVO, OSS/BSS, and NFVI. • Open and adaptable NFV ecosystem to accelerate the deployment of NFV by communications service providers.

Table 8.1.   (*Continued*)

Project Name	Conducting Organization	Description
5GEx [51]	European Union	• Focuses on VIM, NFVO, OSS/BSS, and NFVI. • Concentrates on 5G infrastructure and aims towards unified multi-domain orchestration to support heterogeneity.
Blue Planet [52]	Nuage and Ciena	• Focuses on VIM, NFO, and OSS/BSS • Enables multi-domain and multi-tenant end-to-end services and intelligent development and delivery of services using orchestration.
ClickOS [53]	European Union	• Focuses on VNFs and VNFM. • Virtualised high-performance software middle-box platform that enables rapid and lightweight NFV applications.
Gohan [54]	NTT Data	• Focuses on VNFM, MANO, and NFVO • Unified and simple cloud service architecture that enables micro-services in one minute and provides a single unified method for developers to create and manage REST-style APIs.
Kubernetes [55]	Google	• Focuses on VIM, MANO, and NFVO. • A system for automating the deployment, scaling, and management of containerised apps. • It lets fast-paced business and enterprise computing environments schedule and coordinate tasks in advance.
OpenSource MANO (OSM) [56]	ETSI	• Focuses on VNFM, VIM, MANO, and NFVO. • MANO software stack is coordinated with ETSI information models to achieve commercial deployment of NFV networks.
Sonata NFV [57]	European Union Horizon 2020	• Focuses on VNFM, VIM, MANO, and NFVO. • Additionally, promotes the development of tools for virtualised services, flexible software network programming, and integrated platforms for development and operation (DevOps) service delivery and orchestration.
Tacker [58]	OpenStack	• Focuses on VNF, VNFM, MANO, and NFVO. • Enables NFV orchestration for the OpenStack platform using the ETSI MANO framework.

(*Continued*)

Table 8.1.   (*Continued*)

Project Name	Conducting Organization	Description
Open Baton [59]	Fraunhofer Berlin	• Focuses on VNFM, VIM, MANO, and NFVO. • Designs the flexible and adaptable orchestration of network services in a variety of network topologies. • Aims to support features such as openness, interoperability, and extensibility in an NFV environment.
Cloudify [60]	GigaSpaces	• Focuses on VNFM, MANO, and NFVO. • TOSCA-based cloud orchestration platform for automating network services and streamlining the orchestration of multiple cloud stacks and hybrid cloud deployments.

Exercises

Q.1. Discuss the architectural components of the NFV framework proposed by ETSI.

Q.2. How is the orchestration managed by NFV?

Q.3. Discuss how static network chaining evolved into virtualised functions.

Q.4. Discuss the disadvantages of static network chaining and compare it with dynamic service chaining.

Q.5. Discuss how virtualised middleboxes came into existence and evolved from service chaining and virtualised functions.

Q.6. Discuss the issues and challenges of implementing service chaining in NFV.

Q.7. Discuss some open solutions that must be adapted by vendors in order to integrate service chaining into NFV.

Q.8. Discuss the implementation of the firewalling service as a virtualised function in the network.

Q.9. Discuss the implementation of load balancing service as a virtualised function in the network.

Q.10. Discuss how NFV can contribute to enhancing the scalability of cloud computing.

Q.11. How does dynamic service chaining help businesses cut CAPEX and OPEX?

References

[1] Clarke, M. C. D., Willis, P., Reid, A., Feger, J., Bugenhagen, M., Khan, W., Fargano, M., Cui, C., Deng, H., and Benitez, J., *et al.* (2012). Network functions virtualisation: An introduction, benefits, enablers, challenges and call for action. In *SDN and OpenFlow World Congress*, October (Vol. 48, pp. 1–16). Available at: https://portal.etsi.org/NFV/NFV_White_Paper.pdf.

[2] Chayapathi, R., Hassan, S. F., & Shah, P. (2016). *Network Functions Virtualization (NFV) with a Touch of SDN: Netw Fun Vir (NFV EPub_1.* Addison-Wesley Professional, Boston, MA.

[3] NFV, Network Functions Virtualisation (2013). "ETSI GS NFV 001 V1. 1.1 (2013-10)." " Network Functions Virtualisation (NFV); Architectural Framework." Available at: https://www.etsi.org/deliver/etsi_gs/NFV/001_099/002/01.01.01_60/gs_NFV002v010101p.pdf.

[4] Manzalini, A., Saracco, R., Buyukkoc, C., Chemouil, P., Kukliński, S., Gladisch, A., Fukui, M., Shen, W., Dekel, E., Soldani, D., Ulema, M., Cerroni, W., Callegati, F., Schembra, G., Riccobene, V., Mas, M. C., Galis, A., & Mueller, J. (2014). Software-Defined Networks for Future Networks and Services. In *White Paper Based on the IEEE Workshop SDN4FNS*. 11–13 Nov. 2013, Trento, Italy.

[5] Adamuz-Hinojosa, O., Ordonez-Lucena, J., Ameigeiras, P., Ramos-Munoz, J. J., Lopez, D., & Folgueira, J. (2018). Automated network service scaling in NFV: Concepts, mechanisms and scaling workflow. *IEEE Communications Magazine, 56*(7), 162–169.

[6] Rehman, A. U., Aguiar, R. L., & Barraca, J. P. (2019). Network functions virtualization: The long road to commercial deployments. *IEEE Access, 7*, 60439–60464.

[7] Ersue, M. (2013). ETSI NFV management and orchestration — An overview. Presentation at the IETF, Volume 88 (2013).

[8] Duan, Q., Ansari, N., & Toy, M. (2016). Software-defined network virtualization: An architectural framework for integrating SDN and NFV for service provisioning in future networks. *IEEE Network, 30*(5), 10–16.

[9] Suriano, A., Striccoli, D., Piro, G., Bolla, R., & Boggia, G. (2020). Attestation of trusted and reliable service function chains in the ETSI-NFV framework. In *2020 6th IEEE Conference on Network Softwarization (NetSoft)*, 29 June–3 July 2020, Ghent, Belgium (pp. 479–486). IEEE.

[10] Ventre, P. L., Pisa, C., Salsano, S., Siracusano, G., Schmidt, F., Lungaroni, P., & Blefari-Melazzi, N. (2016). Performance evaluation and tuning of virtual infrastructure managers for (micro) virtual network functions. In *2016 IEEE Conference on Network Function Virtualization and Software Defined Networks (NFV-SDN)*, 7–10 Nov. 2016, Palo Alto, CA (pp. 141–147). IEEE.

[11] Addis, B., Belabed, D., Bouet, M., & Secci, S. (2015). Virtual network functions placement and routing optimization. In *2015 IEEE 4th International Conference on Cloud Networking (CloudNet)*, 5–7 Oct. 2015, Niagara Falls, ON, Canada (pp. 171–177). IEEE.

[12] Yang, S., Li, F., Trajanovski, S., Chen, X., Wang, Y., & Fu, X. (2019). Delay-aware virtual network function placement and routing in edge clouds. *IEEE Transactions on Mobile Computing, 20*(2), 445–459.

[13] Kaur, K., Mangat, V., & Kumar, K. (2022). A review on Virtualized Infrastructure Managers with management and orchestration features in NFV architecture. *Computer Networks, 217*, 109281.

[14] Chen, J., Cao, H., & Yang, L. (2019). NFV MANO based network slicing framework description. In *2019 IEEE International Conference on Consumer Electronics-Taiwan (ICCE-TW)*, 20–22 May 2019, Yilan, Taiwan (pp. 1–2). IEEE.

[15] Gonzalez, A., Gronsund, P., Mahmood, K., Helvik, B., Heegaard, P., & Nencioni, G. (2015). Service availability in the NFV virtualized evolved packet core. In *2015 IEEE Global Communications Conference (GLOBECOM)*, 6–10 Dec. 2015, San Diego, CA (pp. 1–6). IEEE.

[16] Zhang, T., Qiu, H., Linguaglossa, L., Cerroni, W., & Giaccone, P. (2020). NFV platforms: Taxonomy, design choices and future challenges. *IEEE Transactions on Network and Service Management, 18*(1), 30–48.

[17] Anwer, B., Benson, T., Feamster, N., & Levin, D. (2015). Programming slick network functions. In *Proceedings of the 1st Acm Sigcomm Symposium on Software Defined Networking Research*, 17–18 June 2015, Santa Clara, CA (pp. 1–13).

[18] Li, T., Zhou, H., & Luo, H. (2017). A new method for providing network services: Service function chain. *Optical Switching and Networking, 26*, 60–68.

[19] Wilhelm, U. G., Staamann, S. M., & Buttyán, L. (2000). A pessimistic approach to trust in mobile agent platforms. *IEEE Internet Computing, 4*(5), 40–48.

[20] Quinn, P. & Nadeau, T. (2013). Service Function Chaining Problem Statement. IETF Internet Draft, Informational.

[21] Blendin, J., Rückert, J., Leymann, N., Schyguda, G., & Hausheer, D. (2014). Position paper: Software-defined network service chaining. In *Proceedings of the 3rd Workshop on EWSDN*, 1–3 Sept. 2014, Budapest, Hungary (pp. 109–114).

[22] Salman, O., Elhajj, I. H., Kayssi, A., & Chehab, A. (2016). SDN controllers: A comparative study. In *2016 18th Mediterranean Electrotechnical Conference, MELECON* (pp. 1–6). IEEE.

[23] Singh, G., Behal, S., & Taneja, M. (2015). Advanced memory reusing mechanism for virtual machines in cloud computing. *Procedia Computer Science, 57*(5), 91–103.

[24] Ning, Z., Wang, N., & Tafazolli, R. (2020). Deep reinforcement learning for NFV-based service function chaining in multi-service networks. In *2020 IEEE 21st International Conference on High Performance Switching and Routing, HPSR*, Newark, NJ (pp. 1–6), IEEE.

[25] Kitada, H., Kojima, H., Takaya, N., & Aihara, M. (2014). Service function chaining technology for future networks. *NTT Technical Review, 12*(8), 1–5.

[26] Dominicini, C. K., Vassoler, G. L., Valentim, R., Villaca, R. S., Ribeiro, M. R. N., Martinello, M., & Zambon, E. (2020). KeySFC: Traffic steering using strict source routing for dynamic and efficient network orchestration. *Computer Networks, 167*, 106975.

[27] Yan, W., Zhu, K., Zhang, L., & Su, S. (2017). Efficient dynamic service function chain combination of network function virtualization. In *2017 IEEE 37th International Conference on Distributed Computing Systems Workshops, ICDCSW*, 5–8 June 2017, Atlanta, GA (pp. 163–168). IEEE.

[28] Ziri, S. R., Samsudin, A. T., Fontaine, C. (2017). Service chaining implementation in network function virtualization with software defined networking. In *Proceedings of the 5th International Conference on Communications and Broadband Networking*, 20–22 Feb. 2017, Bali, Indonesia (pp. 70–75).

[29] Fountoulakis, E., Liao, Q., & Pappas, N. (2020). An end-to-end performance analysis for service chaining in a virtualized network. *IEEE Open Journal of the Communications Society, 1*, 148–163.

[30] Medhat, A. M., Carella, G. A., Pauls, M., Monachesi, M., Corici, M., & Magedanz, T. (2016). Resilient orchestration of service functions chains in a NFV environment. In *2016 IEEE Conference on Network Function Virtualization and Software Defined Networks (NFV-SDN)*. 7–10 Nov. 2016, Palo Alto, CA (pp. 7–12). IEEE.

[31] Li, Y. & Chen, M. (2015). Software-defined network function virtualization: A survey. *IEEE Access, 3*, 2542–2553.

[32] Hawilo, H., Shami, A., Mirahmadi, M., & Asal, R. (2014, November/ December). NFV: State of the art, challenges, and implementation in next generation mobile networks (vEPC). *IEEE Network, 28*(6), 18–26.

[33] Nguyen, V. G., Brunstrom, A., Grinnemo, K. J., & Taheri, J. (2017). SDN/ NFV-based mobile packet core network architectures: A survey. *IEEE Communications Surveys & Tutorials, 19*(3), 1567–1602.

[34] Bronstein, Z. & Shraga, E. (2014). NFV virtualisation of the home environment. In *2014 IEEE 11th Consumer Communications and Networking Conference (CCNC)*, January, Las Vegas, NV (pp. 899–904). IEEE.

[35] Sridharan, S. (2020). A literature review of network function virtualization (NFV) in 5G networks. *International Journal of Computer Trends and Technology, 68*(10), 49–55.

[36] Papavassiliou, S. (2020). Software defined networking (SDN) and network function virtualization (NFV). *Future Internet, 12*(1), 7.

[37] Souza, R., Dias, K., & Fernandes, S. (2020). NFV data centers: A systematic review. *IEEE Access, 8,* 51713–51735.

[38] Combining Cloud, NFV, and Service Provider SDN (2014). The real-time cloud. Ericsson, Stockholm, Sweden, White Paper Uen 284 23–3219.

[39] Derakhshan, F., Grob-Lipski, H., Roessler, H., Schefczik, P., & Soellner, M. (2013). Enabling cloud connectivity using SDN and NFV technologies. In *Mobile Networks and Management* (pp. 245–258). Springer International Publishing, California.

[40] Basile, C., Valenza, F., Lioy, A., Lopez, D. R., & Perales, A. P. (2019). Adding support for automatic enforcement of security policies in NFV networks. *IEEE/ACM Transactions on Networking, 27*(2), 707–720.

[41] Mukherjee, B. K., Pappu, S. I., Islam, M., & Acharjee, U. K. (2020). An SDN based distributed IoT network with NFV implementation for smart cities. In *International Conference on Cyber Security and Computer Science*, February (pp. 539–552). Springer, Cham.

[42] Internet research task force. IRTF [Online]. Available at: https://irtf.org/ (Accessed on 19 September 2022).

[43] Lopez, D. & Krishnan, R. (2015). The nfvrg network function virtualization research at the irtf. *Journal of ICT Standardization, 3*(1), 57–66.

[44] Network function virtualization resesarch group (NFVRG) IETF. [Online]. Available at: https://datatracker.ietf.org/rg/nfvrg/about/ (Accessed on 21 March 2019).

[45] Service function chaining (SFC) IETF. [Online]. Available at: https://datatracker.ietf.org/wg/sfc/about/ (Accessed on 19 March 2022).

[46] ATIS Overview, ATIS, 1200 G Street, NW Suite 500 | Washington, DC 20005, 2019. [Online]. Available at: https://sites.atis.org/wp-content/uploads/2019/02/ATIS-Overview-2019.pdf.

[47] About BBF, Broadband Forum, 5177 Brandin Court Fremont, CA 94538. [Online]. Available at: https://www.broadband-forum.org/about-bbf (Accessed on 21 March 2019).

[48] Zoom project [Online]. Available at: https://www.tmforum.org/collaboration/zoom-project/ (Accessed on 18 September 2022).

[49] Open platform for NFV (OPNFV) [Online]. Available at: https://wiki.opnfv.org/ (Accessed on 19 September 2022).

[50] Calif, P. (2015). Hewlett Packard Enterprise OpenNFV Solution Portal Brings Telcos Closer to Realizing NFV Benefits, hp. [Online]. Available at: https://www8.hp.com/us/en/hp-news/press-release.html?id=2136079#.Wh3lxdJl82w (Accessed on 19 September 2022).

[51] Sgambelluri, A., Tusa, F., Gharbaoui, M., Maini, E., Toka, L., Perez, J. M., Paolucci, F., Martini, B., Poe, W. Y., Hernandes, J. M., Muhammed, A., Ramos, A., de Dios, O. G., Sonkoly, B., Monti, P., Vaishnavi, I., Bernardos, C. J., & Szabo, R. (2017). Orchestration of network services across multiple operators: The 5g exchange prototype. In *2017 European Conference on Networks and Communications (EuCNC)*, 12–15 June 2017, Oulu, Finland (pp. 1–5).

[52] NFV orchestration [Online]. Available at: http://www.blueplanet.com/products/nfv-orchestration.html (Accessed on 19 September 2022).

[53] Clickos fast and lightweight network functions virtualization [Online]. Available at: http://cnp.neclab.eu/projects/clickos/ (Accessed on 19 September 2022).

[54] Micro services in a minute simple and unified cloud service architecture. [Online]. Available at: http://gohan.cloudwan.io/ (Accessed on 19 September 2022).

[55] Production-grade container orchestration [Online]. Available at: https://kubernetes.io/ (Accessed on 19 September 2022).

[56] What is OSM? [Online]. Available at: https://osm.etsi.org/ (Accessed on 19 September 2022).

[57] [Online]. Available at: http://sonata-nfv.eu/content/about-sonata (Accessed on 19 September 2022).

[58] Tacker openstack NFV orchestration [Online]. Available at: https://wiki.openstack.org/wiki/Tacker (Accessed on 19 September 2022).

[59] Open baton an extensible and customizable NFV manocompliant framework [Online]. Available at: http://openbaton.github.io/ (Accessed on 19 September 2022).

[60] Telco self service — Accelerated with orchestration [Online]. Available at: https://cloudify.co/nfv/ (Accessed on 19 September 2022).

[61] Bhushan, K. & Gupta, B. B. (2019). Distributed denial of service (DDoS) attack mitigation in software defined network (SDN)-based cloud computing environment. *Journal of Ambient Intelligence and Humanized Computing*, *10*, 1985–1997.

[62] Bhushan, K. & Gupta, B. B. (2018). Detecting DDoS attack using software defined network (SDN) in cloud computing environment. In *2018 5th International Conference on Signal Processing and Integrated Networks (SPIN)*, 22–23 Feb. 2018, Noida, India (pp. 872–877). IEEE.

[63] Stergiou, C., Psannis, K. E., Kim, B. G., & Gupta, B. (2018). Secure integration of IoT and cloud computing. *Future Generation Computer Systems*, *78*, 964–975.

[64] Stergiou, C., Psannis, K. E., Gupta, B. B., & Ishibashi, Y. (2018). Security, privacy & efficiency of sustainable cloud computing for big data & IoT. *Sustainable Computing: Informatics and Systems*, *19*, 174–184.

Chapter 9
SDN Security and Challenges

There is no denying the fact that SDN has envisioned innovation in networking applications and significantly reduced the operational and maintenance costs for network operators. Developers rushed to introduce a variety of new SDN-compliant hardware, software, and services due to the exhilaration of unified and global visibility throughout the network and the ability to programme network devices. However, despite all of this activity, one important aspect that developers have left behind is "SDN Security." In this chapter, we discuss some of the major SDN security issues and challenges.

9.1 SDN Security: How Is It Different From Traditional Network Security?

Several of the security challenges that arise in SDN networks are similar to those that are found in traditional networks. When compared to traditional networks, the segregation of the control and data planes allows for multi-tenancy, programmability, and centralised management. Tenants run SDN programmes that interface with the SDN controller, which provides instructions to network elements [1, 2]. The SDN architecture offers definite benefits in terms of security. For instance, data derived from network anomaly detection or traffic analysis can be routinely sent to the central controller. The central controller can examine and correlate this network feedback with a comprehensive network view enabled by SDN to retrieve useful insights. This might help an organisation frame new security policies to prevent or mitigate an attack. It is a common belief among researchers that an SDN-enabled global network view and programmability help in controlling network security threats to a great extent [3].

On the negative side, the SDN platform might introduce a slew of new security issues. These include an increased risk of denial-of-service (DoS) attacks due to network device centralised control, flow-table limitations, a lack of trust between network elements due to the open programmability of the network, and a lack of best practices related to SDN functions and components [4].

9.1.1 Centralised Management

Networking devices typically undergo individual management and monitoring in traditional networks. However, network management has grown difficult in the absence of universal protocols that can communicate with all network devices, regardless of their manufacturer. SDN enables distributed network devices to be monitored and managed, leading to a more adaptable network management process. Although there is a chance that the SDN control plane will become a bottleneck, the fact that it can see the complete network gives it the ability to dynamically mitigate any reported incident [5]. By isolating questionable traffic, networks, or hosts, for instance, DDoS attacks can be promptly identified and handled. Traditional DDoS appliances typically only have a local perspective of the network, whereas centralised elements have a much larger understanding of network structure and performance. This makes the SDN an ideal option for the dynamic enforcement of a cohesive security posture. However, this feature of centralisation has rendered SDN controllers a host of several exploitable vulnerabilities that might pose a serious security issue to any organisation.

9.1.2 Programmability

Programmability, the capacity to quickly, securely, and effectively configure a network, is one of the major advantages brought forth by SDN. There are different levels of complexity and abstraction existing for SDN programmability [6]. Flexible control is the main advantage that programmability offers for SDN-based networks. A network becomes more agile when it can be managed and changes can be implemented quickly. The network can be more secure due to its flexibility because it is always being watched over. Moreover, the network can be designed to stop malicious activity in almost real time. However, flexibility induced by programmability can make network open to several network attacks and threats. When SDN grants users programmatic access, the hazards are increased. Think about a scenario where consumers are compelled to "trust" and rely on third-party applications or solutions built on standards in order to access the network. If isolation is not correctly implemented, control information and network element management may also be misused.

9.1.3 Multi-Tenancy

When networks are created utilising the SDN approach, it is possible for numerous tenants to use the same physical network. Further, these virtual networks are managed and monitored irrespective of the existence of each other. With multi-tenancy, network resources can be used more effectively, resulting in a lower total capital cost. By automatically scaling resources, for example, SDN enables tenants to respond more quickly to network modifications, i.e., automatic resource scaling [7]. Tenants shouldn't be able to interfere with one another's networks in order to maintain a reasonable level of security, and they shouldn't even need to be aware that they are sharing network resources with other tenants. Tenant isolation is an important factor to be considered for ensuring security for an SDN network [8].

9.2 SDN Security Analysis

In order to perform security analysis work, the SDN security issues are categorised by type and with respect to the SDN layer/interface affected by each issue/attack [9]. In this section, we discuss SDN security issues with respect to SDN layers. In the following sections, we cover every layer and its corresponding potential attack points.

9.2.1 Data Layer

The data layer of SDN is composed of several switches, routers, and other networking devices with a table of flow entries. These flow entries direct these physical devices as to what appropriate action should be taken for an incoming data packet [10, 11]. A switch serves as the end user's direct entry point into the network. As a result, it's crucial to identify the security risks associated with these switches and develop countermeasures to mitigate them. These physical devices can be an easy target for attackers to infiltrate into an SDN network.

The OpenFlow client, Flow Table, and Flow Buffer are the three components that typically make up an OpenFlow switch. When a packet is received by the switch from an input port, it stores the packet in the flow buffer and searches the flow table for the appropriate rule for this packet [12]. The packet is routed to the appropriate output port if the rule is discovered. If the rule cannot be discovered, a request for a new rule will be issued to the controller through the OpenFlow client [13]. A number of attack scenarios are possible on this layer.

(a) **Unauthorised access:** Since an SDN controller communicates with the data layer through a southbound API, there exist numerous proprietary and vendor-specific APIs and protocols for this, for example, OpenFlow (OF), Interface to the Routing System (I2RS), Path Computation Element Communication Protocol (PCEP), Open vSwitch Database Management Protocol (OVSDB), BGP-LS, OpenStack Neutron, and Open Management Infrastructure (OMI). These protocols are quite new in this domain and have several inbuilt vulnerabilities that could be exploited by the attacker. These are data-control layer interface protocols [14].

Further, the data layer consists of numerous physical devices, and these devices need to be protected by a proper authorisation and authentication mechanism. If not secured properly, then these devices can be accessed by any unauthorised user, which might result in malfunctioning of the device. Additionally, these devices can also be hijacked if the attacker directly hits the SDN controller. Through the SDN controller, he can hit these devices directly, resulting in data leakage and modification.

(b) **Data leakage:** Side channel attacks are another type of attack possible on network components in the data plane. This attack is usually performed to anticipate the flow rules associated with a particular type of traffic. In order to successfully execute this attack, the attacker uses certain network data, such as timing information (i.e., information about how long it took to forward a packet to the next hop or controller), to determine whether or not a flow rule is present. Considering an OpenFlow switch, there are numerous actions available to be taken on an incoming packet, for example, forward, drop, or send to the controller. In this case, it is possible for an attacker to perform timing analysis on the incoming traffic to determine what action had been applied to the particular packet [15]. It's not a difficult task for an attacker to observe that a packet that has been forwarded to the outport interface would take less time as compared to a packet that has been forwarded to the SDN controller. Further, by sending a set of malformed packets, an attacker could get more precise information about the traffic pattern and the switching device [16]. Next, by reading the complete pattern, an attacker could generate a voluminous set of malformed packets that would be directed towards the controller by the switching device, resulting in a DoS attack [17, 18] on the controller.

The secure storage of credentials (such as keys and certificates) for numerous logical networks in the programmable data plane is another unresolved issue in the SDN architecture. In the cloud environment, the possibility of cross-VM side channel attacks has been illustrated in the literature. In this attack, a malicious VM searches for vulnerable VMs and uses the targeted resource to obtain useful information. Similarly, in an SDN environment, such type of data leakage is possible. For example, on top of an OpenFlow-enabled switch, OF-Config creates several OF-Logical switches [6, 9]. Every logical switch has been allocated to a different user. The operation of the logical network instance may be jeopardised if the logical networks and the credentials they are linked to (such as keys and certificates) are not properly separated or containerised.

(c) **Data modification:** A man-in-the-middle (MITM) attack is a common network assault, and its main goal is to place an agent device between two nodes in order to intercept and tamper with data communications without the knowledge of either communication party. MITM attack types that are specific to one another include port mirroring, DNS spoofing, and session hijacking. In order to intercept and alter the forwarding rules sent to the switch and to gain control of packet forwarding, a MITM attack between the switch and the controller is a great option for targeting SDN. Moreover, we have already mentioned the fact that an attacker gaining control of the SDN controller can easily alter the existing flow rules or insert new flow rules into the flow table of the underlying switches. Considering an OpenFlow switch, there is a specification which defines the usage of TLS to mutually authenticate the controllers and switches, although the TLS version is not given and the security feature is also optional. Due to the ignorance of security features in the form of TLS adoption by major vendors (and in the majority of open-source controllers and switches), attacks such as a MITM attack are feasible. An attacker might alter the control messages (such as OpenFlow) sent by the controller or may insert reset messages to break the connection between the controller and the switch.

Further, it must also be required to secure the components that lie between the controller and the switch. To ensure this, proper authentication and authorisation mechanisms should be in place to mitigate a MITM attack.

(d) **DoS attack:** The SDN design, which combines the central controller with segregation of the control and data planes, introduces one of the main security flaws of SDN [19–23]. An attacker might overwhelm the controller with packets requiring a flow rule decision and make it inaccessible for legitimate users because of the communication channel between the controller and the network device. The infrastructure level might be subjected to a similar DoS attack by flooding the flow table, which has a finite amount of memory resources. Additionally, DoS attacks might result in fraudulent rule insertion and rule change [10].

(e) **Policy employment:** We have already discussed the issue related to the TLS protocol, i.e., how vendors ignore utilising such types of protocols to ensure a secure channel between different devices and the controller. It is important for vendors to realise that employing these types of protocols can ensure the security of the network to a great extent. SDN facilitates us with programmability, which also makes it possible to create dynamic flow regulations [6]. It is this advantage, in fact, that could result in security flaws. To resolve policy conflicts from numerous programmes installed on various devices, inconsistencies must be checked. In order to resolve interoperability issues among networking devices from different vendors, on several occasions, the interfaces of network devices are left loose intentionally, resulting in numerous vulnerabilities.

(f) **No visibility on global network:** In the industry, it is very important to meet the requirements of an audit process. A network should be able to provide a controlled inventory of networking devices. A controller must know what devices are in the running state and what type of traffic a device is handling. All this information comes from a global view, which the controller has over the complete network. This global view can help the controller remain accountable in the event of a conflict. However, maintaining this global view can also induce so many vulnerabilities.

9.2.2 Control Layer

The SDN controller is the brain of any SDN network, and it is this entity which offers centralised control over the whole network. It is the entity which has a global view of the network and sets flow tables of networking devices accordingly. As it offers centralised control, it is susceptible to various types of attacks. By either faking northbound API messages or southbound messages to the network devices, the attacker would like to spawn new flows. If an attacker is able to effectively spoof flows from the trusted controller, they will have the power to manipulate how traffic moves through the SDN and may even be able to get around security-related restrictions. The controller is subjected to a DoS attack, or the attacker could use other ways to bring it down [24, 25]. The attacker may attempt a resource-consumption attack on the controller to slow it down, make it respond to Packet_In events very slowly and make it send Packet_ Out messages slowly.

Often, Linux-based operating systems (OSs) are used by SDN controllers. However, the vulnerabilities of a general-purpose operating system become weaknesses for the SDN controller if it operates on that OS. Sometimes, the default passwords are used with no security settings to deploy controllers. The SDN engineers managed to "just barely" get it to function, but they were afraid of ruining it, so they didn't want to touch it. As a result, the system was left in production with an insecure configuration.

In the worst case, if an attacker built their own controller and convinced network components that flows came from the legitimate controller [26], the attacker could then add items to the network elements' flow tables, which would prevent the SDN engineers from seeing any suspicious activity. In this scenario, the attacker has full control over the network.

9.2.3 Application Layer

The possible attacks on applications could range from malicious or unauthorised applications to configuration issues, which have already been discussed in the previous section. A pool of controllers may be accessed by programmes from many third-party sources [27]. Due to the abstraction provided by the SDN controller, applications can read and write network states, which is essentially a level of network control. An attacker might access network resources and influence network behaviour if he compromises a controller or application. Apart from this, an unchecked malicious application could induce numerous vulnerabilities in the network.

These are some of the major security concerns related to an SDN network, which are also shown in Figure 9.1.

9.3   SDN Security Solutions

In this section, we discuss the various solutions that can be offered to solve the above-mentioned problems. The solutions that are discussed in this section are general solutions.

9.3.1   Resiliency of Control Plane

Given that network control is centralised, all communications within the control plane must be viewed as vital, as an outage caused by a successful attack may have an unintended impact on business continuity. If, for example, the SDNC is blocked from taking appropriate defensive action to neutralise a DoS attack, the entire network and all of its tenants may suffer. To avoid this, the control plane must be more resilient [28]. The SDNC exposes a number of interfaces for interacting with tenant applications and network components. The type and number of active applications decide the traffic loads on these interfaces. Network components, such as those that forward packets for which they lack forwarding rules, may also have an impact on the traffic on the interfaces. So, traditional networks seem to be more resilient in terms of SDNC dependency [29].

Rate-limiting network elements in terms of bandwidth and resource consumption, such as CPU load, memory usage, and API calls, is an effective way to improve the resilience of the centralised control plane against DDoS attack and to prevent it from disseminating the rest of the network [30].

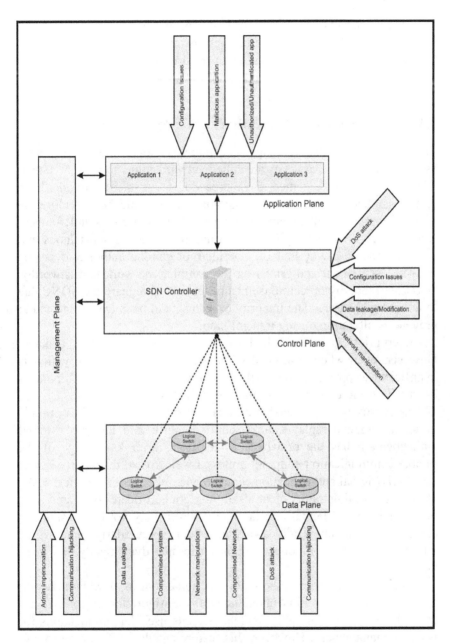

Figure 9.1. Attacks possible on different layers of SDN.

Resilience can be increased further by properly dedicating resources, in which the SDNC authenticates each resource request and then verifies these incoming requests against strong authorisation control policies.

9.3.2 Authentication and Authorisation Mechanism

The procedures needed to recognise an unknown source and subsequently establish its access privileges are called authentication and authorisation. When properly implemented, these procedures can shield networks from particular attack types [31, 34]. The attack type could be providing the system incorrect feedback and tricking it into thinking it is under attack, causing the system to deploy countermeasures that are superfluous and use resources in a way that isn't optimal, or gaining authority over one network component and rendering the complete network untrustworthy. Additional security precautions must be taken to safeguard the SDNC due to its essential nature. The integrity of data should be at least protected to prevent its alteration during transmission.

Encryption is one method of preventing control data leakage. However, even when combined with integrity protection, encryption is insufficient to protect against MITM attacks. Therefore, all communications within the control plane must be mutually authenticated. TLS and IPSec security protocols enable mutual authentication as well as provide protection against replay attacks, confidentiality, and integrity. Mutual authentication has the drawback of requiring prior knowledge of the remote communication endpoint, unless a well-trusted third party is present [32]. Mutual authentication can be manually done on a modest scale. To do this, administrators must instal the right certificates or shared keys on all endpoints. Manual installation, however, may not be possible for complicated and physically separate systems, particularly in networks where many SDN components might be formed dynamically and managed by many parties.

The SDN controller is the main functional unit of an SDN network, as it provides information about network configuration to its services through API calls. This process helps tenants use SDN applications for network management. However, this feature enables different tenants to use the same hardware, which is a very alarming situation. In order to prevent this, basic security measures should be in place, such as argument validation [33]. Apart from this, strong authentication and authorisation measures should be employed, especially for the SDN controller. If proper identity and access management mechanisms are in place, then it would be easy to trace back the main culprit unit after any security breach. Role based access control (RBAC) can help restrict the access of unauthorised entities to the SDN controller. RBAC has its own disadvantages due to the loosely defined roles and the systems where changes are made frequently. System log management can help in this direction.

9.3.3 Data Plane Isolation

Tenants operating businesses on virtual networks are prone to the same type of network attacks, as in the case of traditional networks. There is no denying the fact that the impacts of a network attack or security breach would be distributed among all the tenants, be they even or uneven. No tenant wants to operate his business on the infrastructure where another tenant who is more susceptible to network attacks resides [35, 36]. To deal with this situation, data plane isolation is required so that no tenant could interfere in the business operations of another.

So, on the data plane, the flows for each tenant must remain segregated. Isolation can be done logically with overlay networks and employed through network elements of a physical network. For example, each tenant's traffic can be routed over a shared infrastructure once it has been tagged with the owner of the traffic. Tunnels that have been marked for a certain tenant are then routed to that tenant's virtual network. For this form of encapsulation, many alternative (and complimentary) approaches are available, including Generic Routing Rncapsulation (GRE), Multiprotocol Label Switching (MPLS), and IPSec. Tagging is one method of achieving logical isolation; however, IP addresses can also be used, eliminating the need for specialised tagging procedures. Given that distinct network function instances are not required to support different tenants, tenants can share certain network functionality as long as isolation is maintained and enforced. Apart from logical isolation, encrypting the tenant's traffic with tenant-specific keys can also be done to ensure data plane isolation. This can be called as traffic isolation. This practice is more robust than just tagging, as it would prevent data leakage during the logical isolation breach/violation.

Resource management is another aspect that must be considered to perform logical isolation on any network. Apart from traffic isolation, shared resource isolation is also required. For example, a programming discrepancy with one tenant can lead to overloading of the underlying shared resource, which would definitely create problem for other tenants. Measures such as rate limiting and shared resource isolation must be employed to deal with these kinds of issues.

9.3.4 Control Plane Isolation

As we have already mentioned in the previous section, isolation is a very important aspect to consider when tenants are using the services provided by same SDN controller. SDN provides data isolation at the data link layer, but what if the working tenants have loose security controls? This may lead to data leakage at higher layers, where tenants operate and run their businesses [37, 38]. For instance, a malicious SDN application with access beyond isolation boundaries may compromise the whole network security by diverting traffic to a different party (information disclosure), overcharging or undercharging (service theft), or even dropping data (DoS). Further, the centralised nature of the SDN controller worsens the situation by amplifying the impact scale. Therefore, the complete responsibility of data and traffic isolation cannot be burdened only on the SDN controller.

9.3.5 Dynamicity

Networks constructed utilising the SDN technique have a dynamic and responsive nature, which creates new opportunities for defending against network threats. Some of the methods that can be used include black hole routing, honeypot forwarding, and automated network management. Another method that makes use of SDN characteristics is service chaining, which may be used to check for malicious payload and start mitigating actions. An SDN-enabled network can perform lower-layer and upper-layer analyses: a lower-layer analysis is in terms of data rate, source of traffic, and packet size, whereas an upper-layer analysis is in terms of transport ports, protocols, and payload fingerprints. Once the SDN network becomes suspicious of any malicious activity, it can make use of this analysis in its selective approach to choosing defensive actions against the malicious activity.

SDN is based on the segregation of control and data planes, but the communication between these two undermines this very fundamental feature of SDN. This would render the data plane a stepping stone for the attacker to attack the SDN controller. Therefore, this communication between the control and data planes must be managed and secured properly.

9.3.6 Configuration Consistency

The feature of programmability might eliminate human intervention in network configuration, but it makes networks more prone to errors. Automatic network reconfiguration is possible only when the SDN controller has a global picture of the network. Moreover, it must allow sanity checks and regression testing so that new networks may be quickly deployed. The flexibility offered by programmability, however, enables tenants to make changes to the shared environment, which can impede the functioning of the entire network — either wittingly or unwittingly as a result of false information. Consistency in configuration among various SDN apps must be considered when we talk about SDN security. Consider a case of coherency conflict arising where the load-balancing system and security controls get initiated because of one tenant. Now, security control decides to isolate the server while the load-balancing service decides to offload some tasks to this server. These types of conflicts need to be addressed by the SDN controller. Here, the SDN controller must ensure that each tenant must accept the network changes made before initiating any SDN service. Methods must be put in place to guarantee that all traffic is covered because the traffic, or portions of it, may be routed along multiple paths. As a result, monitoring is required along every path. Similar problems occur in conventional networks as well; however, the faster service delivery provided by the SDN architecture may exacerbate this kind of conflict.

The advent of software-defined networks has eliminated the need for secure, trustworthy, flexible, and well-managed networks. However, because the two planes are separated, SDN is more exposed to attack vectors than traditional networks. This means that network and control traffic's availability, consistency, authenticity, secrecy, and integrity may be severely compromised. The SDN architecture provides a virtualised network that transforms today's networks into programmable and flexible platforms. The future of networking will increasingly rely on software, and SDN will become the new network norm. However, before the SDN can be deployed securely, significant security risks related to the SDN controller and applications need to be addressed.

Exercises

Q.1.   How is maintaining SDN security different from maintaining security on a traditional network?

Q.2.   How do the important features of SDN turn into disadvantages when security is considered in the network?

Q.3.   Discuss how the data-plane layer of SDN induces some serious vulnerabilities for attackers.

Q.4.   How is a side channel attack possible on switches and routers placed at the data plane of SDN?

Q.5.   Discuss how storing the credentials of numerous logical networks in a programmable data plane is a serious threat.

Q.6.   Discuss how attackers perform MITM attacks between a switch and the SDN controller.

Q.7.   Discuss how a DoS attack on the SDN controller leads to fraudulent rule insertion or rule modification.

Q.8.   Discuss the importance of securing communication channels between devices on the data plane and the SDN controller.

Q.9.   Discuss how northbound and southbound interfaces make an SDN controller more vulnerable to cyberattacks.

Q.10.   Discuss how choosing the right operating system for an SDN controller can be a major factor in ensuring network security.

Q.11.   Discuss how the application layer induces vulnerabilities in an SDN network.

Q.12.   Discuss how data plane and control plane isolation can be a major preventive measure against serious threats in a multi-tenant environment.

Q.13.   Discuss the importance of having an authentication and authorisation mechanism in place for ensuring the security of devices on the data plane.

Q.14.   Discuss some major solutions that can be adopted by SDN vendors to make their services more resilient against cyberattacks.

References

[1] Slavov, K., Migault, D., & Pourzandi, M. (2015). Identifying and addressing the vulnerabilities and security issues of SDN. *Ericsson Technology Review, 92*(7).

[2] Open Networking Foundation (2014). SDN architecture overview. Available at: http://www.opennetworking.org/images/stories/downloads/sdn-resources/technical-reports/TR_SDN-ARCH-Overview-1.1-11112014.02.pdf.

[3] ACM (2013). Proceedings, towards secure and dependable software-defined networks. Abstract. Available at: http://dl.acm.org/citation.cfm?id=2491199.

[4] Mishra, A., Gupta, N., & Gupta, B. B. (2021). Defense mechanisms against DDoS attack based on entropy in SDN-cloud using POX controller. *Telecommunication Systems, 77*(1), 47–62.

[5] Gupta, B. B. (Ed.) (2018). *Computer and Cyber Security: Principles, Algorithm, Applications, and Perspectives*. CRC Press. UK, London.

[6] Scott-Hayward, S., O'Callaghan, G., & Sezer, S. (2013). SDN security: A survey. In *Proceedings of the IEEE SDN4FNS*, 11–13 Nov. 2013, Trento, Italy (pp. 1–7).

[7] Smeliansky, R. (2014). SDN for network security. In *Proceedings of the 1st International Science and Technology Conference MoNeTeC*, 28–29 Oct. 2014, Moscow, Russia (pp. 1–5).

[8] Schehlmann, L., Abt, S., & Baier, H. (2014). Blessing or curse? Revisiting security aspects of software-defined networking. In *Proceedings of the 10th International Conference on Network and Service Management* (CNSM), 17–21 Nov. 2014, Rio de Janeiro, Brazil (pp. 382–387).

[9] Scott-Hayward, S., Natarajan, S., & Sezer, S. (2015). A survey of security in software defined networks. *IEEE Communications Surveys & Tutorials, 18*(1), 623–654.

[10] Costa, V. T. & Costa, L. H. M. K. (2013). Vulnerability study of FlowVisor-based virtualized network environments. In *Presented at the 2nd Workshop Network Virtualization Intelligence Future Internet*. Rio de Janeiro, Brazil.

[11] Ding, A. Y., Crowcroft, J., Tarkoma, S., & Flinck, H. (2014, June). Software defined networking for security enhancement in wireless mobile networks. *Computer Network, 66*, 94–101.

[12] Tsugawa, M., Matsunaga, A., & Fortes, J. A. (2014). Cloud computing security: What changes with software-defined networking? In *Secure Cloud Computing* (pp. 77–93). Springer-Verlag. New York, NY.

[13] Shaghaghi, A., Kaafar, M. A., Buyya, R., & Jha, S. (2020). Software-defined network (SDN) data plane security: Issues, solutions, and future directions. In *Handbook of Computer Networks and Cyber Security* (pp. 341–387). Springer, California.

[14] Gao, S., Li, Z., Xiao, B., & Wei, G. (2018). Security threats in the data plane of software-defined networks. *IEEE Network*, *32*(4), 108–113.
[15] OpenFlow Switch Specification Version 1.4, Open Networking Foundation. [Online]. Available at: https://www.opennetworking.org.
[16] Ristenpart, T., Tromer, E., Shacham, H., & Savage, S. (2009). Hey, you, get off of my cloud: Exploring information leakage in third-party compute clouds. In *Proceedings of the 16th ACM Conference on CCS*, 9–13 Nov. 2009, Chicago, IL (pp. 199–212).
[17] Gupta, B. B. & Badve, O. P. (2017). Taxonomy of DoS and DDoS attacks and desirable defense mechanism in a cloud computing environment. *Neural Computing and Applications*, *28*(12), 3655–3682.
[18] Gupta, B. B. & Dahiya, A. (2021). *Distributed Denial of Service (DDoS) Attacks: Classification, Attacks, Challenges and Countermeasures*. CRC Press.
[19] Natarajan, S., Ramaiah, A., & Mathen, M. (2013). A software defined cloudgateway automation system using OpenFlow. In *Proceedings of the IEEE 2nd International Conference on CloudNet*, 11–13 Nov. 2013, San Francisco, CA (pp. 219–226).
[20] Shin, S., Yegneswaran, V., Porras, P., & Gu, G. (2013). AVANT-GUARD: Scalable and vigilant switch flow management in software-defined networks. In *Proceedings of the ACM SIGSAC Conference on Computer and Communications Security*, 4–8 Nov. 2013, Berlin, Germany (pp. 413–424).
[21] Fonseca, P., Bennesby, R., Mota, E., & Passito, A. (2012). A replication component for resilient OpenFlow-based networking. In *Proceedings of the IEEE NOMS*, 16–20 April 2012, Maui, HI (pp. 933–939).
[22] Yao, G., Bi, J., & Xiao, P. (2011). Source address validation solution with OpenFlow/NOXarchitecture. In *Proceedings of the 19th IEEE ICNP*, 17–20 Oct. 2011, Vancouver, BC, Canada (pp. 7–12).
[23] Naous, J., Stutsman, R., Mazieres, D., McKeown, N., & Zeldovich, N. (2009). Delegating network security with more information. In *Proceedings of the 1st ACM Workshop Research Enterprise Network*, 21 August 2009, Barcelona, Spain (pp. 19–26).
[24] Braga, R., Mota, E., & Passito, A. (2010). Lightweight DDoS flooding attack detection using NOX/OpenFlow. In *Proceedings of the IEEE 35th Conference on LCN*, 10–14 Oct. 2010, Denver, CO (pp. 408–415).
[25] Yan, Q. & Yu, F. R. (2015). Distributed denial of service attacks in software-defined networking with cloud computing. *IEEE Communications Magazine*, *53*(4), 52–59.

[26] Nguyen, T. H. & Yoo, M. (2017). Analysis of link discovery service attacks in SDN controller. In *2017 International Conference on Information Networking (ICOIN)*, 11–13 Jan. 2017, Da Nang, Vietnam (pp. 259–261). IEEE.

[27] Mishra, A., Gupta, N., & Gupta, B. B. (2021). Defense mechanisms against DDoS attack based on entropy in SDN-cloud using POX controller. *Telecommunication Systems, 77*(1), 47–62.

[28] Feghali, A., Kilany, R., & Chamoun, M. (2015). SDN security problems and solutions analysis. In *2015 International Conference on Protocol Engineering (ICPE) and International Conference on New Technologies of Distributed Systems (NTDS)*, 22–24 July 2015, Paris, France (pp. 1–5). IEEE.

[29] Hussein, A., Elhajj, I. H., Chehab, A., & Kayssi, A. (2016). SDN security plane: An architecture for resilient security services. In *2016 IEEE International Conference on Cloud Engineering Workshop (IC2EW)*, 4–8 April 2016, Berlin, Germany (pp. 54–59). IEEE.

[30] Vizarreta, P., Machuca, C. M., & Kellerer, W. (2016). Controller placement strategies for a resilient SDN control plane. In *2016 8th International Workshop on Resilient Networks Design and Modeling (RNDM)*, 13–15 Sept. 2016, Halmstad, Sweden (pp. 253–259). IEEE.

[31] Mattos, D. M. F., Ferraz, L. H. G., & Duarte, O. C. M. B. (2014). AuthFlow: Authentication and access control mechanism for software defined networking. University of Federal Rio Janeiro, Rio de Janeiro, Brazil.

[32] Soares, A. A., Lopes, Y., Passos, D., Fernandes, N. C., & Muchaluat-Saade, D. C. (2021). 3AS: Authentication, Authorization, and Accountability for SDN-Based Smart Grids. *IEEE Access, 9*, 88621–88640.

[33] Oktian, Y. E., Lee, S., Lee, H., & Lam, J. (2015). Secure your northbound SDN API. In *2015 Seventh International Conference on Ubiquitous and Future Networks*, 7–10 July 2015, Sapporo, Japan (pp. 919–920). IEEE.

[34] Bhushan, K. & Gupta, B. B. (2019). Distributed denial of service (DDoS) attack mitigation in software defined network (SDN)-based cloud computing environment. *Journal of Ambient Intelligence and Humanized Computing, 10*, 1985–1997.

[35] Bhushan, K. & Gupta, B. B. (2018). Detecting DDoS attack using software defined network (SDN) in cloud computing environment. In *2018 5th International Conference on Signal Processing and Integrated Networks (SPIN)*, 22–23 Feb. 2018, Noida, India (pp. 872–877). IEEE.

[36] Gupta, B. B. & Chaturvedi, C. (2019). Software defined networking (SDN) based secure integrated framework against distributed denial of service (DDOS) attack in cloud environment. In *2019 International Conference on Communication and Electronics Systems (ICCES)*, 17–19 July 2019, Coimbatore, India (pp. 1310–1315). IEEE.

[37] Mishra, A., Gupta, B. B., Peraković, D., Yamaguchi, S., & Hsu, C. H. (2021). Entropy based defensive mechanism against DDoS attack in SDN-Cloud enabled online social networks. In *2021 IEEE International Conference on Consumer Electronics (ICCE)*, 10–12 Jan. 2021, Las Vegas, NV (pp. 1–6). IEEE.

[38] Prathiba, S. B., Raja, G., Bashir, A. K., AlZubi, A. A., & Gupta, B. (2021). SDN-assisted safety message dissemination framework for vehicular critical energy infrastructure. *IEEE Transactions on Industrial Informatics*, *18*(5), 3510–3518.

Chapter 10

SDN and NFV with Other Technologies

Virtualisation is a stride in the direction of modern technology. In the course of the most recent decades, there has been a concerted shift away from hardware and towards a software-centric strategy for approaching technological problems. The Internet and the plethora of capabilities that it has brought to traditionally run businesses are mostly responsible for this development. Enterprises are lured to software-based solutions because of their flexible, agile, and scalable characteristics; as a result, enterprises are willing to adapt and use these solutions. For example, the storage infrastructure has seen how the data centre (DC) has changed to become a cloud, hybrid, or multi-cloud environment. On the other hand, the distinction between hardware and software is becoming hazier due to innovations such as edge computing and the Internet of Things (IoT).

10.1 Introduction

The networking architecture is another area that has felt the effects of the ongoing digital transformation. In the past, networks relied on a convoluted physical infrastructure of switches and routers that had to be manually configured. The older networking infrastructure was complex and static, with separate protocols handling different aspects of the network. This made transferring the network and scaling up or down more difficult. Another restriction of the conventional networking architecture was the inconsistency of the systems that were distributed across different sites without centralised supervision [1, 2]. All of these factors together caused the traditional networking architecture to fall short of the shifting demands of modern businesses.

Social media, the cloud, mobile devices, and big data analytics all present fresh prospects for expansion and differentiation for agile businesses. The network provides the foundation for these advanced technologies to function [3]. The exponential growth of Internet-enabled gadgets is placing an increasingly heavy burden on the infrastructure supporting these connections. Organisations that are unable to rapidly and frequently deploy new IT configurations may suffer from the negative effects of using traditional networking in the face of this high pace of change. Networks that are flexible, secure, and able to handle frequent changes in configuration can be a game-changer for cloud and mobile services. As service providers try to maintain levels of network capabilities that enable them to easily accommodate the expanding number of users on the network, SDN emerges as the best option available in terms of current technology. The rising mobility of businesses requiring easy accessibility to streamlined operations is a further factor. The ability of SDN solutions to reduce capital and operational costs is an additional factor contributing to the increasing demand for SDN in the market [4, 5].

In the case of IoT, for example, as it becomes a business reality, network managers are under enormous pressure to accommodate the rising number of devices/users on the network without compromising bandwidth quality [6, 7]. Therefore, any business considering embracing IoT must first implement an SDN system [8, 9]. When it comes to cloud computing, the recent decade has marked a major paradigm shift in the field of computing. Virtualised cloud DCs have gradually replaced physical servers because they are more flexible, scalable, and cost-effective [10].

SDN is well suited for use as the underpinning layer of a blockchain architecture because of its ability to facilitate real-time application performance. As an alternative to exchanging data between nodes, blockchain-enabled SDN would facilitate a cryptocurrency exchange. While the concept of an SDN powered by blockchain technology is exciting, only a select few vendors actually provide this service [11]. Additionally, SDN isn't the only field where blockchain technology can be useful. Blockchain technology has the potential to disrupt established systems, including the IoT and cloud computing [12].

In this section, we discuss how SDN supports these modern technologies, what issues and challenges these SDN-enabled technologies encounter, and what could be the possible solutions.

10.2 SDN and NFV with Cloud Computing

The potential of cloud computing to provide infrastructure resources, such as computing, networking, storage, and software as services, has revolutionised a sizable section of the IT business. SDN offers programmable and virtualised networks in place of traditional tightly coupled network infrastructure [13]. NFV offers physical telecommunications infrastructures and network functions to be turned into virtualised network functions and services. Virtualisation is essential for the provisioning and delivery of virtual resources and services in cloud, SDN, and NFV technologies, and their related software-defined infrastructures [14]. Traditional security flaws are always present, while these technologies always introduce their own security vulnerabilities.

Cloud computing, SDN, and NFV all rely on virtualisation because it makes it possible to abstract the underlying resources for usage by multiple tenants, to separate users inside the same cloud/network, and to separate services and functions on the same hardware [15]. Moreover, it is crucial in the process of creating and managing a provider's services. Typically, a hypervisor is used to introduce virtualisation as a software abstraction layer between operating systems and the underlying hardware (including compute, network, and storage). Since the hypervisor controls the hardware resources in cloud DCs, several virtual machines (VMs), each running their own operating system, set of apps, and network services, can coexist on a single piece of hardware [16]. Consequently, virtualisation enables multitenancy, provides workload isolation, increases server utilisation, and gives customers access to elastic and scalable resources and services.

SDN capabilities, such as the ability to adjust to fluctuating workloads, programmable control planes, heightened network security, network virtualisation, a global view of DCN, and the integration of a hypervisor and a cloud computing manager, can have a profound effect on the utility and efficiency of cloud computing. SDN was developed out of a desire for scalability and cost-efficiency in cloud computing that supports several tenants across complex networking. As SDN can manage both the network forwarding plane and the centralised control plane, network elements become dynamically programmable and configurable. With the capabilities of SDN controllers to monitor the entire network, numerous research projects [17–21] have been done to increase quality of service (QoS) and energy efficiency, including bandwidth allocation per flow, traffic consolidation, and dynamic configuration.

Before further discussing the integration between SDN, NFV, and cloud computing, we are assuming that readers have primitive knowledge about cloud computing.

10.2.1 Current Trends/Research in SDN-Enabled Cloud

In this section, we discuss the current research trends in an SDN-enabled cloud according to the categories of aim, application model, configuration, etc., as shown in Table 10.1.

Table 10.1.   Recent trends/research domain in an SDN-enabled cloud.

Category	Sub-Category	Description	SDN Controllers
Objective	Performance	• SDN can improve it by offering granular control over the entire network. • SDN is one method for speeding up the deployment of many VMs in a massive DC. • Throughput, latency, and error rate are some of the metrics that can be used to quantify a network's performance.	OF-SLB [22], QoSFlow [23], AQSDN [24], SDN-Orch [25], C-N-Orch [26], Orch-Opti [27], B4 [28], OpenQoS [29], CNG [30], ADON [31], CometCloud [32], SD-IC [33], Orch-IC [34], VIAS [35], CL-Orch [36], SVC [37], BDT [38], SDN-TE [39].
	Energy efficiency	• A DC's energy consumption is primarily determined by host servers, networking devices, and cooling systems and is proportional to usage level. • In addition to compute elasticity, SDN allows for network elasticity. • During low network utilisation, SDN can combine network traffic into fewer switches, allowing unused switches to be turned off.	ElaticTree [40], CARPO [41], DISCO [42], FCTcon [43], GETB [44], VMPlanner [45], VMRouting [46], PowerNetS [47, 48], S-CORE [49], QRVE [50], SLAEE-DO [51], ODM-BD [52].

Table 10.1.   (*Continued*)

Category	Sub-Category	Description	SDN Controllers
	Security	• SDN is widely utilised in cloud DCs to protect against DDoS attacks. • Due to its ability to handle the entire DC network, the SDN controller requires a very high level of security.	GBSF [53], Brew [54].
	Virtualisation	• In a cloud DC, numerous tenants may share a single instance of a network's underlying hardware, such as a switch or a physical link, using virtualisation provided by SDN. • NFV is also another example of SDN utilisation in virtualisation.	FairCloud [55], QVIA-SDN [56], Opti-VNF [57], Dyn-NFV [58], E2E-SO [59].
Target architecture	Intra DCN	• In a DC, SDN is used for intra-host communication. • DC networking can be fine-tuned according to bandwidth usage for incoming and outgoing packets.	OF-SLB [22], QoSFlow [23], AQSDN [24], SDN-Orch [25], C-N-Orch [26], Orch-Opti [27].
	Inter DCN	• Network connectivity between DCs in different locations can be optimised with SDN. • Cloud providers with several DCs can use SDN to manage the WAN between them by developing their own SDN controller.	OpenQoS [29], B4 [28], CNG [30], ADON [31], CometCloud [32], SD-IC [33], Orch-IC [34], VIAS [35], CL-Orch [36], SVC [37], BDT [38], SDN-TE [39].

(*Continued*)

Table 10.1.   *(Continued)*

Category	Sub-Category	Description	SDN Controllers
Application model	Batch processing	• Constant bandwidth is more important than latency or response time in most batch processing operations; therefore, the SDN controller has to follow a slightly different approach.	ADON [31].
	Map reduce	• A large task is divided into smaller tasks and processed on numerous devices at the same time, which requires large bandwidth and computing power. • If jobs are evenly distributed and processed at the same speed, network bursts between mappers and reducers can be a bottleneck. • With suitable SDN control logic, burst traffic can be dynamically dispersed resulting in reduced bottleneck effects.	
	Web application	• The upper- and lower-tier servers connect with several levels of the web application model, such as load balancers, application servers, and databases, which require quick response times and low latency.	SLAEE-DO [51], CARPO [41], PowerNetS [47].

Table 10.1. *(Continued)*

Category	Sub-Category	Description	SDN Controllers
	Streaming	• This is for applications that constantly produce new data, which then must be transferred in big quantities across networks. These applications are time sensitive.	CometCloud [32], AQSDN [24].
Configuration	Homogeneous	• In a DC, all the machines and switches in an edge rack have the same hardware specs, and all the racks have the same number of hosts and switches. • To achieve energy efficiency in a DC, a homogenous environment can be helpful.	ElaticTree [40], CARPO [41], DISCO [42], FCTcon [43], GETB [44], VMPlanner [45], VM-Routing [46], PowerNetS [47, 48], S-CORE [49].
	Heterogeneous	• Since the internetworking system includes many distinct networking operators, each of which may employ a somewhat different set of networking devices, studies of inter-DCN network performance often assume a heterogeneous setup.	Orch-Opti [27], B4 [28], CNG [30], ADON [31], CometCloud [32], SD-IC [33].

10.2.2 Challenges in SDN-Enabled Cloud Computing

The emergence of SDN with dynamic controllability has the potential to deliver numerous benefits to cloud DCs, as requirements and utilisation vary dynamically on demand. In this section, we discuss the challenges faced by both of these technologies when merged.

10.2.2.1 *Programmability*

When a network is programmable, it can support more complex network services. Existing DC hardware and management architectures are frequently inflexible. This requires administrators to adhere to vendor- and hardware-specific rules. The management of high-performance packet flows to provide communication between servers presents difficulties for conventional DCs. Scaling and server overbooking can be utilised to reduce service costs. Two prominent examples of hybrid packet and circuit-switched DC network designs are presented in C-Through [60] and Helios [61]. By allowing circuit-switched networks to provide more bandwidth to applications, these topologies boost the networks' performance. This would help in retaining balance between intra- and inter-DC networking. Intelligent switching techniques are regarded as extremely successful since they consolidate switching data into a single logical file system for analysis [62, 63]. By utilising best-fit switching hardware devices, intelligent switching techniques reduce network asset use. In a software-defined data centre (SDDC), self-adaptive services and the composition of those services make it easier for network administrators to handle load shifts, traffic routing, and control features. In clouds and distributed systems, ideas about self-adaptability are becoming more important as middleware infrastructure becomes a big part of self-adaptive service composition. Software-defined cloud computing ideas allow application developers to regulate network elements and data flows according to their interests, for example, by writing apps. Google connects cluster routers using a virtual network overlay and switching fabric [64].

In Ref. [65], a novel energy-efficient flow scheduling and routing method is suggested for SDN-enabled DC networks. OpenStack Neat [66] can aid DC admins in cutting energy use in hybrid and pure SDDC prototypes by adding programmability tools to the control management interface. It's essentially an augmented version of OpenStack designed to cut costs by dynamically reassigning VMs in real time. Taking this similar strategy and expanding it to SDDC results in even better power savings.

SLAs need close monitoring to make sure all service activities and rules are being followed. Multiple issues with SLA monitoring and compliance can be handled with the use of a programmable management framework, as outlined in Ref. [67], that is based on SDN principles.

10.2.2.2 *Scalability*

The objective of SDN-enabled cloud computing is to make cloud infrastructure design, operation, and administration simpler. This paves the way for the creation of networks that are adaptable to the ever-evolving needs of systems. Large-scale parallel processing methods are used by cloud providers, such as Google and Yahoo, to handle scalability issues [68]. Moreover, many businesses rely on high-performance network services to ensure swift data transfers between their physical servers. Hyperscalability provided by SDN-based cloud computing architectures in DCs can help fix these issues, which could lead to better DC performance overall [69]. In the following, we take a closer look at how the advances in scalability brought about by SDN-defined cloud computing are affecting the norms of cloud DC design.

A DC's VM applications must be scalable. The number of necessary VMs for handling a growing workload rises in parallel with the need for scalability [70]. For these apps to be seamlessly integrated and processed, SDN controllers must handle any issues that may arise due to the workload. Network administrators are aided by SDN controllers in creating and tailoring testbeds for traffic engineering strategies in a simulated network environment [71]. In SDC, the functions of controlling a network are pushed to a single location. This raises certain issues with scalability. As networks grow, more network requests are sent to the controller, and eventually, there will come a point where it will no longer be able to handle all of the requests. Parallelism can be used to address this issue [72].

When the operations of an SDN-enabled DC are performed on a massive scale, they can quickly overwhelm a centralised controller. Incorporating policies on network routers and switches will fix this issue. By enforcing switching policies, scalability bottlenecks are eliminated before they may slow down the system. These issues can be resolved by the proposed solutions, such as Onix [73], Hyperflow [74], and Kandoo [75]. The deployment and migration of applications between various cloud tenants are supported by cloud architectures. The cloud manager enables this to happen. A software-defined virtualization idea called AutoSlice [76] automates the implementation of SDN capabilities for intermediary mediation services. This makes it easier for cloud managers to support and accommodate many tenants.

10.2.2.3 *Security*

SDCC aggregates numerous services for monitoring and managing network security into a unified interface. This orchestration is absolutely necessary in order to fulfil the regulatory standards. It's because security events associated with SDCs can be incorporated into a real-time policy-based system. As a result, security overheads on shared resources will be reduced. It is noteworthy that using conventional DC-based methods to achieve the same outcomes is expensive and difficult. Adaptability, virtualisation, and on-demand availability of resources in SDN-enabled DCs are largely responsible for their dynamicity. In the cloud, SDN helps admins spot suspicious behaviour with little effort by storing historical data, correlating it with policies, and optimising it depending on the observed results. Further, it also helps with the management of services in order to allocate bandwidth according to specified standards.

Access to a system is restricted to authorised users via role-based authorisation services. In massive network applications, they are becoming increasingly popular. Although these authorisation services have frequently been criticised for their complexity in establishing an initial role structure, they have nonetheless proven effective in dispersed environments. DevoFlow [77], Beacon [78], NOX [79], and Maestro [80] controllers are currently extending their role-based authorisation capabilities to address real-time authorisation-based security risks.

Threat modelling can aid in eliminating severe security threats. As the main threat modelling approaches lack automation, scaling them in large DCs is extremely difficult. Techniques such as STRIDE and Process for Attack Simulation and Threat Analysis (P.A.S.T.A.) can be applied in an SDN-based cloud to execute automated security functions. Utilising P.A.S.T.A. [82] in the cloud can decrease the high costs associated with security vulnerabilities. Alternatively, STRIDE evaluates a network's vulnerability to attacks.

Extensive planning is required prior to the implementation of an acceptable use policy (AUP) that is based on service-level agreements. The reason for this is that detecting rule conflicts in typical cloud technologies is a laborious procedure. FortNOX [79] is a role-based security enforcement kernel for the NOX OpenFlow controller. For inconsistencies in the flow rules, it immediately alerts the user. Instances of policy breaches are identified by the security kernel.

It will take a long time for DCs to completely adapt to software-defined practices. Existing DC transformation projects concentrate on standardisation/consolidation, virtualisation, automation, and security upgrades. Numerous obstacles exist in the transformation process because of the current static status of DCs.

10.2.2.4 *Interoperability*

Concerns around interoperability of SDN-enabled cloud computing continue to be a barrier for the IT sector. Transitioning from a typical cloud environment to SDE is facilitated by standardisation efforts. Deploying a completely new software-defined controller is simple and convenient because all of its elements and devices are software defined. However, it does not seem feasible when transformations of huge DCs are considered. Traditional networking hardware is abundant, making it impossible to replace it all with software-defined networking infrastructure. In confined settings, such as a testbed or campus network, the ability to swap components out is typically a viable choice. Organisations should understand the requirement for inter-DC traffic designs and policies/rules in order to guarantee a rapid transition from traditional DCs to DCs based on SDN. After the necessary adjustments have been made in corporate SLAs, these regulations can be enforced on DCs. A corporation needs to establish a product development agenda in order to be successful in achieving a comprehensive transformation solution.

Without uniform standardisation, SDN controllers from different vendors can act in unexpected ways. Also, bottlenecks in network traffic might arise due to the use of many controllers. These complications might be simplified with the use of an interoperability standard solution. In order to resolve questions about controller interoperability in software-defined DCs, a standard or multi-vendor-supported SDN controller is essential. Telecommunication service providers are moving towards a network architecture that is built on an orchestrated ecosystem of vendor-neutral hardware and multi-vendor virtualised network operations.

10.3 SDN and NFV with IoT

In the context of current wireless communications, the IoT is a concept that is quickly gaining traction. The idea is predicated on the widespread presence of various "smart things" or devices, such as radio-frequency identification (RFID) tags, sensors, actuators, and smart mobile phones, all of which are individually addressable and thus capable of intelligently interacting with one another and working together to achieve shared goals [83]. Wireless networking advancements have enabled these hundreds of smart devices to connect to the Internet from anywhere and at any time. The amount of data created per day is increasing dramatically with the introduction of IoT [84]. The features of diversity and dynamics, as well as the explosion of big data, present a significant obstacle to the design of IoT architecture in the era of the cloud and big data. To fulfil the requirements of diversity and dynamics, networks should now be more intelligent, powerful, efficient, secure, consistent, and scalable. We believe that SDN [9] and NFV [13, 85] are two promising technologies that could help overcome these challenges to developing the IoT architecture.

10.3.1 How SDN Benefits IoT?

IoT offers a wide range of use cases and dedicated applications and platforms by different vendors, which induces redundancy in the data generated by IoT [86, 87, 127]. An IoT network is made up of a collection of sensor and actuator networks, as well as end-user sensor nodes, all of which run at the edge network. Meanwhile, a few gateways and access points back up the edge network (access network). The DC and core networks are also crucial components of the IoT. Furthermore, SDN technologies have a wide variety of applications across many different kinds of networks. There are several use cases for the IoT too. Following are some of the use cases:

(a) **Network policing:** SDN can provide a global picture of the entire network. This feature allows for two methods to be used in SDN to monitor the network: controller-initiated probing, and switch-reported network state changes. Probing is performed by the SDN controller sending out probe messages to the network devices, such as routers and switches, in order to collect data at regular intervals. Larger networks have been shown to have significantly better optimised operational expenditure (OPEX) [88]. While relying on switches to actively transmit network information may reduce overhead, it may also lead to compromised accuracy. As a result, we see that there is a cost–benefit analysis between control complexity and accuracy.

By taking advantage of a global picture of the network and a centralised data management system, SDN technology enables the efficient management of data traffic flows, with minimal impact on the network's latency and capacity. Through network load balancing and swift message transport, SDN applied to IoT networks will maximise the utilisation of the available bandwidth.

(b) **Data aggregation:** SDN controllers play a pivotal role in OpenFlow-based flow placement by capitalising on their global network view [89]. Flows can now be tracked and analysed for more informed decision-making. Since an IoT network typically contains a wide variety of devices, SDN makes it practical and viable to exert unified control over the entire network.

(c) **Mobility:** Billions of gadgets will be connected in the IoT in the next few years, and users must be able to make full use of their devices at any time and from any location without encountering any kind of restriction. The SDN technology enables smooth management of users' mobility via control of these devices.

(d) **Energy management:** Since the billion connected devices to the IoT network will generate a massive amount of data, it would take a large number of DCs to process all of this information. These DCs require a significant amount of electrical energy to operate. Therefore, it will be necessary to build DCs that are both energy efficient and equipped with an intelligent energy management system. Using the SDN controller to efficiently route network traffic to the appropriate server, the SDN technology will allow for the creation of energy-efficient IoT DCs by dynamically enabling or disabling equipment in response to consumption patterns.

(e) **Network resources utilisation:** Overuse of the network by users increases the load on the network's equipment, which in turn decreases the latter's performance. To improve the network's efficacy, it is necessary to create a prior plan for the QoS requested by the users and to configure the network devices for optimised traffic engineering. The SDN controller makes use of the global picture of the network to determine the most efficient route for data flowing into the network and to determine the rules that must be applied to that data flow. It would help reduce the amount of energy and money needed to operate the network and increase its productivity.

(f) **Traffic-aware NFV deployment:** VMs are the central computational element in networked DCs. With SDN, the controller has a global view of all traffic, and monitoring is possible for each VM running IoT analysis software in the DC. This would ensure scalability in SD IoT while matching the best practice of NFV. Consequently, VMs must be deployed in a dynamic and efficient manner, including placement issues and resource allocation limits.

(g) **Security:** Distributed systems and centralised systems are two typical architectures. A network intrusion detection system (NIDS) is used at the network's nerve centre to provide centralised security. The NIDS is deployed at the core of the network to ensure security at the centralised level. However, the performance is not satisfactory in some instances. As an example, the overhead may increase due to the need for additional dedicated middleware; furthermore, a network operator has limited views of the network due to the traditional network architecture, which means the host-band solution approaches are OS specific, likely resulting in different contention between solutions [90]. Thus, SDN should be viewed as an alternate strategy at the core network to attain various key performance indicators (KPIs) of a network.

10.3.2 Recent Trends of SDN Enabled IoT

Wireless sensor networks (WSNs) have limited functionalities due to some challenges and issues. WSNs are more difficult to deploy and administer since they need specific adaptations for specific applications. To get around this, SD IoT was developed by merging the benefits that SDNs bring with those of WSNs. Additionally, an SDN-WSN is vulnerable to security risks that negatively affect the system's QoS performance and vulnerability. System unreliability, for instance, would result from denial-of-service (DoS) attacks or malicious attacks using misleading data and parameters [128]. For this reason, widespread WSN deployment is challenging and fraught with challenges. When running applications which have unique requirements for adaptability and control, operators must implement special adaptation methods.

In this section, we discuss some current trends in this particular domain, as shown in Table 10.2.

Table 10.2. Recent trends/research domains of SDN-driven IoT.

Objective	Refs.	Description
IoT Security	[91]	• A framework has been designed. for network layer attacks. • Framework has low computation cost. • Communication cost is not considered while designing framework. • Storage cost is also not considered. • Data security has been proposed as the countermeasure.
	[92]	• A framework has been designed. for network layer attacks. • Framework has low computation cost. • Communication cost is moderate, i.e., not too high nor too low. • Storage cost is also low. • Communication security has been proposed as the countermeasure.
	[93]	• A framework has been designed. for network and perception layer attacks. • Framework has low computation cost. • Communication cost is high. • Storage cost is low. • Data, device, and communication securities have been proposed as the countermeasures.
	[94]	• A framework has been designed. for perception layer attacks. • Framework has high computation cost. • Communication cost is high. • Storage cost is also not considered. • Device security has been proposed as the countermeasure.
	[95]	• A framework has been designed for network layer attacks. • Framework has high computation cost. • Communication cost is not considered while designing framework. • Storage cost is also not considered. • Communication security has been proposed as the countermeasure.
	[96]	• A framework has been designed. for network layer attacks. • Framework has high computation cost. • Communication cost is not considered while designing framework. • Storage cost is also not considered. • Communication security has been proposed as the countermeasure.

(Continued)

Table 10.2. *(Continued)*

Objective	Refs.	Description
IoT Manage-ment	[97]	• Authors have proposed a virtualised network-based solution for IoT management by utilising NFV. • The suggested architecture is split up into distinct layers, each responsible for a different function: service, global OS, NFVO, SDN controller, and virtualisation. • The proposed framework is very generic and does not have any detailed working of the components.
	[98]	• Authors have proposed a SDN-driven IoT management framework with NFV implementation. • Control layer of SDN consists of distributed OS which maintains IoT network view to be provided at the physical layer, where IoT devices are present for data forwarding. • Virtualisation overhead is present which needs to be addressed.
	[99]	• Authors have proposed a message-oriented publish and subscribe middleware incorporated with SDN principles. • The control layer of SDN is an integrated data distribution service (DDS), which acts as an interface between IoT and the rest of the network. • SDN and DDS offer reconfigurable wireless data plane, dynamic channel configuration, swift client alliance, and mobility management. • High computation overhead of DDS middleware.
	[100]	• Authors proposed an SDN-driven publish and subscribe system with minimum cost topic connected overlay (MCTCO) algorithm to optimise routing schema through traffic engineering. • Overhead of computing topic tree and forming clusters in the network.
	[101]	• Authors have proposed an SDN-based stateful solution for wireless sensor network called as SDN-WISE. • SDN-WISE employs tree data structures to record the actions of its states array, accepted IDs array, and WISE flow table. • Proposed architectures include a topology discovery protocol to help manage IoT which is an overhead.
Cellular Network	[102]	• Authors have proposed SoftRAN, which supports resource management, mobility support, traffic off loading, and reduced delay. • Virtualisation and centralised control plane are not defined properly. • Interaction between core network and RAN is also not defined.

Table 10.2. *(Continued)*

Objective	Refs.	Description
	[103]	• Authors have proposed SoftCell for fine grain policy management in an IoT network, which supports dynamic traffic offloading and efficient routing. • Minimal virtualisation has been attained. • OpenFlow API has been utilised as a controller. • Scalability is also high. • Defining fine grain policies is a bit difficult.
	[104]	• Authors have proposed SoftAir, which is a flexible platform for partial and full centralisation. • Fine grain virtualisation has been achieved. • Security issue has not been addressed.
	[105]	• Authors have proposed cellSDN, which supports mobility management and fine grain control. • It offers basic support for virtualisation. • Inefficient traffic engineering using MPLS and VLAN tags.

The prerequisites for industrial use are examined in Ref. [106], with an emphasis on systems that have used SDN, allowing the authors to establish the extent to which each need is satisfied by SDN. Meanwhile, it was established that SDN was not necessary for usability or communication across public networks. One of the main benefits of software-defined networks is that they allow for the use of a wide variety of communication technologies while still allowing for unified, technology-agnostic network management. SDNs have been shown to be effective in IIoT networks, which means that the latter can take advantage of their low cost and simple setup.

The research in Refs. [107, 108] demonstrates how SDN's centralised software control can reduce the amount of hardware needed for management networks. In Ref. [28], the authors investigate whether or not SDN can be used to build sophisticated access rules for devices with granular permissions at different levels of authorisation. Many IIoT devices pose a high security risk because of their inherent limitations. Numerous attacks, including denial of service (DOS), man in the middle (MIM), and floods, are frequently directed at such devices. For mission-critical programmes, such as those used in business, it becomes increasingly important to secure these devices. Certain security issues of this type, especially those occurring at the network level, can be addressed using SDNs.

The IIoT, and especially new industrial networks, require flexibility. To accomplish this, it is proposed in Ref. [29] that the entire IIoT, not only the network, must be defined in software. With regard to the network itself, SDN can be utilised by both internal and external networks related to industries. In this approach, there is no need for a widespread upgrade of the existing protocols and procedures pertaining to the hardware used in such networks.

10.3.3 Open Research Issues of SDN and IoT integration

In this section, we discuss the open research issues of SDN integration with IoT. Following are some research challenges:

(a) **Policy enforcement:** It is difficult to ensure that policies are being enforced consistently across the entire network, although some potential ways have been offered. Multiple SDN controllers are expected to cooperate in a distributed way [109, 129]. As a result, there may be problems with concurrent policy enforcement due to differences in SDN policies and specifications for each controller. Therefore, concurrency concerns at the data plane of network switches may emerge from concurrent policy enforcement. That's why it's so important to develop effective methods of policy enforcement to deal with these issues,

(b) **Real-time deployment:** There are multiple solutions utilising SDN and IoT together that have been proposed so far, but only in theoretical aspects. There is a gap in the literature between theoretical considerations and actual implementations [110, 130]. Deploying the proposed schemes requires thorough research into a variety of challenges, including deployment policies, problems with different vendor-specific services, and the integration of multiple devices. Therefore, before proceeding with the real deployment, it is necessary to understand a variety of open challenging issues, such as a clear market policy and how the old devices may be supported by the new technology.

(c) **Issues with mobility:** Heterogeneous devices, which can be either mobile or stationary, constitute an IoT environment. Additionally, the mobility pattern of one gadget may differ from that of another. As a result, while making changes to the devices' forwarding rules, network operators must take mobility into account as well. Nonetheless, most of the current SDN-based solution approaches lack investigation into updating forwarding rules in the presence of mobile devices. In addition, the IoT is anticipated to enable the connectivity of billions of devices. Consequently, it is difficult to efficiently and reliably process requests from billions of devices while also adapting the forwarding rules in real time to account for the mobility of the devices. Therefore, it is necessary to address a number of issues, such as optimal rule placement, traffic flow optimisation, controller placement problems, and dynamic resource allocation, while taking both the stationary and dynamic nature of an IoT environment into account.

(d) **Interoperability:** With SDN technology, the built-in control logic in network devices may be extracted and reprogrammed as required. Therefore, effective management of present hardware devices is required so that they may be customised or reconfigured without requiring specialised hardware or protocols from their manufacturers. With the current SDN technologies, however, supporting the old networking devices is challenging. Therefore, we need SDN-based solution approaches that can handle traditional networking devices in an abstracted fashion while still taking hardware-specific concerns into account.

10.4 SDN with 5G/6G

Information technology is advancing at a breakneck pace, and the network management systems for 5G and 6G networks are progressing in the direction of integration, distribution, diversity, and intelligence. For example, the Internet automotive industry's rapid growth depends heavily on network speed, which has become a major factor behind the development of 5G/6G networks. Network programmability is an area of prospective innovation in this regard, allowing for highly abstracted network management. Since SDN technology allows for flexible adjustment according to diverse use cases, flexibility is an essential prerequisite for 5G/6G network architecture.

In this section, we study the benefits yielded by SDN to 5G/6G, major research work in this particular domain, and finally the open research challenges when these two technologies meet.

10.4.1 How SDN benefits 5G/6G?

The first generation (1G) introduced us to cell phones; the second generation (2G) made it possible for us to send and receive text messages; the third generation (3G) gave us access to the Internet; and the fourth generation (4G) brought us the speed and capabilities that form the backbone of our digital lives. By adhering to bringing advancements to the telecom network, where the NFV architecture serves as the foundation, 5G asserts to be genuinely software defined in terms of its key functions and being end to end. With an ever-increasing number of endpoints, it's likely that 4G will soon be pushed to its performance and capacity limits. The short-comings of current telecommunications networks are considered to be remedied by the introduction of 5G architecture. Network slicing is a necessary tool for operators to use in order to meet the growing need for more rapid network speeds, to automate their networks, and to streamline their network infrastructure. In this way, SDN can serve as 5G's true underpinning.

Now, we see how the telecom sector is benefiting from SDN technology.

(a) **Network programmability:** Fifth-generation mobile networks stand out due to their programmable networks. There will be a wide variety of new communication requirements in the 5G era, coming from a wide variety of devices, users, and businesses. 5G networks will need to be programmable, adaptable, modular, software-driven, and managed in such a way that they enable a wide variety of services if they are to effectively meet these demands. The SDN technology's ability to facilitate network programming is a crucial factor in this regard. A programmable 5G network offers service agility by shortening the time it takes to create and adapt services, service diversity by providing a single infrastructure for multiple services with varying requirements, and resource efficiency by allocating the appropriate amount of resources at the right time and place.

(b) **Network slicing:** Network slicing is another game-changing idea that will come with 5G. Network slicing refers to the process of partitioning a single 5G physical network into numerous independent logical networks of various sizes and architectures that are dedicated to various services. This would allow operators to create distinct levels of services for different enterprise verticals, empowering them to customise their operations. Apart from customisation, network slicing aids operators in guaranteeing QoS. Network operators can enhance network performance by decreasing latency and tightening security by tuning QoS as per the requirements.

(c) **Improved performance:** High-speed 5G services improve reliability, rapid provisioning, and high-speed bandwidth for remote organisations when used in conjunction with SD-WAN.

(d) **Virtualisation:** With NFV, service providers may deploy a wide variety of networked endpoints without having to shell out a tonne of money for expensive, specialised hardware. In contrast to proprietary hardware, which can take months to instal, these network features can be up and running in just a few weeks. When talking about 5G, NFV helps virtualise many different layers. In particular, 5G network slicing is made possible by NFV, which allows for many virtual networks to run atop the same physical infrastructure. NFV also lets service providers create new services on the fly. Depending on the type of 5G service, the network will have several service chains. This gives service providers flexibility and makes it possible for them to scale up or down their services to meet changing customer needs. It also cuts their capital and operating costs by making their network infrastructure more flexible and less expensive, and it cuts the time it takes to set up new network services.

(e) **Mobility:** Multi-homing, or exposing the end host to numerous networks at once so that consumers can move freely across wireless infrastructures and the provider can sustain them, is a significant difficulty in wireless and broadband networks. This method will develop as a result of deploying relays with SDN capabilities between a central network and an external network perimeter. Using SDN and NFV between a residential gateway and an access network would result in an architecture that offloads the majority of the gateway's functions to a virtualised runtime.

(f) **M2M communications:** End users will need to be able to interact not just with one another but also with surrounding items and machines, such as sensors embedded in objects, in order to participate in future wireless networks. The management of M2M networks will be greatly aided by the concept of wireless SDN (WSDN). Drivers for a WSDN must be adaptable enough to facilitate topology discovery, self-configuration, and self-organisation of network nodes.

(g) **Cooperation:** SDN and NFV will have further direct effects on cooperative networks. SDN can enable enhanced caching solutions for data on the perimeter network to meet the high capacities required by 5G systems for seamless data flow between networks.

10.4.2 Recent Trends of SDN Enabled 5G

It has been the overarching ambition and vision of both the business and academic communities to create a 5G network that can accommodate a wide range of industries while also meeting the expectations of end users in terms of service quality. In this section, we discuss some major research projects that utilise SDN and NFV to deliver 5G networks with fine orchestration across multiple domains and multi-vendor heterogeneous networks. Table 10.3 shows some major projects that intend to integrate SDN and 5G.

Table 10.3.   List of some major 5G projects based on SDN.

Project Name	Description
5G-MEDIA [111]	• An SDN- and NFV-based flexible network architecture that enables the dynamic and adaptable distribution of UHD content over 5G content delivery networks (CDNs), immersive media, and virtual reality. • It aims to utilise and appropriately expand the useful outcomes of ongoing 5G PPP projects in order to provide an agile development, verification, and orchestration platform for services.
5G-NORMA [112]	• It is an SDN- and NFV-based novel 5G mobile network architecture which supports mobility management, orchestration mechanisms, and QoE/QoS. • Multi-service and context-aware adaption of network functions to support multiple services and their respective QoE/QoS requirements.
5G TANGO [113]	• Proposed a 5G programmable network with NFV-driven service development kit (SDK) to support virtual network functions (VNFs). • Does not support video streaming.
5G MoNArch [114]	• It intends to leverage network slicing which uses SDN, NFV, the orchestration of access network, core network functions, and analytics to facilitate a wide range of use cases in vertical industries, such as automotive, healthcare, and media.
MATILDA [115]	• Programmable network infrastructure allows for the creation and orchestration of 5G-ready applications and network services through network slicing.

Table 10.3.   (*Continued*)

Project Name	Description
SESSAME [116]	• It revolves around three concepts: (a) use of NFV and edge cloud computing to place network intelligence and applications at the network edge; (b) the significant evolution of the small cell idea, which is common in 4G but is anticipated to reach its full potential in the challenging high-density 5G scenarios; (c) multi-tenancy in the communication network.
5G-XHAUL [117]	• A programmable network solution to wireless and optical 5G networks which supports reconfigurable, software-defined cognitive control plane with the capacity to predict traffic demand in both time and space.
5G-Transformer [118]	• It is an SDN/NFV-based mobile transport and computing (MTC) paradigm which utilises network slicing to provision and orchestrate MTC slices as per the requirement.
5G-Crosshaul [119]	• It allows multi-tenancy through network slicing that supports efficient and flexible allocation of network resources.
CHARISMA [120]	• To create a multi-technology, multi-operator, software-defined, and convergent fixed 5G mobile network architecture.
SAT5G [121]	• Integration of network slice management and orchestration in 5G SDN/NFV-based satellite networks.
CogNet [122]	• VNF network resources must be dynamically adjusted while reducing performance degradations in order to meet SLA/ELAs standards.
SONATA [123]	• An integrated management and control system is incorporated into the dynamic design of the software-defined architecture of the 5G network.
SLICENET [124]	• Developed a framework for the control, management, and orchestration of a cognitive network that permits the sharing of infrastructure between different operator domains in SDN/NFV-enabled 5G networks.
COHERENT [125]	• Modelling and managing radio resources effectively in programmable radio access networks.
5G Exchange [126]	• Enabling cross-domain service orchestration across different administrations or across multi-domain single administrations.

10.4.3 Open Research Issues of SDN/NFV and 5G Integration

Despite the many advantages that can be gained, implementing SDN and NFV technologies poses certain challenges, which are discussed as follows:

(a) **Network slicing:** In 5G networks, transitioning from hardware- to software-based platforms could render flexible multi-tenancy support, where numerous applications/services from different use cases may be accommodated across a shared SDN/NFV-based infrastructure. In addition, the evolution of the network sharing paradigm to the network slicing idea, which enables several VNFs to be setup on the same NFV platform, poses numerous administration issues for big slices. Notably, despite the fact that dynamic resource sharing between slice tenants would increase network resource usage, it requires intelligent scheduling algorithms that can distribute resources among these slices. In addition, the placement of network functions (NFs) within the slice, intra-slice management, and inter-slice management still require substantial work to establish and actualise the notion of network slicing in 5G networks.

(b) **Orchestration and integration in hybrid networks:** Despite the fact that NFV is advertised as being built on industry-standard hardware and software, service providers still experience vendor lock-in on occasion. To deal with this issue, it is essential that all software components function in an interoperable way. The resulting network ought to be adaptable and scalable through the dynamic allocation of resources. To meet this requirement, a flexible, automated, and programmable orchestration platform is necessary.

(c) **Lack of capabilities:** Given that both SDN and NFV are still in their infancy, it should not come as a surprise that NFV offers the possibility of reducing operating expenditures while simultaneously improving client experiences. One of the obstacles is the absence of vendor solutions as well as the decreased acceptance of technologies that enable service providers to leverage the capabilities that are necessary to operationalise SDN and NFV. By adopting SDN and NFV, service providers may transform their networks from static, hardware-centric connectivity systems to agile, software-driven service platforms.

(d) **Security and privacy:** Security is another significant issue for SDN- and NFV-based networks. Virtualised evolving packet cores, IP multimedia services, residential gateways, and even next-generation firewalls are just some of the virtualised network parts that operators have begun introducing in their access and core networks. Unfortunately, the security aspects of virtualisation have received almost no consideration.

(e) **QoS and quality of experience (QoE) on demand:** A 5G network is expected to satisfy various QoS parameters, such as reliability, latency, jitter, and throughput. While WSNs have stringent requirements for packet loss, mobile surveillance applications can typically function with a higher bit error rate and latency, but require large bandwidth to operate. Similarly, the QoE of a service depends on its architecture (such as the capabilities of servers, caches, and their locations), the performance of the core mobile network, and the RANs. QoS and QoE pose a significant challenge which needs to be addressed every time a new application or service runs on the SDN-enabled 5G network.

(f) **Scalability:** Multiple scalability and compatibility concerns may arise due to the fact that a 5G network is expected to support a diverse range of controller applications running on different pieces of hardware. For instance, when an application is running, it may need to respond quickly to changes in the underlying physical infrastructure. Otherwise, it will be difficult to assign and schedule the physical resources to the several applications running at the same time, and that might reduce the network capacity. In order to ensure smooth functioning of the NFV, SDN controller, and data plane, it is necessary to employ an orchestration method.

Exercises

Q.1.   Discuss the real-time applications of the integration of SDN, NFV, and cloud computing.

Q.2.   What features of SDN and NFV can be best utilised for making cloud computing scalable, energy efficient, and secure?

Q.3.   Discuss some major research projects undergoing to efficiently integrate SDN/NFV and the cloud.

Q.4.   What are the challenges and issues that can hinder the implementation of SDN/NFV in a cloud computing environment?

Q.5.   Discuss the real-time applications of the integration of SDN, NFV, and IoT.

Q.6.   What benefits can SDN/NFV provide to the IoT to make it more resource and energy efficient and secure? Also, discuss some use cases.

Q.7.   Discuss some recent trends/projects underway to integrate IoT and SDN/NFV.

Q.8.   What are the challenges and issues that can hinder the implementation of SDN/NFV in an IoT environment?

Q.9.   How is the mobility of a cellular network well supported by SDN and NFV?

Q.10.   Discuss in detail how network slicing is supported by SDN and NFV.

Q.11.   Discuss some major ongoing research projects aimed at efficiently integrating SDN/NFV and 5G.

Q.12.   What are the challenges and issues that can hinder the implementation of SDN/NFV in 6G?

References

[1] Yousaf, F. Z., Bredel, M., Schaller, S., & Schneider, F. (2017). NFV and SDN — Key technology enablers for 5G networks. *IEEE Journal on Selected Areas in Communications*, *35*(11), 2468–2478.

[2] Ray, P. P. & Kumar, N. (2021). SDN/NFV architectures for edge-cloud oriented IoT: A systematic review. *Computer Communications*, *169*, 129–153.

[3] Okwuibe, J., Haavisto, J., Kovacevic, I., Harjula, E., Ahmad, I., Islam, J., & Ylianttila, M. (2021). SDN-enabled resource orchestration for industrial IoT in collaborative edge-cloud networks. *IEEE Access*, *9*, 115839–115854.

[4] Stallings, W. (2015). *Foundations of Modern Networking: SDN, NFV, QoE, IoT, and Cloud.* Addison-Wesley Professional, Boston, MA.

[5] Nguyen, T. G., Phan, T. V., Nguyen, B. T., So-In, C., Baig, Z. A., & Sanguanpong, S. (2019). SeArch: A collaborative and intelligent NIDS architecture for SDN-based cloud IoT networks. *IEEE Access*, *7*, 107678–107694.

[6] Conti, M., Kaliyar, P., & Lal, C. (2019). CENSOR: Cloud-enabled secure IoT architecture over SDN paradigm. *Concurrency and Computation: Practice and Experience*, *31*(8), e4978.

[7] Muñoz, R., Vilalta, R., Yoshikane, N., Casellas, R., Martínez, R., Tsuritani, T., & Morita, I. (2018). Integration of IoT, transport SDN, and edge/cloud computing for dynamic distribution of IoT analytics and efficient use of network resources. *Journal of Lightwave Technology*, *36*(7), 1420–1428.

[8] Mishra, A., Gupta, N., & Gupta, B. B. (2021). Defense mechanisms against DDoS attack based on entropy in SDN-cloud using POX controller. *Telecommunication Systems*, *77*(1), 47–62.

[9] Gaurav, A., Gupta, D. D., Hsu, C, H., Yamaguchi, S., & Chui, K. T. (2021). Fog layer-based ddos attack detection approach for internet-of-things (IoTs) devices. In *2021 IEEE International Conference on Consumer Electronics (ICCE)*, 10–12 Jan. 2021, Las Vegas, NV (pp. 1–5). IEEE.

[10] Mishra, A., Gupta, B. B., Peraković, D., Yamaguchi, S., & Hsu, C. H. (2021). Entropy based defensive mechanism against DDoS attack in SDN-Cloud enabled online social networks. In *2021 IEEE International Conference on Consumer Electronics (ICCE)*, 10–12 Jan. 2021, Las Vegas, NV (pp. 1–6). IEEE.

[11] Gupta, B. B. & Dahiya, A. (2021). *Distributed Denial of Service (DDoS) Attacks: Classification, Attacks, Challenges and Countermeasures*. CRC Press, London, UK.

[12] Tselios, C., Politis, I., & Kotsopoulos, S. (2017). Enhancing SDN security for IoT-related deployments through blockchain. In *2017 IEEE Conference on Network Function Virtualization and Software Defined Networks (NFV-SDN)*, 6–8 Nov. 2017, Berlin, Germany (pp. 303–308). IEEE.

[13] Jain, R. & Paul, S. (2013). Network virtualization and software defined networking for cloud computing: A survey. *IEEE Communications Magazine*, *51*(11), 24–31.

[14] Son, J. & Buyya, R. (2018). A taxonomy of software-defined networking (SDN)-enabled cloud computing. *ACM Computing Surveys (CSUR)*, *51*(3), 1–36.

[15] Duan, Q., Ansari, N., & Toy, M. (2016). Software-defined network virtualization: An architectural framework for integrating SDN and NFV for service provisioning in future networks. *IEEE Network*, *30*(5), 10–16.

[16] Battula, L. R. (2014). Network security function virtualization (NSFV) towards cloud computing with NFV over openflow infrastructure: Challenges and novel approaches. In *2014 International Conference on Advances in Computing, Communications and Informatics (ICACCI)*, 24–27 Sept. 2014, Delhi, India (pp. 1622–1628). IEEE.

[17] Li, H., Ota, K., & Dong, M. (2018). Virtual network recognition and optimization in SDN-enabled cloud environment. *IEEE Transactions on Cloud Computing*, *9*(2), 834–843.

[18] Casado, M., Foster, N., & Guha, A. (2014). Abstractions for software-defined networks. *Communications of the ACM*, *57*(10), 86–95. http://dx.doi.org/10.1145/2661061.2661063.

[19] Jin, H., Cheocherngngarn, T., Levy, D., Smith, A., Pan, D., Liu, J., & Pissinou, N. (2013). Joint host-network optimization for energy-efficient data center networking. In *Proceedings of the 2013 IEEE 27th International Symposium on Parallel Distributed Processing (IPDPS'13)*, 20–24 May

2013, Cambridge, MA (pp. 623–634). http://dx.doi.org/10.1109/IPDPS. 2013.100.

[20] Tomovic, S. & Radusinovic, I. (2018). A new traffic engineering approach for QoS provisioning and failure recovery in SDN-based ISP networks. In *2018 23rd International Scientific-Professional Conference on Information Technology (IT)*, 19–24 Feb. 2018, Zabljak, Montenegro (pp. 1–4). IEEE.

[21] Li, F., Cao, J., Wang, X., & Sun, Y. (2017). A QoS guaranteed technique for cloud applications based on software defined networking. *IEEE Access, 5,* 21229–21241.

[22] Wang, R., Butnariu, D., & Rexford, J. (2011). OpenFlow-based server load balancing gone wild. In *Proceedings of the 11th USENIX Conference on Hot Topics in Management of Internet, Cloud, and Enterprise Networks and Services (Hot-ICE'11)*, USENIX Association, Berkeley, CA (pp. 12–12). Available at: http://dl.acm.org/citation.cfm?id=1972422. 1972438.

[23] Ishimori, A., Farias, F., Cerqueira, E., & Abelem, A. (2013). Control of multiple packet schedulers for improving QoS on openflow/SDN networking. In *Proceedings of the 2013 2nd European Workshop on Software Defined Networks (EWSDN'13)* (pp. 81–86). http://dx.doi.org/10.1109/EWSDN.2013.20.

[24] Wendong, W., Qinglei, Q., Xiangyang, G., Yannan, H., & Xirong, Q. (2014). Autonomic QoS management mechanism in software defined network. *Communications, China 11*(7), 13–23. http://dx.doi.org/10.1109/CC.2014.6895381.

[25] Martini, B., Adami, D., Gharbaoui, M., Castoldi, P., Donatini, L., & Giordano, S. (2016). Design and evaluation of SDN-based orchestration system for cloud data centers. In *Proceedings of the 2016 IEEE International Conference on Communications (ICC'16)* (pp. 1–6). http://dx.doi. org/10.1109/ICC.2016.7511144.

[26] Gharbaoui, M., Martini, B., Adami, D., Giordano, S., & Castoldi, P. (2016). Cloud and network orchestration in SDN data centers: Design principles and performance evaluation. *Computer Networks, 108*(Supplement C), 279–295. http://dx.doi.org/10.1016/j.comnet.2016.08.029.

[27] Spadaro, S., Pagès, A., Agraz, F., Montero, R., & Perelló, J. (2016). Resource orchestration in SDN-based future optical data centres. In *2016 International Conference on Optical Network Design and Modeling (ONDM'16)* (pp. 1–6). http://dx.doi.org/10.1109/ONDM.2016. 7494057.

[28] Jain, S., Kumar, A., Mandal, S., Ong, J., Poutievski, L., Singh, A., Venkata, S., Wanderer, J., Zhou, J., Zhu, M., Zolla, J., Hölzle, U., Stuart, S., & Vahdat, A. (2013). B4: Experience with a globally-deployed software defined wan. In *Proceedings of the ACM SIGCOMM 2013 Conference on*

SIGCOMM (SIGCOMM'13) (pp. 3–14). ACM, New York. http://dx.doi.org/10.1145/2486001.2486019.

[29] Egilmez, H. E., Tahsin Dane, S., Tolga Bagci, K., & Murat Tekalp, A. (2012). OpenQoS. An openflow controller design for multimedia delivery with end-to-end quality of service over software-defined networks. In *Proceedings of the 2012 Asia-Pacific Signal Information Processing Association Annual Summit and Conference (APSIPA ASC'12)*, Hollywood, CA (pp. 1–8).

[30] Mechtri, M., Houidi, I., Louati, W., & Zeghlache, D. (2013). SDN for inter cloud networking. In *Proceedings of the 2013 IEEE SDN for Future Networks and Services (SDN4FNS'13)* (pp. 1–7). http://dx.doi.org/10.1109/SDN4FNS.2013.6702552.

[31] Seetharam, S., Calyam, P., & Beyene, T. (2014). ADON: Application-driven overlay network-as-aservice for data-intensive science. In *Proceedings of the 2014 IEEE 3rd International Conference on Cloud Networking (CloudNet'14)* (pp. 313–319). http://dx.doi.org/10.1109/CloudNet.2014.6969014.

[32] Petri, I., Zou, M., Reza Zamani, A., Diaz-Montes, J., Rana, O., & Parashar, M. (2015). Integrating software defined networks within a cloud federation. In *Proceedings of the 15th IEEE/ACM International Symposium on Cluster, Cloud and Grid Computing (CCGrid'15)* (pp. 179–188). http://dx.doi.org/10.1109/CCGrid.2015.11.

[33] Cahyadi Risdianto, A., Shin, J.-S., & Won Kim, J. (2016). Deployment and evaluation of software-defined inter-connections for multi-domain federated SDN-cloud. In *Proceedings of the 11th International Conference on Future Internet Technologies (CFI'16)* (pp. 118–121). ACM, New York. http://dx.doi.org/10.1145/2935663.2935683.

[34] Kim, Y., Kang, S., Cho, C., & Pahk, S. (2016). SDN-based orchestration for interworking cloud and transport networks. In *2016 International Conference on Information and Communication Technology Convergence (ICTC'16)* (pp. 303–307). http://dx.doi.org/10.1109/ICTC.2016.7763490.

[35] Jeong, K. & Figueiredo, R. (2016). Self-configuring software-defined overlay bypass for seamless inter- and intra-cloud virtual networking. In *Proceedings of the 25th ACM International Symposium on High-Performance Parallel and Distributed Computing (HPDC'16)* (pp. 153–164). ACM, New York. http://dx.doi.org/10.1145/2907294.2907318.

[36] Cerroni, W., Gharbaoui, M., Martini, B., Campi, A., Castoldi, P., & Callegati, F. (2015). Crosslayer resource orchestration for cloud service delivery: A seamless SDN approach. *Computer Networks, 87*(Supplement C), 16–32. http://dx.doi.org/10.1016/j.comnet.2015.05.008.

[37] Azizian, M., Cherkaoui, S., & Senhaji Hafd, A. (2017). Vehicle software updates distribution with SDN and cloud computing. *IEEE Communications Magazine, 55*(8), 74–79. http://dx.doi.org/10.1109/MCOM.2017.1601161.

[38] Wu, Y., Zhang, Z., Wu, C., Guo, C., Li, Z., & Lau, F. C. M. (2017). Orchestrating bulk data transfers across geo-distributed datacenters. *IEEE Transactions on Cloud Computing*, 5(1), 112–125. http://dx.doi.org/10.1109/TCC.2015.2389842.

[39] Amarasinghe, H., Jarray, A., & Karmouch, A. (2017). Fault-tolerant IaaS management for networked cloud infrastructure with SDN. In *Proceedings of the 2017 IEEE International Conference on Communications (ICC'17)* (pp. 1–7). http://dx.doi.org/10.1109/ICC.2017.7996342.

[40] Heller, B., Seetharaman, S., Mahadevan, P., Yiakoumis, Y., Sharma, P., Banerjee, S., & McKeown, N. (2010). ElasticTree: Saving energy in data center networks. In *Proceedings of the 7th USENIX Conference on Networked Systems Design and Implementation (NSDI'10)* (pp. 249–264). USENIX Association, Berkeley, CA. Available at: http://dl.acm.org/citation.cfm?id=1855711.1855728.

[41] Wang, X., Yao, Y., Wang, X., Lu, K., & Cao, Qing (2012). CARPO: Correlation-aware power optimization in data center networks. In *Proceedings of the 2012 IEEE INFOCOM (INFOCOM'12)* (pp. 1125–1133). http:// dx.doi.org/10.1109/INFCOM.2012.6195471.

[42] Zheng, K., Wang, X., & Liu, J. (2017). DISCO: Distributed traffic flow consolidation for power efficient data center network. In *Proceedings of the 16th International IFIP TC6 Networking Conference, Networking*, IFIP Open Digital Library, 12–16 June 2017, Stockholm, Sweden. Available at: http://dl.ifip.org/db/conf/networking/networking2017/1570334940.pdf.

[43] Zheng, K. & Wang, X. (2017). Dynamic control of flow completion time for power efficiency of data center networks. In *Proceedings of the 2017 IEEE 37th International Conference on Distributed Computing Systems (ICDCS'17)* (pp. 340–350). http://dx.doi.org/10.1109/ICDCS.2017.138.

[44] Dias de Assunção, M., Carpa, R., Lefévre, L., & Glýck, O. (2017). On designing SDN services for energy-aware traffic engineering. In *Proceedings of the 11th International Conference on Testbeds and Research Infrastructures for the Development of Networks and Communities*. http://dx.doi.org/10.1007/978-3-319-49580-4_2.

[45] Fang, W., Liang, X., Li, S., Chiaraviglio, L., & Xiong, N. (2013). VMPlanner: Optimizing virtual machine placement and traffic flow routing to reduce network power costs in cloud data centers. *Computer Networks*, 57(1), 179–196. http://dx.doi.org/10.1016/j.comnet.2012.09.008.

[46] Jin, H., Cheocherngngarn, T., Levy, D., Smith, A., Pan, D., Liu, J., & Pissinou, N. (2013). Joint host-network optimization for energy-efficient data center networking. In *Proceedings of the 2013 IEEE 27th International Symposium on Parallel Distributed Processing (IPDPS'13)* (pp. 623–634). http://dx.doi.org/10.1109/IPDPS.2013.100.

[47] Zheng, K., Wang, X., Li, L., & Wang, X. (2014). Joint power optimization of data center network and servers with correlation analysis. In *Proceedings of the 2014 IEEE INFOCOM (INFOCOM'14)* (pp. 2598–2606). http://dx.doi.org/10.1109/INFOCOM.2014.6848207.

[48] Zheng, K., Zheng, W., Li, L., & Wang, X. (2017). PowerNetS: Coordinating data center network with servers and cooling for power optimization. *IEEE Transactions on Network and Service Management, 14*(3), 661–675. http://dx.doi.org/10.1109/TNSM.2017.2711567.

[49] Cziva, R., Jout, S., Stapleton, D., Po Tso, F., & Pezaros, D. P. (2016). SDN-based virtual machine management for cloud data centers. *IEEE Transactions on Network and Service Management, 13*(2), 212–225. http://dx.doi.org/10.1109/TNSM.2016.2528220.

[50] Habibi, P., Mokhtari, M., & Sabaei, M. (2016). QRVE: QoS-aware routing and energy-efficient VM placement for software-defined datacenter networks. In *Proceedings of the 8th International Symposium on Telecommunications (IST'16)* (pp. 533–539). http://dx.doi.org/10.1109/ISTEL.2016.7881879.

[51] Son, J., Vahid Dastjerdi, A., Calheiros, R. N., & Buyya, R. (2017, April). SLA-aware and energyefficient dynamic overbooking in SDN-based cloud data centers. *IEEE Transactions on Sustainable Computing, 2*(2), 76–89. http://dx.doi.org/10.1109/TSUSC.2017.2702164.

[52] Singh Aujla, G., Kumar, N., Zomaya, A. Y., & Rajan, R. (2018). Optimal decision making for big data processing at edge-cloud environment: An SDN perspective. *IEEE Transactions on Industrial Informatics, 14*(2), 778–789. http://dx.doi.org/10.1109/TII.2017.2738841.

[53] Chowdhary, A., Pisharody, S., Alshamrani, A., & Huang, D. (2017). Dynamic game based security framework in SDN-enabled cloud networking environments. In *Proceedings of the ACM International Workshop on Security in Software Defined Networks & Network Function Virtualization (SDN-NFVSec'17)* (pp. 53–58). ACM, New York. http://dx.doi.org/10.1145/3040992.3040998.

[54] Pisharody, S., Natarajan, J., Chowdhary, A., Alshalan, A., & Huang, D. (2017). Brew: A security policy analysis framework for distributed SDN-based cloud environments. *IEEE Transactions on Dependable and Secure Computing.* http://dx.doi.org/10.1109/TDSC.2017.2726066.

[55] Popa, L., Kumar, G., Chowdhury, M., Krishnamurthy, A., Ratnasamy, S., & Stoica, I. (2012). FairCloud: Sharing the network in cloud computing. In *Proceedings of the ACM SIGCOMM 2012 Conference on Applications, Technologies, Architectures, and Protocols for Computer Communication (SIGCOMM'12)* (pp. 187–198). ACM, New York. http://dx.doi.org/10.1145/2342356.2342396.

[56] Rodrigo de Souza, F., Christian Miers, C., Fiorese, A., & Piegas Koslovski, G. (2017). QoSaware virtual infrastructures allocation on SDN-based clouds. In *Proceedings of the 17th IEEE/ACM International Symposium on Cluster, Cloud and Grid Computing (CCGrid'17)* (pp. 120–129). IEEE Press, Piscataway, NJ. http://dx.doi.org/10.1109/CCGRID.2017.57.

[57] Leivadeas, A., Falkner, M., Lambadaris, I., & Kesidis, G. (2017). Optimal virtualized network function allocation for an SDN enabled cloud. *Computer Standards & Interfaces*, *54*(P4), 266–278. http://dx.doi.org/10.1016/j.csi.2017.01.001.

[58] Callegati, F., Cerroni, W., Contoli, C., Cardone, R., Nocentini, M., & Manzalini, A. (2016). SDN for dynamic NFV deployment. *IEEE Communications Magazine*, *54*(10), 89–95. http://dx.doi.org/10.1109/MCOM.2016.7588275.

[59] Bonafiglia, R., Castellano, G., Cerrato, I., & Risso, F. (2017). End-to-end service orchestration across SDN and cloud computing domains. In *2017 IEEE Conference on Network Softwarization (NetSoft'17)* (pp. 1–6). http://dx.doi.org/10.1109/NETSOFT.2017.8004234.

[60] Foerster, K.-T., Pacut, M., & Schmid, S. (2019). On the complexity of non-segregated routing in reconfigurable data center architectures. *ACM SIGCOMM Computer and Communications Review*, *49*(2), 2–8.

[61] Shao, E., Wang, Z., Yuan, G., Tan, G., & Sun, N. (2019). Wormhole optical network: A new architecture to solve long diameter problem in exascale computer. *CCF Transactions on High Performance Computing*, *1*, 73–91.

[62] Wu, R., Huang, L., & Zhou, H. (2019). RHKV: An RDMA and HTM friendly key–value store for data-intensive computing. *Future Generation Computer Systems*, *92*, 162–177.

[63] Calcaterra, C., Carmenini, A., Marotta, A., & Cassioli, D. (2019). Hadoop performance evaluation in software defined data center networks. In *Proceedings of the International Conference Computing, Network Communications (ICNC)*, Lanzhou, China (pp. 56–61).

[64] Kaur, G., Bala, A., & Chana, I. (2019). An intelligent regressive ensemble approach for predicting resource usage in cloud computing. *Journal of Parallel and Distributed Computing*, *123*, 1–12.

[65] Xu, G., Dai, B., Huang, B., Yang, J., & Wen, S. (2017). Bandwidth-aware energy efficient flow scheduling with SDN in data center networks. *Future Generation Computer Systems*, *68*, 163–174.

[66] Ponraj, A. (2019). Optimistic virtual machine placement in cloud data centers using queuing approach. *Future Generation Computer Systems*, *93*, 338–344.

[67] Hawilo, H., Jammal, M., & Shami, A. (2019). Network function virtualization-aware orchestrator for service function chaining placement in the cloud. *IEEE Journal on Selected Areas in Communications, 37*(3), 643–655.

[68] Cokic, M. & Seskar, I. (2019). Software defined network management for dynamic smart GRID traffic. *Future Generation Computer Systems, 96*, 270–282.

[69] Gou, Z., Yamaguchi, S., & Gupta, B. B. (2017). Analysis of various security issues and challenges in cloud computing environment: A survey. In *Identity Theft: Breakthroughs in Research and Practice*, edited by Information Resources Management Association (pp. 221–247). IGI Global, Hershey, PA. https://doi.org/10.4018/978-1-5225-08.

[70] Bhushan, K. & Gupta, B. B. (2019). Distributed denial of service (DDoS) attack mitigation in software defined network (SDN)-based cloud computing environment. *Journal of Ambient Intelligence and Humanized Computing, 10*(5), 1985–1997.

[71] Persico, V., Grimaldi, D., Pescape, A., Salvi, A., & Santini, S. (2017). A fuzzy approach based on heterogeneous metrics for scaling out public clouds. *IEEE Transactions on Parallel and Distributed Systems, 28*(8), 2117–2130.

[72] Liu, W., Wang, Y., Zhang, J., Liao, H., Liang, Z., & Liu, X. (2020). AAMcon: An adaptively distributed SDN controller in data center networks. *Frontiers of Computer Science, 14*. 146–161.

[73] Son, J. & Buyya, R. (2019). SDCon: Integrated control platform for software defined clouds. *IEEE Transactions on Parallel and Distributed Systems, 30*(1), 230–244.

[74] Nobre, J. C., de Souza, A. M., Rosario, D., Both, C., Villas, L. A., Cerqueira, E., Braun, T., & Gerla, M. (2019). Vehicular software-defined networking and fog computing: Integration and design principles. *Ad Hoc Network, 82*, 172–181.

[75] Nayyer, A., Sharma, A. K., & Awasthi, L. K. (2019). Laman: A supervisor controller based scalable framework for software defined networks. *Computer Network, 159*, 125–134.

[76] Jain, V., Yatri, V., & Kapoor, C. (2019). Software defined networking: State-ofthe-art. *Journal of High Speed Networks, 25*(1), 1–40.

[77] Cokic, M. & Seskar, I. (2019). Software defined network management for dynamic smart GRID traffic. *Future Generation Computer Systems, 96*, 270–282.

[78] Chaipet, S. & Putthividhya, W. (2019). On studying of scalability in single-controller software-defined networks. In *Proceedings of the 11th International Conference on Knowledge Smart Technology (KST)*, Tokyo, Japan (pp. 158–163).

[79] Birkinshaw, C., Rouka, E., & Vassilakis, V. G. (2019). Implementing an intrusion detection and prevention system using software-defined networking: Defending against port-scanning and denial-of-service attacks. *Journal of Network and Computer Applications*, *136*, 71–85.

[80] Chuang, C.-C., Yu, Y.-J., & Pang, A.-C. (2018). Flow-aware routing and forwarding for SDN scalability in wireless data centers. *IEEE Transactions Network Service Management*, *15*(4), 1676–1691.

[82] UcedaVelez, T. & Morana, M. M. (2015). *Risk Centric Threat Modeling: Process for Attack Simulation and Threat Analysis*. Wiley, Hoboken, NJ.

[83] Harbi, Y., Aliouat, Z., Refoufi, A., & Harous, S. (2021). Recent security trends in internet of things: A comprehensive survey. *IEEE Access. 9*, 113292–113314.

[84] Li, J., Altman, E., & Touati, C. (2015). A general SDN-based IoT framework with NVF implementation. *ZTE Communications*, *13*(3), 42–45.

[85] Brief, ONF Solution. (2014). OpenFlow-enabled SDN and Network Functions Virtualization. *Open Networking Found*, *17*, 1–12.

[86] Gupta, B. B. & Quamara, M. (2020). An overview of Internet of Things (IoT): Architectural aspects, challenges, and protocols. *Concurrency and Computation: Practice and Experience*, *32*(21), e4946.

[87] Adat, V., Dahiya, A., & Gupta, B. B. (2018). Economic incentive based solution against distributed denial of service attacks for IoT customers. In *2018 IEEE International Conference on Consumer Electronics (ICCE)*, 12–14 Jan. 2018, Las Vegas, NV (pp. 1–5). IEEE.

[88] Hernandez-Valencia, E., Izzo, S., & Polonsky, B. (2015). How will NFV/SDN transform service provider opex? *IEEE Network*, *29*(3), 60–67.

[89] Das, S., Sahni, S. (2014). Network topology optimization for data aggregation. In *2014 14th IEEE/ACM International Symposium on Cluster, Cloud and Grid Computing*, Piscataway, NJ (pp. 493–501). IEEE.

[90] Sekar, V., Egi, N., Ratnasamy, S., Reiter, M. K., & Shi, G. (2012). Design and implementation of a consolidated middlebox architecture. In *9th fUSE-NIXg Symposium on Networked Systems Design and Implementation (fNS-DIg 12)*, 25–27 April 2012, San Jose, CA (pp. 323–336).

[91] Ma, D. & Shi, Y. (2019). A lightweight encryption algorithm for edge networks in software-defined industrial Internet of Things. In *Proceedings of the IEEE 5th International Conference on Computer and Communication (ICCC)*, 6–9 Dec. 2019, Chengdu, China (pp. 1489–1493).

[92] Salman, O., Abdallah, S., Elhajj, I. H., Chehab, A., & Kayssi, A. (2016). Identity based authentication scheme for the Internet of Things. In *Proceedings of the IEEE Symposium on Computer and Communications (ISCC)*, 27–30 June 2016, Messina, Italy (pp. 1109–1111).

[93] Kalkan, K. & Zeadally, S. (2017). Securing Internet of Things with software defined networking. *IEEE Communications Magazine, 56*(9), 186–192.

[94] Wang, X., Xu, K., Chen, W., Li, Q., Shen, M., & Wu, B. (2020). ID-based SDN for the Internet of Things. *IEEE Network, 34*(4), 76–83.

[95] Bhunia, S. S. & Gurusamy, M. (2017). Dynamic attack detection and mitigation in IoT using SDN. In *Proceedings of the 27th International Telecommunications Networks and Application Conference (ITNAC)*, 22–24 Nov. 2017, Melbourne, VIC, Australia (pp. 1–6).

[96] Bull, P., Austin, R., Popov, E., Sharma, M., & Watson, R. (2016). Flow based security for IoT devices using an SDN gateway. In *Proceedings of the IEEE 4th International Conference on Future Internet Things Cloud (FiCloud)*, 22–24 Aug. 2016, Vienna, Austria (pp. 157–163).

[97] Omnes, N., Bouillon, M., Fromentoux, G., & Le Grand, O. (2015). A programmable and virtualized network & IT infrastructure for the internet of things: How can NFV & SDN help for facing the upcoming challenges. In *Proceedings of the 2015 18th International Conference on Intelligence in Next Generation Networks, ICIN 2015*, 17–19 Feb. 2015, Paris, France (pp. 64–69).

[98] Li, J., Altman, E., & Touati, C. (2015). A General SDN based IoT Framework with NVF Implementation. *ZTE Communications, 13*(3), 42–45.

[99] Hakiri, A., Berthou, P., Gokhale, A., & Abdellatif, S. (2016). Publish/subscribe-enabled software defined networking for efficient and scalable IoT communications. *IEEE Communications Magazine, 53*(9), 48–54.

[100] Wang, Y., Zhang, Y., & Chen, J. (2016). SDNPS: A load-balanced topic-based publish/subscribe system in software-defined networking. *Applied Sciences, 6*(4), 1–21.

[101] Galluccio, L., Milardo, S., Morabito, G., & Palazzo, S. (2015). SDN-WISE: Design, prototyping and experimentation of a stateful SDN solution for WIreless SEnsor networks. In *2015 IEEE Conference on Computer Communications (INFOCOM)*. 26 April–1 May 2015, Hong Kong China (pp. 513–521). IEEE.

[102] Gudipati, A., Perry, D., Li, L., & Katti, S. (2013). SoftRAN: Software defined radio access network. In *Proceedings of the Second ACM SIGCOMM Workshop on Hot Topics in Software Defined Networking*. 16 August 2013, Hong Kong, China.

[103] Jin, X., Li, L., Vanbever, L., & Rexford, J. (2013). Softcell: Scalable and flexible cellular core network architecture. In *Proceedings of the Ninth ACM Conference on Emerging Networking Experiments and Technologies*, 9–12 Dec. 2013, Santa Barbara, CA (pp. 163–174).

[104] Akyildiz, I., Wang, P., & Lin, S. (2015). SoftAir: A software defined networking architecture for 5G wireless systems. *Computer Networks, 85*, 1–18.

[105] Li, L. E., Mao, Z. M., & Rexford, J. (2012). Toward software-defined cellular networks. In *2012 European Workshop on Software Defined Networking (EWSDN)*, 9–12 Dec. 2013, Santa Barbara, CA (pp. 7–12).

[106] Ehrlich, M., Krummacker, D., Fischer, C., Guillaume, R., Perez, S., Frimpong, A., Meer, H., Wollschlaeger, M., Schotten, H., & Jasperneite, H. (2018). Software-defined networking as an enabler for future industrial network management. In *Proceedings of the 2018 IEEE 23rd International Conference on Emerging Technologies and Factory Automation (ETFA)*, 4–7 Sep. 2018, Turin, Italy (Vol. 1, pp. 1109–1112).

[107] Chen, B., Wan, J., Shu, L., Li, P., Mukherjee, M., & Yin, B. (2018). Smart factory of industry 4.0: Key technologies, application case, and challenges. *IEEE Access, 6*, 6505–6519.

[108] Hossain, M. S., Muhammad, G., Abdul, W., Song, B., & Gupta, B. B. (2018). Cloud-assisted secure video transmission and sharing framework for smart cities. *Future Generation Computer Systems, 83*, 596–606.

[109] Gupta, B. B. & Quamara, M. (2020). An overview of Internet of Things (IoT): Architectural aspects, challenges, and protocols. *Concurrency and Computation: Practice and Experience, 32*(21), e4946.

[110] Tewari, A. & Gupta, B. B. (2020). Security, privacy and trust of different layers in Internet-of-Things (IoTs) framework. *Future Generation Computer Systems, 108*, 909–920.

[111] 5G media: Programmable edge-to-cloud virtualization fabric for the 5G Media industry, CORDIS EU research results, Grant agreement ID: 761699.

[112] Gramaglia, M., Digon, I., Friderikos, V., Von Hugo, D., Mannweiler, C., Puente, M. A., Samdanis, K., & Sayadi, B. (2016). Flexible connectivity and QoE/QoS management for 5G Networks: The 5G NORMA view. In *2016 IEEE International Conference on Communications Workshops (ICC)*, 23–27 May 2016, Kuala Lumpur, Malaysia (pp. 373–379). IEEE.

[113] 5GTANGO Project Consortium (2019). 5GTANGO: 5G development and validation platform for global industry-specific network services and apps [Online]. Available at: https://5gtango.eu.

[114] Gutierrez-Estevez, D. M., Dipietro, N., Dedomenico, A., Gramaglia, M., Elzur, U., & Wang, Y. (2018). 5G-MoNArch use case for ETSI ENI: Elastic resource management and orchestration. In *2018 IEEE Conference on Standards for Communications and Networking (CSCN)*, Honolulu, HI (pp. 1–5). IEEE.

[115] MATILDA — A holistic, innovative framework for design, development and orchestration of 5G-ready applications and network services over sliced programmable infrastructure. Available at: http://www.matilda-5g.eu/.

[116] SESAME Project. Available at: http://www.sesame-h2020-5g-ppp.eu/.

[117] Camps-Mur, D., Gutierrez, J., Grass, E., Tzanakaki, A., Flegkas, P., Choumas, K., Giatsios, D., Beldachi, A., Diallo, T., Zou, J., Legg, P., Bartelt, J., Chaudhary, J. K., Betzler, A. Aleixendri, J. J., Gonzalez, R., & Simeonidou, D. (2019). 5G-XHaul: A novel wireless-optical SDN transport network to support joint 5G backhaul and fronthaul services. *IEEE Communications Magazine, 57*(7), 99–105.

[118] Mangues-Bafalluy, J., Baranda, J., Pascual, I., Martínez, R., Vettori, L., Landi, G., Zurita, A., Salama, D., Antevski, K., Martín-Pérez, J., Andrushko, D., Tomakh, K., Martini, B., Li, X., & Salvat, J. X. (2019). 5G-TRANSFORMER Service Orchestrator: design, implementation, and evaluation. In *2019 European Conference on Networks and Communications (EuCNC)*, 18–21 June 2019, Valencia, Spain (pp. 31–36). IEEE.

[119] Li, X., Casellas, R., Landi, G., de la Oliva, A., Costa-Perez, X., Garcia-Saavedra, A., Deiss, T., Cominardi, L., & Vilalta, R. (2017). 5G-crosshaul network slicing: Enabling multi-tenancy in mobile transport networks. *IEEE Communications Magazine, 55*(8), 128–137.

[120] Parker, M. C., Koczian, G., Adeyemi-Ejeye, F., Quinlan, T., Walker, S. D., Legarrea, A., Siddiqui, M. S., Escalona, E., Spirou, S., Kritharidis, D., Habel, K., Jungnickel, V., Trouva, E., Kourtis, A., Liu, Y., Frigau, M. S., Point, J. C., Lyberopoulos, G., Theodoropoulou, E., Filis, K., Rokkas, Th., Neokosmidis, I., Levi, D., Zetserov, E., Foglar, A., Ulbricht, M., Peternel, B., & Gustincic, D. (2016). CHARISMA: Converged heterogeneous advanced 5G cloud-RAN architecture for intelligent and secure media access. In *2016 European Conference on Networks and Communications (EuCNC)*, 27–30 June 2016, Athens, Greece (pp. 240–244). IEEE.

[121] Liolis, K., Geurtz, A., Sperber, R., Schulz, D., Watts, S., Poziopoulou, G., Evans, B., Wang, N., Vidal, O., Tiomela Jou, B., Fitch, M., Sendra, S. D., Khodashenas, P. S., & Chuberre, N. (2019). Use cases and scenarios of 5G integrated satellite-terrestrial networks for enhanced mobile broadband: The SaT5G approach. *International Journal of Satellite Communications and Networking, 37*(2), 91–112.

[122] Xu, L., Assem, H., Buda, T.S., López, D.R., Yahia, I. G. B., Smirnov, M., Raz, D., Uryupina, O., Martin, A., Mozo, A., Gallico, D., & Mullins, R. (2013). Cognet: A network management architecture featuring cognitive capabilities. In *Proceedings of the European Conference on Networks and Communications (EuCNC)*, Lisbon, Portugal (pp. 325–329).

[123] Soenen, T., Van Rossem, S., Tavernier, W., Vicens, F., Valocchi, D., Trakadas, P., Karkazis, P., Xilouris, G., Eardley, P., Kolometsos, S., Kourtis, M.-A., Guija, D., Siddiqui, S., Hasselmeyer, P., Bonnet, J., & Lopez, D. (2018). Insights from SONATA: Implementing and integrating a microservice-based NFV service platform with a DevOps methodology. In *NOMS 2018 — 2018 IEEE/IFIP Network Operations and Management Symposium*, 23–27 April 2018, Taipei, Taiwan (pp. 1–6). IEEE.

[124] Wang, Q., Alcaraz-Calero, J., Weiss, M. B., Gavras, A., Neves, P. M., Cale, R., Bernini, G., Carrozzo, G., Ciulli, N., Celozzi, G., Ciriaco, A., Levin, A., Lorenz, D., Barabash, K., Nikaein, N., Spadaro, S., Morris, D., Chochliouros, J., Agapiou, Y., Patachia, C., Iordache, M., Oproiu, E., Lomba, C., Aleixo, A. C., Ro-Drigues, A., Hallissey, G., Bozakov, Z., Koutsopoulos, K., & Walsh, P. (2018). SliceNet: End-to-end cognitive network slicing and slice management framework in virtualised multi-domain, multi-tenant 5G networks. In *2018 IEEE International Symposium on Broadband Multimedia Systems and Broadcasting (BMSB)*, 6–8 June 2018, Valencia, Spain (pp. 1–5). IEEE.

[125] Kostopoulos, A., Agapiou, G., Kuo, F.-C., Pentikousis, K., Cipriano, A., Panaitopol, D., Marandin, D., Kowalik, K., Alexandris, K., Chang, C.-Y., Nikaein, N., Goldhamer, M., Kliks, A., Steinert, R., Mämmelä, A., & Chen, T. (2016). Scenarios for 5G networks: The COHERENT approach. In *2016 23rd International Conference on Telecommunications (ICT)*, 16–18 May 2016, Thessaloniki, Greece (pp. 1–6). IEEE.

[126] Sgambelluri, A., Tusa, F., Gharbaoui, M., Maini, E., Toka, L., Perez, J. M., Paolucci, F., Martini, B., Poe, W. Y., Melian Hernandes, J., Muhammed, A., Ramos, A., de Dios, O. G., Sonkoly, B., Monti, P., Vaishnavi, I., Bernardos, C. J., & Szabó, R. (2017). Orchestration of network services across multiple operators: The 5G exchange prototype. In *2017 European Conference on Networks and Communications (EuCNC)*, 12–15 June 2017, Oulu, Finland (pp. 1–5). IEEE.

[127] Stergiou, C., Psannis, K. E., Kim, B. G., & Gupta, B. (2018). Secure integration of IoT and cloud computing. *Future Generation Computer Systems, 78*, 964–975.

[128] Stergiou, C., Psannis, K. E., Gupta, B. B., & Ishibashi, Y. (2018). Security, privacy & efficiency of sustainable cloud computing for big data & IoT. *Sustainable Computing: Informatics and Systems, 19*, 174–184.

[129] Gupta, B. B. & Badve, O. P. (2017). Taxonomy of DoS and DDoS attacks and desirable defense mechanism in a cloud computing environment. *Neural Computing and Applications, 28*, 3655–3682.

[130] Bhushan, K. & Gupta, B. B. (2019). Distributed denial of service (DDoS) attack mitigation in software defined network (SDN)-based cloud computing environment. *Journal of Ambient Intelligence and Humanized Computing, 10*, 1985–1997.

Index

Printed in the USA
CPSIA information can be obtained
at www.ICGtesting.com
LVHW020724010224
770406LV00002B/14